Michael Matthews is a police officer with the London Metropolitan Police, currently working at Scotland Yard. He is a keen traveller, writer and photographer and has had articles published in travel and police magazines. His photographs have been used around the world to illustrate everything from national newspapers to book covers. Michael likes real ale, lobster roll and ballet (yes, ballet). He is 40 years old and lives just outside London. *We Are The Cops* is his first book.

WE ARE THE COPS

MICHAEL MATTHEWS

SILVERTAIL BOOKS • *London*

First published in Great Britain in 2015 by Silvertail Books
www.silvertailbooks.com
Copyright © Michael Matthews 2015
1
The right of Michael Matthews to be identified as the author
of this work has been asserted by him in accordance
with the Copyright, Design and Patents Act 1988
A catalogue record of this book is available from the British Library
Typeset in Ehrhardt Monotype by Joanna Macgregor
Printed in the UK by CPI Group (UK) Ltd, Croydon, CR0 4YY
ISBN 978-1-909269-22-4

This book is dedicated to law enforcement officers, past, present and future and to those who have given their lives or who may never recover from their injuries.

CONTENTS

INTRODUCTION

'We're the police. We're not fucking social workers.'

Crazy stuff happens in the States, and more often than not it's the cops who end up dealing with it. As a result, policing in America stands alone, because of its environment (natural and man-made), its attitudes and approach, its extremes, its dangers, its excitement and its contrasts. Here is a group – a family – of men and women who are to be admired and at times even envied. These are people who face and do the extraordinary, whose job it is to run towards danger for the sake of other people.

This book is intended to be a window into their lives, a way of showing the world what it is really like to be a cop in the US by using the words of the people who know it best – the cops themselves. The voices in this book are all different, from different cities, states and counties, male and female, rookies and veterans. But they are also all the same, because they are all cops.

There are close to eight hundred thousand law enforcement officers in the United States of America which, considering the population of the country, actually isn't that many (the UK has more per capita) and, leaving out Federal Agencies, they are generally spread over three different types of agency: state troopers, county sheriffs and local police departments. All enforce the law in one way or another, but it is not that straightforward. Each is distinct and even within their own kind there are numerous variations and differences. So although this might not be entirely correct in all cases, put most simply, this is how I see them: State Troopers (known in some states as State Police, Highway Patrol or Department of Public Safety) are paid for by the state and have jurisdiction over the entire state. Each state is then split into a number of counties (although Alaska doesn't have any) and each county has its sheriff's department (although Connecticut has state marshals instead), who have law enforcement responsibility throughout their own county. Then there are the local police departments that are generally paid for by the towns and cities they police. Some of these local police departments are actually 'Public Safety Departments', where the officers are trained and act as both police and firefighters. It's a good way of keeping down costs, I guess.

But not all towns and cities have their own police department because if they want one, they have to pay for it themselves, and in these circumstances the sheriffs and/or the troopers serve them. For example, if Los Angeles decided that it no longer wanted or could no longer afford a police department, the LAPD wouldn't exist and so the Los Angeles County Sheriff's Department, (the city and the county have the same name in this instance), would take over the full time policing of the city.

But a city would never let its police department go, right? Wrong.

This does happen. I myself have seen it first hand in Michigan, where the Highland Park Police Department was dissolved in 2001 because the city could no longer afford them. Shortly afterwards, I was shown around this poor, rundown city by the handful of county sheriffs who were tasked with keeping some kind of law and order in a city where the police had simply been there one day then gone the next. The abandoned police station and police cars had been vandalized and destroyed in what looked like an orgy of anarchy. Fortunately the department has since been re-established.

There are a staggering amount of different law enforcement agencies in America, close to 18,000, including over 12,000 police departments (the NYPD being the largest with 34,500 officers); literally thousands of separate agencies and departments – state, county, city, university and school departments, federal agencies and special districts such as airport, harbour and transit departments. Although there are other things to take into consideration such as size and population (the UK population is roughly five times smaller than the US – 64 million compared to 318 million), by comparison, the UK has 51. I questioned why some smaller departments didn't amalgamate (I know of a department where the Chief of Police is in charge of himself) and a cop in New England told me that the local communities had no appetite for it. They liked having their own, dedicated departments. Like a gated community with private security, I thought. But the amount of departments and agencies – along with the variations within them – can be mind-boggling.

Despite all this, the model for 'modern' policing in the US came from Great Britain, Sir Robert Peel and the London Metropolitan Police. But policing in America goes back further than Peel and although there were previous 'watches' and patrols, the first city to employ 'police' was Philadelphia in 1751. And the first recorded officer death was as far back as 1791, when Constable Darius Quimly of the Albany County Constables Office in New York was shot dead during an arrest. Over two hundred years later, the wall at the National Law Enforcement Officers Memorial in Washington DC now contains nearly 20,000 names.

Since the turn of the twentieth century, the number of officer deaths per year has almost always been in triple figures. The figures vary, depending on the recording methods, but according to the National Law Enforcement Officers Memorial, the 1970s were a particularly deadly decade with 2,301 recorded deaths – an average of 230 a year. 1974, the year of my birth, was the decade's most lethal, with 280 officers killed, which was just shy of the 293 officer deaths recorded for 1930. Elsewhere it is recorded as 313 officers but either way, it is the highest ever year. The 1920s were even worse than the 1970s, with an average of 235 officers killed a year and a total of 2,355. I find these figures shocking. But then the figures for all years are always astounding, even though they can fluctuate wildly. 106 deaths were recorded for 2013 – the lowest figure since 1944 – and although it's down from the 123 that were recorded for 2012, it is still tragically and shockingly high.

The causes of officer deaths range from stabbings to vehicle accidents. Many are recorded as 'gunfire'. Four of the officers who died in 2012 were New York Police Department officers who finally succumbed to the effects of 9/11 and the toxins they breathed in during the rescue and recovery operation. On other years that number has been higher. It is obviously a dangerous job and police officers also kill hundreds of people a year in the US, in what is classed as 'justifiable homicides'; The difference being that one set of people are legally in the right and the other are in the wrong.

I remember being acutely aware of the dangers of being a cop in the US when I was growing up and watching American cop shows such as TJ Hooker, CHiPS, Hill Street Blues and movies like Lethal Weapon, Turner and Hooch, Stakeout and even Smokey and the Bandit. However, I was convinced that American cops were the coolest guys in the world, all ass-kickin', cigar-chomping, gun-toting men of action with endless attitude and a bottomless collection of sharp wisecracks. For me, an English kid in the genteel London suburbs, they couldn't have been more different to our own British Bobbies. Nowhere did policing seem so extreme and as much fun as it did in America.

A few years on, having finally reached the required age, I phoned the American Embassy in London in a state of great excitement, and asked about joining the NYPD. It had to be the NYPD because to my TV-educated teenage mind they were the craziest of the bunch (later I would learn for myself that really was true).

'Hi,' I said to the female operator, my voice full of enthusiasm. 'I want to join the NYPD.' For some reason I half-expected her to hand me a gun and a badge through the telephone receiver.

'Join the what?' she said.

'The New York Police Department.'

'You want to be a cop?'

'Yes,' I said. 'In America.'

'Are you American?'

'No.'

She hung up.

As much as I loved her show of real American attitude, I was deeply disappointed. I immediately resolved to make a life for myself which was as close as I could get to the NYPD: I became a British cop, or rather, a British policeman (I quickly learned that using the term 'cop' in the UK makes you seem ridiculous).

Over the next ten years or so, my obsession with the American police grew, and eventually I began travelling to the United States to find out more. I quickly learned about the 'ride-along' programs, which allow private citizens – usually with an interest in joining the police – to experience the life of a cop by going out on patrol with an officer in their local town. Despite not even being American, and often not even being understood, I was always allowed to ride. And the experience was everything I hoped for and dreamed of, because it really was like being in a US cop show. Car chases, foot chases, drawn guns, fist-fights, drugs, arrests, attitude – from both the cops and the perps – and even 'dip', which I learnt was a way of taking tobacco by placing a wad of damp black stuff under your lip, sucking it and then pretty much making yourself sick.

As the years went on, I travelled to the States more and more, always hooking up with officers right across the country, going on ride-alongs and learning what life was like for the men and women who work in law enforcement. My fascination with their work and their lives was obvious, and they would often tell me about their experiences. That is where the idea for this book came from – the officers themselves.

Over the years that I have been patrolling and meeting with

American officers, I have laughed so hard that I have hurt myself, cried for and cried with officers and the people they come into contact with. I have rolled around on the ground with violent suspects, assisted in arrests, chased criminals and helped those in need. I have been more scared than I had ever been before or have felt since, and have feared for my life on more than one occasion. I have felt extreme happiness, hope and joy but also reached rock-bottom despair, distress and terror – experiences and emotions that cops feel and go through every single day.

At the end of days like that, cops get a pay cheque and a pension – if they are lucky. As you will read, some will not make it that far. Many will come away scarred for life physically or mentally, or both. Some will also get to take memories and experiences away with them that most people could not dream up in the wildest parts of their imagination. Many of these are shared in the following pages.

Other books of this type have been written before, but they often related to a single officer or focused on small geographical areas, perhaps just one force. I wanted to put a book together that gave the reader a wider view of policing in America. Although there is much that may be similar in the work of a cop in New York and a trooper in, say, Alaska, there are many differences. For one, you don't get moose in Times Square.

I wanted this book to be different, to be more than just funny tales or stories of gunfights, although they would be important parts. I also wanted to know what made cops tick. I wanted to get under the uniform, out of the handcuffs and find out how they really felt about their job, their colleagues, the politics and the public. I wanted to know what a cop really thinks about and how they feel, to get a broad and deep understanding of modern police in America today. The project proved to be exhausting, but man, what an adventure.

The finished book is not separated into departments or individual officers. Instead it is arranged under specific subject headings with officers' tales all mixed together, and starts where all police officers careers start – The Rookie. I have then attempted to roughly follow the career path of some, but not all, police officers: working on patrol, moving into specialist departments and then, perhaps, if the officer was career minded in that way, moving into detective divisions such as Homicide and Vice. There are some stories that would easily fit into more than one category but I have placed these in the chapters where I felt they were best suited. The job, as you will read, can and does take its toll and the chapters Officer Down and The Negatives show this only too well. Emotionally, they were the toughest to write.

Towards the end of the book is one officer's experiences from 9/11, an incident like no other and an attack that took the lives of many thousands of people including sixty police officers. Firefighters had a reason to climb those towers (a staggering 343 of them were killed, including a chaplain and two paramedics). But police officers, who were not carrying breathing apparatus, hoses or fire resistant clothing, just did what cops do; they went there to do whatever they could to help, no matter what that might turn out to be. Heroes, every one of them. Cigar-chomping heroes with attitude, I like to think.

So here it is; America's police, telling it like it is.

1

The Rookie

'*What's it like being a rookie?*' *I asked the cop, as the patrol car he was driving dipped and bumped along a wide, potholed alleyway.*

'*Nobody knows you, nobody trusts you, nobody likes you,*' *he said.*

'*Other officers or the public?*'

'*Everyone.*'

Although this was not the experience of every new cop I spoke with, it did seem that each generation of police officer looks at the next generation with a level of suspicion and distrust. Times change, people change and cops change, and if there is one thing cops don't seem to like, it's change. So it can be tough being the new recruit – being the rookie.

Usually, one of two things would happen when I asked cops about their days as a rookie: either their eyes would light up and a broad grin would stretch across their face as they thought back to those early and exciting days in their careers, or else their faces would drop as they recalled the struggle and torment that came with being a new cop. You have to prove yourself and even then, that may not be enough. Time

9

served – time on the job – can mean everything, and that's the one thing a rookie doesn't have.

Being brand new, fresh out of the academy, with a pristine uniform, sparkling, unused equipment and a head full of the official line as taught by instructors who are just following the curriculum is one thing, but the reality of actually being out on the streets is – as I was told many times – something completely different.

Everyone has their own reasons for becoming a cop – family tradition, paycheque, something different – and many will have similar fears when they are the new kid: how will people treat me? Will I get shot on my first day? Will I have to shoot somebody on my first day? Will I screw up so badly I have to resign immediately?

There are some officers, however, who will not worry about any of those things. They will turn up with buckets of bravado, plenty of attitude and act like they have been doing the job longer than the Chief. These officers are usually brought down to size very quickly, if not by the realities of the job, then by other officers.

It can be a rough and extremely sharp learning curve, where even your own family and friends can turn against you. In the space of just a few weeks, days, even hours, you can go from a clueless, immature idealist to a hard-assed, streetwise sceptic. There are probably few jobs in the world where your very character and values can change so significantly and so quickly. The fact is, not everyone has what it takes and not all police officers make it past being a rookie.

―――――――――――――――

When I joined the police it was the worst day of my mother's life. Jews didn't become cops. I was the only Jew in my precinct for a long time. It wasn't a big thing but I was the only one. But it was weird, Jews in this country, you know, don't take menial labour jobs or stuff like that. Having a blue-collar job as a Jew is frowned upon in the United States. Well, we can't all be doctors and lawyers. I think it's changed a lot though, because the precinct I work in now has lots of Jews. I think the whole atmosphere has changed. But my mother thought it was the worst day of my life. She was very distraught.

Almost everybody in my academy class was Irish. Their families were just so proud but my mother was like, 'Oh my God! A cop?' I guess she got over it eventually, but I don't know.

This is also the woman who told me my whole life that I would grow up to be a ditch digger. I'm not sure being a cop was much better.

****

I joined the police department because I grew up in a bad neighbourhood of Staten Island, New York – predominately black and Hispanic – and whilst we were growing up we were burglarised nine times and I saw a lot of despair in the community and really, truthfully, I just wanted to become a cop. No family history, I'm the first. My mother didn't want it; my father didn't care. My mother thought it would make me very jaded. She wanted me to be a fireman. They get better pay because they steal. All firemen are thieves. I had a fireman tell me that you should 'never let good money burn'.

But my father was just happy that I had a paying job. That I was working and I have a pension. He just wanted to make sure that his kids were set for the rest of their lives with work, but my mother wanted me to be something more.

****

11

I had no burning desire to be a cop; didn't grow up my whole life saying, 'I'm gonna be a cop'. Nothing. I was a truck mechanic. I was a happy truck mechanic. I had a bad run of luck on trucks; I got run over, had a transmission fall on me, but still, never thought I was gonna be a cop.

I was on my way to an engagement party in New Jersey with a friend of mine. He didn't get the gift, I didn't get the gift, so we stop at this mall in Queens. As we're walking in, there's this cop standing there handing out applications to take the police test. I take it, fill out the application, took the test three months later and nine months after that I was hired as a cop. That's how I became a cop; I walked into a department store where a guy handed me a piece of paper. Twenty-four years later, if I could find that guy I would give him the biggest kiss. It was the greatest move that I ever took, but back then I didn't know it was the greatest move. In fact, I almost quit on my first day after getting to my precinct.

My first assignment ever – finished my training, finished the academy – my first assignment was to sit on a hospitalised prisoner. He was in the intensive care unit; I never saw so many wires and tubes coming out of a human being in my entire life. Everything you can imagine was hooked up to him.

I'm like, 'What the fuck am I doing here?'

He was handcuffed to the bed – this guy ain't going nowhere. He's going nowhere. Even if he wakes up, he ain't going nowhere!

I left that day saying, 'I just wasted eight hours of my fucking life.'

Back then I was a very active guy. I was within a hair's breadth of quitting. I was absolutely disgusted. I worked in a precinct with old timers, guys with a lot of time – anywhere from eighteen years to thirty years – and these guys would all say that being a cop was the greatest job they ever did. For my first five years on the job I didn't understand how they could possibly say this was the greatest job they ever did. I enjoyed it, but I didn't love it the way these other guys loved it. I couldn't understand loving the job to that level. I mean these guys *loved* the job. But somewhere around twelve years on the force I started to understand why people loved the job. And I'll tell you right now, it's the greatest job I'll ever have my entire life. The people you meet, the things you do; it's just the greatest job ever.

****

I was very, very lucky. My class was the last class before there was a hiring freeze and the precinct I went to was kind of split between younger cops and cops with a lot of time on the job. And because it was such a bad and busy place, everybody looked out for everybody else.

You quickly learnt how to do the job because you were working with guys who had like, fifteen to eighteen years on the force, so you just went out on patrol with them. Granted, they wouldn't let you drive, they wouldn't let you talk on the radio, they wouldn't let you say anything when you went to a job but they didn't treat you bad and if you made a mistake they'd just say, 'Don't ever fucking do that again', and they'd leave it at that.

You got all the shit assignments but in terms of learning how to do police work, they taught you how to do police work the right way, so that nobody was getting hurt. They taught you how to be a real cop. It wasn't like it is today where these kids have no idea; where the blind are leading the blind.

****

Some guys will look for a job in the wanted ads in the newspapers or else they're planning out their careers and going to college or whatever. But they look and they see that being a plumber pays this amount and an accountant pays that amount and a casino worker gets this amount. But the police pay this amount – therefore I'll be police. And if that's how you decided that you wanted to be a policeman, then you fucked up because that's not how it works. As lame as it sounds, the police picks you.

My mum worked for Highway Patrol, my Dad worked for Highway Patrol, my flop stepbrother worked for Highway Patrol but I was never interested in doing that. I was having a perfectly fine time making an ass-load of money building bridges. Then I started reading cop books. Then I started listening to cop stories. And then pretty soon I'm thinking, 'I've got to be a cop'. Do I know when that happened? No idea. But all of a sudden I decided I had to be a cop.

I went and told my boss and said, 'I've been here ten years. I'm leaving. I'm gonna go be a cop.'

'What for?'

'I don't know. I fucking do not know, but that's what I'm going to do.'

And that's how I decided.

A while later, I went to my police oral boards and they ask the question, 'Could you take a life if you had to?'

I say, 'Of course.'

'What makes you want to be a cop?'

And I said, 'Hey, I'm not here with the Miss America speech – I

14

don't wanna save the world. I don't want to work with disadvantaged children. It's a job that you need people to do and I think I can do it. When someone calls the cops for help, I wanna be the guy that shows up. I want to be the guy that fixes it, makes it right. If some little kid's lost and I find his parents, that's a victory to me. The rest after that is gravy, almost.'

Then they've look at my application and they go, 'How much money did you make building bridges last year?'

I said, 'Forty-two thousand dollars.'

They said, 'You know you start at twenty-six thousand here?'

And I said, 'Yeah, I know that.'

They said, 'Well, you're about smart enough to be a cop.'

****

The things that you see with the new generation that we're hiring and the thing that we're losing with our new generation, is the ability to communicate with other people.

One of the biggest things in this job is learning how to talk to people. But this new generation of cops, they don't know how to talk to people. Their interpersonal communication is zero. I mean, I don't know if it's because they are so used to texting rather than talking? The recruits now, they want to email or text rather than talk. I don't know if it's because these kids sit at home and play computer games all the time but they don't want to actually speak to you.

And the other one is, the ability to read and write – it's gone out the window. It's insane. Somehow I think it's all connected but I don't know how. It's so weird.

I give talks in high school and people always ask me, 'What courses should I take? Should I take criminal justice?'

I say, 'No. We'll teach you the law. We'll teach you search and seizure. We'll teach you how to use force. We'll teach you all the police stuff. You need to go out and take courses in English composition, public speaking and things like that because if you show up at my academy, I can't teach you how to talk to people. I can't teach you how to read and write. These are things you should be able to do *before* you become a cop!'

****

When I came on the job I was a reserve officer, I was nineteen and I was viewed as a spy for the Chief – I couldn't be trusted. No one knew who you were or they didn't know if you could do your job – handle yourself on the street – or if you were going to be a complete idiot. So you got the shit assignments. Everyone looked at you a little sceptical, like, 'let's see what this guy's going to be all about'.

Once you worked, you know, a couple of months, people realised that 'this guy's a good guy – he's nice, he knows what he's doing'. And so on. Once you've been to a couple of bar fights or calls with other officers, people accepted you and trusted you. But it took time.

****

The guys that are in The Bronx always say that The Bronx cops are the best and that The Bronx is the best place to work; they think they're really good and granted, they have some pretty decent restaurants and you can eat pretty good and hang out and drink pretty good. But then they sent me to Harlem. They sent six of us to this one place at the same time. We were all pretty much devastated as we all thought that we were staying in The Bronx and would live our lives as Bronx cops - and that would have been great but then you walk into the precinct in Harlem. You drive down the block and it's half abandoned and burnt out. It was a hellhole. Then you walk in the front door and the first thing you see on the wall are thirteen pictures of police officers who had been killed in the line of duty and this particular precinct has more officers murdered than any other precinct in the city.

That was a little bit eye opening and you think, 'Oh boy! What am I getting my hands into here?' But then you kind of get on with it. There ended up being some really good guys there – really sharp, smart, good guys. As far as I was concerned, they blew every Bronx guy I ever knew, away.

You were busy. In Harlem you'll do anywhere between ten and thirty of your own jobs – let alone backing up on jobs – in an eight hour period of time, especially on a weekend or a holiday. You and your partner were going from job to job to job. We're talking about a place that was a mile square, half abandoned and burnt out and they were averaging seventy plus murders a year. One place! And there'd probably be five hundred shootings of people that didn't die. It's not as bad now though. It's way better. They got the murder rate down. One year I think they had three, maybe five, if they even had that many. How did they get in down so low? A little bit of the police taking back the streets, you know? There was a period of time where the whole precinct, everybody, was on the same page. If there were lazy people, nobody would work with them or go near them. Everybody worked.

When you went to work, you knew that somebody was getting arrested, somebody's going to jail and you'd work in groups and teams to make that happen. And so we just took the streets back. And over time, all these really bad guys, well, we'd put them all in jail.

****

Have I seen a difference in the people we're hiring? Yes. The economy collapsing has caused a big problem. It's caused a big problem because people are losing their jobs and the police department has been recruiting. So people are like, 'Hey, the police department's hiring! Where else can I get a job and earn potentially seventy-five to eighty thousand dollars a year? It's enough to still raise a family, I get full benefits and it's a neat job. It's the full package. Where else can I get that? Well, I'm going to go be a police officer!'

So the economy has kind of become our recruiter. Whereas in the past we were recruiting people that were in colleges or coming out of the military and people that wanted to be police officers, now they're coming to us because they need a job. But they don't realise the amount of commitment required or what this job entails. And so they come into the academy and we run them through a myriad of high stress scenarios and they realise very quickly, 'Oh no, this is definitely not what I signed up to do.'

And so that's where our attrition rate also comes from – they just go away because they realise that this is more than a paycheque and some medical benefits. There's a whole other aspect to it that they didn't realise; the dangers, the commitment that it takes. I mean, you get guys in the academy on day one who show up thinking that the second they graduate from the academy, they're going to become homicide detectives. That's the kind of mentality that we're facing right now.

****

A lot of guys don't want to go the supervisor route, as they don't want to supervise these morons, because they are responsible for everything these rookie cops do. And they're morons!

I was taught how to talk, I was taught how to walk, I was taught how to hold myself regardless of what the job was that I responded to. Now you have a guy with two years on the job teaching a guy with six months on the job. How does that work? I got taught by guys with twenty years on the job.

****

You're like a newborn when you go out there. There's no way the academy can prepare you for what you are going to see every day and what you are going to do every day.

When they give you a radio and the car keys and say, 'Well, good luck!' That's a whole different feeling.

And I think you see more in your first year in Baltimore than you would in your whole career in some other jurisdictions. It's like dog years; one year in Baltimore is worth seven years elsewhere.

2

On The Job

*W*hether it's catching thieves, arresting drunks or reporting a traffic accident, day-to-day policing can have its own challenges (I
witnessed the widest range of emotions from officers on this chapter) and
there is a lot of truth in the adage that 'no two days are the same'. Simply
being on the job – out on patrol, doing what people expect police to do – it
is often the case that these are the days when the police officer will encounter the strangest, the funniest or the most dangerous situations. A SWAT
officer told me that he had found working regular patrol to be far more
dangerous than working SWAT because officers often patrolled alone and
were unprepared when the unexpected happened.

Something I often heard officers say was, 'All the stories just blend
into one.' That alone was testament to just how much a police officer does
and sees day in, day out, throughout their career. I would occasionally
see an officer struggling to think back and recall a particularly interesting
tale to tell me about. But the truth is, each and every one of them could
probably give me enough material for an entire book on their own.

Being 'on the job' and working the streets every day, police officers

20

become numb to what it is they are required to do and they often forget just how unusual their job can be. To them it's just another arrest, another car chase, another incident. But to those who do not inhabit their world, it is all funny, fascinating, shocking and new. So I encouraged them to just tell me something – anything – even if they didn't think it was all that interesting. But of course, these stories would be interesting and if that incident, whatever it might have been, had been the one, single thing the officer had told me about in the course of the interview, it would have been worth it for that alone. And by getting the officers to focus on just one of these incidents, it would always lead them to other stories as their memories opened up.

'There are so many times I wished I'd kept a journal, just because everyday something happens that most people would be amazed by,' an officer in Michigan told me.

The tales and experiences I heard were a real mixed bag. Talks with some of these officers would last just a few minutes whereas others would, and did, go on for a good few hours. The stories ranged from funny to sad, routine to outlandish. Officers laughed, officers cried. The interviews varied widely and that, of course, is just how policing is.

Your friends always ask you, 'What's it like being a police officer? Tell me a cool story.'

And you have to wonder, well, what is a cool story? What do you mean by that?

****

Our officers encountered a guy sitting on the kerb, bleeding profusely from the testicles. He had gone to this man to get his balls removed and this guy advertised that he could do that. He did it in his house. So on this dudes kitchen table, he took his balls off and when we did the search of the house we found the balls in the fridge. In a Tupperware bowl. And his name was Dr Wang. I mean you can't make this shit up! Wang, the ball cutter!

The long and the short of it is – no pun intended – the victim had sought out this person through some homosexual website and sought out this guy because he wanted his testicles removed. Apparently there are a lot of people that want this to happen; there are people that want this done. But at the time you couldn't just go into a doctor's office, because they wouldn't do it. So there was this website – eunuch dot com or some crap – which is where he found this cat. So he goes in this guy's house, they have some small talk or whatever and then he jumps up on the dining-room table and this kid proceeds to remove his testicles. Now the kid said that testicles are a delicacy and he actually had them in a Tupperware bowl in the refrigerator with some, like, strawberry pie. And they had even shared some pie. You can't make this shit up! Have some pie and have your balls cut off!

So the officers show up and they see the guy and his jeans are just saturated in blood. At first we were treating this as an assault with intent to maim – this is what we're thinking – but the victim said that he hadn't been assaulted. He said that he had come here for this express purpose.

Well ultimately, you've got to charge somebody with something; you don't call the police and have all this going on without somebody going to jail. So they charged the guy with operating without a medical licence. Wang, the ball cutter.

****

I got called to relieve a swing shift unit – they were doing a standard burglary report but they had to go and do something else – so me and my partner went to take over and we made contact with the two officers.

They're like, 'Yeah, we cleared the house, everything's good. Here's the owner of the building. He's got all the information so that you can take the report or whatnot.'

So we're sitting there and as my partner and I are talking, this stuff starts falling off the roof above us – you know, the popcorn ceiling, so to speak.

I'm thinking, that's odd. And then, ten seconds later, – 'CRASH!' – the suspect comes falling through the ceiling, literally right onto the table in front of us.

The guy had scampered into the roof when the previous two cops came but they didn't go up and check that area.

The burglar was hiding up there and as he was trying to sneak out he just happened to drop right through the roof, right onto the table where we were sat! We were literally sitting down, taking the report and started to see a couple of white things falling and then we look up and CRASH! He comes right down on top of us. And we're like, 'Whoooooa!' and then the scramble was on! We got him into custody but we had a chuckle about it later on.

We told the previous two guys, 'Hey, thanks for the prisoner!'

How about that!

****

I stopped this woman for speeding once. You know what she said to me? She said, 'Oh officer, it's just that I really need to take a shit!'

23

I mean, what are you supposed to say to that?

****

Had this interesting vehicle situation once, where this one-legged guy was having a fight with his girlfriend. It was night and he got out of the car in six lanes of road. He crawled across the first three lanes, got to the median, started to cross the next three and then got run over. Then he got run over again. And then he got run over a third time.

When we arrived we were trying to figure out what happened here, because there is blood splatter but the blood's not disturbed. This doesn't even make sense. How does the blood not get disturbed yet the blood is splattered? Well, finally we found out he got run over and over and over. The blood would collect in pools, cars would run through it, splattering the blood and then the blood would pool back in again. And so the blood looked undisturbed yet it was splattered. He got run over several times and he was quite a way down the road from the initial impact.

I had a brand new trainee with me that was pretty green and was just kind of getting in my way whilst I was trying to deal with this situation – I was there to train him but I had to deal with things and he was getting in the way – so I sent him looking for the guys other leg.

I said to him, 'Obviously a car took off his leg, and this leg has gotta be somewhere, so go find the leg.'

So he spent half-an-hour looking for the leg before I finally explained to him that this one-legged guy never had it to start with.

****

One of the things about police work that I liked was the independence and the autonomy. You're out there by yourself, you don't have anybody sitting there looking over your shoulder, not even your sergeant.

A sergeant will have maybe eight guys to look after and most of the old time sergeants, well, you couldn't even find 'em, much less have 'em show up for a serious call or something. You wouldn't know where in the hell they might be. They were probably with their mistress or who knows where. You couldn't find them.

So, you were on your own and I loved that. I loved that independence, that autonomy of being out there and making my own decisions, deciding how I was going to handle a situation.

Before I became a cop, I used to work on an assembly line. I hated assembly line work. I hated somebody looking over my shoulder. Police work was great, though. You checked your car out and you hit the streets and you were on your own. Sure, you had to answer the radio calls and you went to where they sent you but otherwise you were totally your own boss. You could make your own decisions as to what you were going to do. And back in the day you really had to screw up royally to get into trouble.

I guess I took to it like a duck takes to water. I liked it. I liked being out there by myself.

****

There was always a level of complaints that came with the job. Back in the day, I received a lot of complaints. The reason? Because I didn't take any shit and I made a lot of arrests. The way it was looked at back then was, if you're an active guy and you make a lot of arrests and you're very involved, then you're gonna get a lot of complaints because that's just the nature of the business. People don't like being arrested and being made to do things they don't want to do, so they figure that the only way to get back at you is to make a complaint. So I got a lot of complaints. Some of those complaints may have been legit. Most of them probably were not.

I got this complaint one time and I actually enjoyed going down to testify for it. We were chasing a car with four guys in it and at one point this car got blocked in by other cars at a red light, the car couldn't go anywhere. The passenger in the front seat threw a gun out of the window and then the car proceeded to smash through every car in front of it to get away. I was the passenger in the squad car so I jumped out to recover the gun but at that point the lane ahead of us had cleared, so my partner takes off after the car. So now I am left standing on the corner and I've got the gun but everybody's gone, right? They grabbed these guys twenty blocks away in some building and naturally they got stomped. They tried to get away and they got stomped. You don't try to run from the police. They got their asses kicked. Now I'm twenty blocks away, I'm standing there holding the gun, right? But I became the arresting officer.

One of the kid's mothers didn't like what she saw, so she made a complaint. She thought there was too much force used. I was the arresting officer so I got the complaint. I go down to the complaint review board and I confirm that I was the arresting officer and they ask me to tell them what happened.

'I really can't tell you what happened,' I told them.

'What do you mean you can't tell us what happened?'

'Well, I was twenty blocks away when these guys got apprehended.'

'What do you mean you were twenty blocks away? You're the arresting officer. Who else was at the scene?'

But I really didn't know who was on the scene. There were cops from four different commands on the scene. My partner could testify to the apprehension and I could testify to seeing the guy throw the gun out of the window so it was all good. As far as who beat them? Couldn't tell you.

Nothing ever came from it because everyone knew it was all bullshit. The complaint was just retaliation against the police for arresting these people. The more important the person was on the street, the more likely you were getting a complaint.

****

I had a funny arrest once where there was a local criminal who was kind of a tough guy – a cop fighter. We were in the precinct one day and this other young fellow – who is known locally as being a homosexual – he comes running into the precinct and he's going, 'He's going to kill me! He's going to kill me!'

He's running around the precinct and we are all just staring at this little homosexual guy. Then the criminal – this tough guy – comes in chasing him.

He goes, 'Come here you little faggot! Get over here!'

And the other guy's going, 'He's going to kill me! He's going to kill me!'

The tough guy chases him around and then chases him out of the precinct.

We're all just standing there looking at each other saying, 'What the hell was that?'

So we go running out and the tough guy has got him at the front of the building and he's smacking him around. We arrested the both of them in order to find out what was going on. Turns out the criminal –

the tough guy – he was horny and drunk and he wanted to hit the little homosexual guy in the butt, to get some sex.

But the little guy had said, 'If you don't get some KY Jelly to make it easy on me, I don't want you to do it.'

So they got into an argument and he started chasing him down the block. And you have to stand there and listen to people and go, 'Oh really? Oh…' and be this sensitive person, but inside you are laughing your head off.

This is what you're fighting about? This is why you are running around the precinct? This is why you want to beat this guy up?

You can't make this stuff up!

****

Where I worked it was such a horrible place it was actually called 'The Tomb of Gloom'. The Tomb of Gloom was actually the name of the precinct and it was a horrible, depressed place. The people who lived in the command area had no money but they all had guns and they all had drugs and that's how the place survived.

The one thing the older cops taught you was that you don't take any shit on the street, because if you let somebody take advantage of you, the next guy that comes along, they're going to try and take advantage of them even harder. If you told a group of kids to move off a street corner and they didn't move off the street corner, then you made them move off that street corner with as much force as necessary. If it meant you whacked them over the head to get them to move, you whacked them over the head to get them to move. If they still didn't move, then five more cops showed up, beat the balls off of them and locked them up. Then they never gave you a problem again.

You wouldn't do that now. If you did that now you would probably go to prison.

****

Guys' on the midnight shift were fooling around and accidentally fired a gun and shot a bullet through the Chief's wall. Luckily, one of the guys had family who owned the local hardware store. So they broke into the Chief's office and got the bullet out of the wall. Then they had to get sheet rock, sand over the bullet hole in the wall, get paint, paint the wall real quick and then lock the office before anyone noticed. They spent half the shift doing it.

There were four or five bullet holes in that station from accidental discharges over the years.

****

I almost shot a small kid. We were going to a 'gun run', to a four or five-storey walk up, something like that.

A job came over the radio, we were assigned, there was a man with a gun in a building and we get there and we go into the building and I'm the first guy on the stairs, going up the building. I hear some people above us, hear somebody running down the stairs and it was a twelve-year-old kid with a freaking toy gun in his hand. I came so close to shooting this kid.

They changed the law. Now fake guns are orange or there has to be a certain amount of orange on the gun. But back then they looked real. I could have easily have shot the kid – killed him and probably gotten away with it. He came within arm's length of me and I just grabbed him. And it was a toy gun.

But this was in Harlem and your gun was always out in Harlem. You go to a gun run in Harlem and there's a building and you're walking up the stairs, yeah, your gun's in your hand.

29

****

I had this fight with this one guy where, if I could have got to my gun, I would have shot him.

It was a domestic violence call. We came out and there was a girl in the front yard and she said that her boyfriend – who she was having trouble with – was inside. So I go inside to see if he's in there and as I was looking through the place, he comes charging out of a room and attacks me and we started fighting from there.

He was empty handed but he was high on PCP, very strong – he was a skinny little kid but he was just throwing me around the room. I mean, we had broken through a door, we had broken holes in the wall, we'd broken a waterbed – he was just throwing me around like a rag doll. It's getting to where I am physically tired; I'm losing this fight. I train in combat, I'm second degree black belt in martial arts and I used to teach martial arts for years, so I'm able to handle myself but like I say, he was kicking my butt.

So I finally got to where I'm going to have to shoot him because I just couldn't go any further. But we broke the waterbed and he was half on the bed and half on the floor and I was able to get him trapped down, inside the folds of the waterbed. He couldn't get out – he was stuck inside the weight of the bed. That was the only way that I was able to get him under control or I would have ended up shooting him.

The funny thing is, I had three officers who were outside and this guy's girlfriend was kinda cute. All three of those officers was there flirting with her whilst I'm getting killed inside. They figured that if I needed them, I would get on the radio. But I couldn't get on the radio because I wasn't able to actually get to my radio. So yeah, that was kinda funny.

We Are The Cops

****

I'll tell you a great story. We get called out to an 'Assault One', where the guy was barely alive in an SRO – Single Room Occupancy. My partner and I got out there and there's blood everywhere. The guy was bludgeoned and there was blood all over this place and so we started treating it like a homicide crime scene, the whole nine yards.

We're working on it for a while and one of the uniformed cops grabs us. He says, 'Listen, I'm not sure if I should tell you this or not but when the first two cops got to the scene, there was a guy leaving the building who had red stuff on his pants.'

I'm like, 'You're kidding, right?'

'No. He told them he was doing some painting and he'd got red paint on his pants. So they let him go.'

I'm like, 'You're kidding right? And if you're not kidding, why the fuck did you tell me?'

So now we know that the first two cops on the scene let the perp go. They just let him go. Uniform cops.

So now my partner and I get hold of these two cops and say, 'Tell us about the guy that was leaving the building when you first got here.'

They said, 'He told us he had red paint on his pants.'

'And you believed him? Have you seen the fucking room?'

That was a real struggle. I mean what the fuck do we do with that information? Do we have these two cops get killed? You know what I'm saying? I mean, do we give these two cops up and have them killed? They would have been killed! Luckily we were able to review the videotape and there was a guy on it and we were able to track him down. So we never killed those cops. We just called them morons.

But my partner and I are from a precinct where everybody got on great. I mean we could have ruined their careers but it was handled really discreetly. Granted, at the end of the day everybody knew but it was handled in a way where these two guys didn't get killed.

****

Because we work under such extreme circumstances, when somebody was calling for help everybody would go. If you were processing an arrest in the station and you heard somebody screaming for help over the radio, you ran out the front door. Half the time you ran out the front door without a gun because you had to lock your gun up when you had an arrest. Half the time you would run out the door, jump in a car, you'd get to the scene and go to grab your gun and you wouldn't have it. You'd be like, 'oh fuck'.

So me and my partner are in front of the station house one day and somebody starts screaming over the radio and this other cop jumps into the back of our car. We didn't invite him in – he just jumps into the back of the car. We're like the first or second car on the scene and you know how when a car is still moving and you open the door and put your foot down? Your foot stays there and the car keeps moving? Well, my partner was the driver at the time and this guy does that exact thing from the back of the car. The car hasn't stopped yet, he swings the door open, goes to step out, his right foot hits the ground, stays still and the car runs him over. So he actually gets ripped out of the car because his foot is stuck under the wheel.

So now I get out of the passenger side of the car and I'm like, 'Are you okay?'

And he's like, 'Yeah, yeah, but the wheel is on my foot!'

So I'm like, 'Back the car up! The wheel is on his foot! Back the car up!'

My partner rolls the car forward and runs him over again!

I'm like, 'No, no! You've got to back up!'

So he backs up and rolls over him a third time! Runs him over three times!

****

Cops like overtime; we have these expressions: 'we turn the trash into cash' and 'collars for dollars'.

****

I've been around the world; cops are the same everywhere. They complain about the exact same thing: pay and overtime. If you were just a regular patrolman, you made shit.

There are two guarantees with this job – you're never going to starve but you're never going to be rich either.

****

I remember driving around on 'midnights' and we would be look-ing for collars because you made the most money in overtime on midnights. You made an arrest on a midnight shift and you couldn't process it 'til eight in the morning, so you'd get seven or eight hours overtime.

I remember driving around three cars deep and we would just be going up and down the block jumping out on people, throwing them against the wall, patting them down and going through their pockets. If they had bullshit contraband – like knives or brass knuck-les – we would just take it from them and send them on their way. It was almost like legalised fucking robbery. We never stole anything though; we never stole money or anything, but it was just like, you know, like here's a knife. No, that's not good enough, get rid of it.

He's got brass knuckles. No, no. We need felonies. Get rid of 'em. We were looking for guns; we're looking for drugs. Knives and brass knuckles were not good enough. If we found those we would smack 'em on the back on the head and send them on their way. I remember thinking, 'we're fucking robbing these people'.

That was common; that was every fucking night. And it would only start after three or four in the morning. You couldn't really do it after six – you had to stop by five because there were decent people that lived there. So you had a short window to get this accomplished. Anybody out on the street at three o'clock in the morning in Harlem on like, a Tuesday night, is not a good person.

****

My neighbourhood that I work in is the absolute worst neighbourhood in Boston. But I'm so complacent and so comfortable there that I don't even – and don't tell this to my husband – sometimes I don't even wear my bullet-proof vest. I should wear it at all times but I'm like, 'whatever'. Sometimes my back is hurting or whatever, so I'll just leave it in the locker, you know, give my back a break. But there are certain areas I will not go out to without wearing it.

They don't make the best vests for women either. They're all lumpy and gross. But I have been to The Bronx in New York and I'm like, 'Jesus Christ! I wish I was in a bullet-proof car, never mind a vest!' Everybody over there looks like a criminal. Everybody! It's totally different to Boston.

The vests are bad and they make these pants for the women that go up over your belly whereas the men have pants that sit at their waist, so I buy the men's pants as they fit me better. I don't want to wear pants that are just over my belly button. It's so uncomfortable, you know? It's not the 1970's anymore; it's time to upgrade our uniforms.

****

This woman calls the station. I'm doing a report. It's like two o'clock in the morning.

'Police, can I help you?'

This woman's screaming hysterically and I'm pulling the phone from my ear. This was right before we had Enhanced 911.

'What's the problem ma'am?'

'My baby's not breathing!'

'Okay. Where are you calling from?'

'I don't know where I am. I know the town but I don't know the name of the road.'

I'm then having to multi-task. I don't have any dispatch training. I'm a cop – I'm not a dispatcher. I'm trying to explain how to do child CPR whilst trying to get little bits and pieces of information about where she's calling from to the ambulance, to get them rolling in the right direction. I'm basically doing this for four to five minutes.

'Do you remember what part of town you came into? Keep doing the compressions, keep doing the blows. Did you pass any businesses?'

'We turned left onto a major road.'

'Okay, the main town road, this is good. Do you remember getting to a blinking light?'

'No, we turned off before we got to a blinking light. There was a big picture of a strawberry.'

So now I know roughly where they are. I get the ambulance going in that direction and at the same time she's screaming hysterically doing CPR on an un-breathing infant.

Finally I figure out where she was and she says, 'I can see the ambulance!'

I'm like, 'Thank God! I'm going to let the line go now ma'am.'

I got into the cruiser and started to head up that way and as I'm close by, the ambulance got on the air and… and… and all I could hear was a screaming child. So they managed to get the kid back. So…

(At this point the officer broke down and began to cry)

It certainly makes up for long nights of bullshit and drunks. You don't mind getting banged up physically every now and then; it's just the emotional toll that this job can take on you if you are not careful. It's awful.

****

Anybody you put cuffs on instantly becomes the toughest guy in the world – 'I'll fuck you!' or 'I'll beat your ass!' – because they know you're not going to touch them when they're in handcuffs.

So we used to have this thing where I'd say to my partner, 'Hey, he's got my cuffs on and I need them back.'

Then we'd take the cuffs off and as soon as the cuffs were off we'd say, 'Okay motherfucker, what are you going to do now motherfucker?'

They'd always back down.

****

The department has changed its ways a little bit. It's been up and down over the years but now they're actually letting us defend ourselves and use some offence. If someone throws a freaking punch at your face, you don't have to risk trying a twist lock or an evasive move or run back and pull you're stick out. Now you can block the punch and pop them right in the freaking pie-hole. But not everyone has these skills; everyone wasn't raised in a bar or everyone doesn't go to the gym and do the 'Billy Blanks' or MMA practice or anything.

What this job all boils down to, to me – after twenty-two years – is if you've got to kick someone's ass, you've got to kick someone's ass and you can't let your own ass get kicked because you've got too much shit on. If you get knocked out by someone, that person suddenly has a taser and a stick and a gun to fuck up all your friends with. So you can't lose. We won't lose and we will survive. I was always told, 'If you get shot, fight through it.'

They show all those inspirational officer safety films now but our shit is mostly, simply dealing with staying on top of things. I always say to officers, 'Kick ass! Kick ass!'

Being able to defend yourself, being able to protect yourself, that's important but unfortunately there're people on the department who couldn't fight their way out of a wet paper sack.

****

I carry a knife. In fact I carry a bunch of knives. I have one just for when I go to the bathroom, because we had an officer once, go to the bathroom and a guy came up behind him and he was on a head and this guy comes in and the next thing you know, BOOM! He jams him in and starts going for his gun. So the officer grabbed his knife, reached back and caught that artery in the guy's thigh; he sliced it wide open.

So I carry one knife in my vest, two on my belt and another one on my hip. You're not going to be good friends with a guy if you use a knife but it's legal for us to carry them. I also carry two guns, one as a back-up weapon, here inside my shirt. So I carry two guns – and I've got another one in the car – four knives and pepper spray. I don't carry a taser.

Most of the knives I use can be defensive but also used at scenes, you know? If I need to cut a branch out of the way, I've got a knife that saws. But some knives are for defence. This one in my vest is an attention getter. It's a conversational piece. Some people carry a knife on the back of their neck too – on the back of their vest. You just reach up, grab it and come down. But most times, if you pull your knife out, that means you can't get to your gun. But that's why I also have a second, back-up gun. I used to keep it on my left side, under the shirt. Now I keep it on my right side. It's a 40 calibre.

I've had one time where a guy tried to get my gun and I'm holding my gun in the holster to stop him from pulling it out whilst I'm fighting him. But I couldn't get my second gun because if I went for my backup I'd have to release the other gun and leave it open. So now I keep it on this side where I can reach it and shoot through my shirt. Bang, bang, bang. I've done that before - I have shirts with holes in them – just to practice.

****

We have moose accidents quite a bit. There's certainly a lot of wildlife in Alaska and it seems that moose have a habit of going out on the roadway when you don't want them to be on the roadway, especially if you're in a little car.

One of the accidents I dealt with – where someone hit a moose – was a teacher on her way to the school. It was still wintertime and it was dark out and she was in a little four-door sedan car and ended up hitting this moose that had run out into the road in front of her.

The moose just came up and hit the car, smashed in the hood and after it hit the hood it rolled up and smashed the window and started to cave in the roof a little bit, so it was certainly a scary moment for that driver. Kind of like, 'Oh my God! Here's a moose! And now it's crushing my car!' That driver escaped any injury but it sure did a number on her car.

A lot of time with the moose, we'll have to shoot them and put them down. But we'll call a charity to come salvage the moose meat and the moose meat will get dispersed to different people that the charity feels are in need of moose meat. It's quite a thing up here – we have our dispatch centres that usually have a list of who the on-call charity is for the night, in case we end up dealing with a moose accident. So we'll call them up and say, 'Hey, we have a moose accident. We've got a moose here on Mile 90 of the Sterling Highway, come meet us and pick up the moose.' And they'll have a couple of people come out and do their thing, pick up the moose and take it back to where they have a place set up. Then they'll butcher the moose and take care of it.

I've shot moose a couple of times. Sometimes the moose are pretty badly injured when they get hit by a vehicle - but they're still alive. So we would dispatch the moose, call the charity and have them come pick it up. The troopers, they issue us a shotgun, so they give us a large enough weapon to dispatch a moose.

It's interesting because I'm not really a big hunter; my idea of getting meat is going to the store. I get my meat there. So it was quite a different experience for me when I started dealing with these accidents involving moose and I had to shoot the moose. I'd look at that poor injured moose and I'd have to kill it so it's not suffering. But it was a different experience for me not being a hunter or having killed an animal before.

****

On one side of the street is the city and the other side of the street is the county. So a lot of the times we will donate our problems to the city. And it's literally, 'Get the fuck out of the county and go across the street if you want to be a dickhead.'

Or we'll put them in our car and drive them ten or fifteen blocks up the road into the city and kick them out, or something like that.

****

Prisons – a lot of them are not rehabilitating people. A lot are actually making them better criminals or harder criminals or smarter criminals, stronger criminals. And they do it with taxpayers' money.

I believe people can turn around but for some people there's no hope; they're just hardened criminals – career criminals – they're not going to change, they're not going to come out and get a 9 to 5 job. They're going to come out and if they want your iPod, they're going to beat you or they're going to shoot you and they're going to take it. And that's the way they are. So those people should be locked up, kept away.

It's not about rehabilitating them, it's just about keeping them away from innocent people.

****

This woman took her dog into court. The magistrate shouts at her to take the dog out.

She said, 'But your honour, this dog is my witness!'

The judge went crazy. There were four cops dragging her out, an arm and leg each, with her dog snarling and snapping at them.

****

Our old booking facility had the old, electronic sliding doors that close real slow; big heavy doors, in the custody area. This one part of it was kind of a holding cell for all different kinds of people; you'd bring somebody in, you'd swipe your card, the door would open and you'd put your guy - your prisoner - in there and the door would close. Then another door would open to a room and your guy would go sit in there with multiple other people.

I was working on paperwork for one of my own prisoners. I went to get my guy out of the holding cell and the door opened real slow. Once I got my guy out, the door started to close again, real slow.

As it was closing there was somebody else's prisoner inside and he wants to ask me a question and he goes, 'O... o... off... officer. O... o... officer.' And I could tell that he's got a stutter when he's talking. So the door is starting to close and he's stuttering and he's like, 'O...o...o...officer, l...le...le...let me ask you a question officer.'

And the door's closing and I go, 'Dude, you'd better hurry up.'

And he's like, 'I... I... I just want to ask, I... I... d... d... do... do... do you know... do... do you k... k... know...' And it's just getting closer and closer - it's just inches from being closed. And right before it closes he goes, 'I... I... I... j... j... just... a... a... a... ah fuck it!' And the door closes.

****

I don't know if it's an average but I think most police officers do about twenty-five years service. Most of them figure, twenty-five is enough and then get out, although it depends on a person's attitude and what they're doing, I guess.

They did away with age limits in the States and we just had a

41

guy – a colleague of mine – retire at fifty years. Fifty years service! He's seventy-five years old. He came on in 1962. He was a patrol sergeant and he worked the streets right up to the end – up to the time he retired. It was incredible but he stayed in good health and good shape.

At fifty years he gets a hundred percent of his salary. The way it works is you get two percent for every year you work. So at fifty years, he retires at one hundred percent.

I don't know how long he'll live to enjoy it thought!

****

One of our traffic cars hit a deer and it scurried off into the woods. Well, it damaged the vehicle and as Crime Scene Investigators, we had to go take pictures of it. In the process of going out there and doing all that, they had to shoot the deer and put it down and everything.

So we go out there and I pull out my knife and I field dressed the deer, got all the meat off of it. That meat is in my freezer. I did it the redneck way – no blood involved. The way I do it, there's hardly any blood. I go in through the back. I do it inside out. I leave all the guts right inside. One side we didn't get though. One side was pretty tore up from the accident.

My partner said, 'That only took you ten minutes.'

I said, 'It would only have taken five minutes if you'd keep your flashlight turned off.' Because, you know, poaching in the backwoods, you do it in the dark.

Deer meat is really good meat. There's no fat in it. It's good-for-you meat.

But my partner had his flashlight on, so I was actually concentrating on what I was doin'. Normally I'd just do it in darkness and do it by feel.

But I'm no redneck. A hillbilly is a redneck that graduated high school. And I graduated high school.

****

Midnights are always a good time to play jokes on each other, like putting pepper spray on the toilet seats, so when someone takes a dump they get their ass on fire.

People have also been known to take a little nap on the night shift. That's usually when the jokes start. We had a guy that fell asleep on the midnight shift; he's out, he's drooling.

One of our local residents came to the station and rang the bell. I opened it up and said, 'What's up?

'That cop is sleeping in front of the station again!'

Now, a friend of mine is a heavy equipment operator and he's got a ten-wheel dump truck. So I called him and asked, 'Are you up right now? I'll buy you a cup of coffee, I need you for something.'

He got his truck and we inched it up as quietly as possible. He got within ten feet of this cop's cruiser.

I said, 'Okay, when I tell you to, I want you to turn the bright lights on and get on the air horn.'

So he puts the high beams on and pulls the air horn - UUUR-RGGGHHHHHHH!

All I see is this cop waking up, eyes the size of dinner plates and he's going at the steering wheel trying to turn the car, thinking he fell asleep at the wheel and he's about to die! Hahahahahahahaha!

****

After twenty-two years on the force I can only think of about three guys – cops – that were beaters and bullies. But I'm sure there're many, many more.

In my twenty-two years I've hit three people in handcuffs – in twenty-two years. The first one was as a rookie. I was working 'graveyard' on my own and everything's a fight. You're working graveyard, you're in Vegas and just north of here was my neighbourhood – it was Paradise and Flamingo. There were titty bars and there were redneck bars and everything was a fight, which was fun; so I went through uniforms like mad because you're always rolling around on the ground.

Well, back to my first guy, punching him in handcuffs: I've got a guy and I'm taking him to jail and this is before we had cages, so he's sitting on the passenger side. I opened the back door – because when you get to the jail you have to take your gun, weapons and all your other crap off and drop them in the back of your car – I'd opened up the back door to put my gun and stuff in and as I leaned inside, this guy's sitting in the front seat – on the passenger side – and he just leaned back from the front seat and spat right in my face. It was less than a second after that that I went BANG! – I just drove his head right straight back, down into the seat. Then I put my stuff back in my holsters, closed the car door, went back around, got into the car and drove him to the frigging hospital. That was the end of that. It was that simple. I didn't sit there and hammer on him for ten minutes, I didn't call him names, I didn't kick him; it was just 'spit', 'smack' and off we go to stitch you up.

****

Where else are they going to give you a gun, a badge, a fast car and tell you to go play with ten of your best friends every night?

3

K-9

*D*riving down the interstate, the cop sitting next to me was fairly quiet. He was expecting a 'ride-along' but he wasn't expecting to tell his life story to the English guy holding the small, slightly sinister looking, digital recorder. In between dealing with a traffic accident, reporting a hit-and-run against a garden fence and looking for a missing ten-year-old child (whose mother suggested we locked him up when we found him, which we did), I did my best to assure the officer that everything was above board and that he could speak to me openly and in confidence. Even so, he remained quiet and seemed to have little to tell me. That happened sometimes.

I asked him about his career and in particular, the various roles he had taken on, in an attempt to find something we could discuss. He casually mentioned that he had been a K-9 handler and I was about to skip onto something else when suddenly he started talking. And he didn't stop talking – or smiling. The officer's face beamed as he talked about his dog and it was obvious just how much his dog had become a part of his career. For some other officers I spoke with, it was career defining.

Obviously many of these dogs are genuinely brave and smart but it was when one particular officer was telling me about just how incredibly stupid his dog was, that I became struck by what was a real sense of loyalty, not just dog to handler, but handler to dog. The crazier the dog behaved, it seemed, the bigger the grin that would develop across the officer's face as he recounted past glorious – and not so glorious – incidents.

In many states across America, K-9's – police dogs – carry the same status as police officers themselves. Many dogs will even have their own badge. Each year, many police officers are killed in the line of duty in the United States. Many K-9s are too and each year the duty deaths for police dogs, reaches double figures. To their handlers, to their departments and to their fellow officers, police dogs are one of the team.

I'd just become a K-9 officer – one of the first that the department had had for years – and I had this dog that was a 'green' dog, which means it can't do anything; it can bite the shit out of you and that's about it.

That dog just ate me alive for about eight week on the training course until they eventually got rid of it. I still have the scars to prove it. He didn't like to give up his toy and he didn't like to release when it came to the bite work. He would get pissed off – like, 'you're taking something away from me and I don't like it!' So his way of lashing out was to bite the shit out of me. I liked the dog but I didn't like the fact that he was biting me all the time.

So they got rid of that dog and they got me a second dog. I had him for a week but that dog *didn't* bite. So then I get my third dog. This one was 'titled' and it did everything that I needed it to do.

Then about a month later I ended up getting bit by another dog, on the hand, just a few days before we graduated. We were doing release work and I was wearing a training sleeve, which had an open end with a wooden dowel on the inside so that you could hold onto it and it wouldn't get pulled off your hand. But the dog came up, missed my arm and caught my hand and just ripped the skin, basically. So I was out of work for four months. I had an infection, so the skin didn't heal and I had this big, giant hole in my knuckle.

So after four months I go back to work and I'm on the streets with my dog and one night he was supposed to bite somebody but when I gave him the command, he kind of looked at me like, 'bite who?' That was the icing on the cake for me and that dog.

So I got rid of him and I called the trainer the next day and I told him about the incident and he said he'd call the broker, who was the guy who would get dogs for our department.

I said, 'Look, I'm about ready to put a fucking bullet into this dog and throw him in the fucking river. This is bullshit. He ain't worth a damn. He's taking up space in the back of the car.'

So I told them that I wanted a Malinois. I ain't fucking around this time. So I get this Malinois and it was a total retard – I probably shouldn't have been in K-9 because I had nothing but issues. Anyway, I get this dog and the head trainer says to me, 'I hope they give you a pretty decent sized Malinois because you're so tall.'

Well, he gets this motherfucker out and it's a standard sized Malinois. Forty-four pounds. And it's sick, you could see ribs and everything. This dog had come right from Slovakia. They picked him up at Newark – at the airport – and then brought him to me. So I'm thinking that they obviously don't take care of the dogs, especially if they're getting rid of them. And they do say that the K-9's in the States are the rejects from Europe. But so what, he was skinny, whatever.

So next thing you know, they start evaluating him and he does okay and everything. So it was like, 'Here he is. Here's your dog.'

Well, I put him in the car and for the next twelve weeks it proceeds to pee out of his ass in my fuckin' car about twenty times a day. Every time he goes in the back of the car, he shits all over it. Diarrhoea. Well, being the retard that he was, he circled. I don't know if you're familiar with Malinois but they pick one way and then they go around in circles, so he would do that in the car and the shit would end up all over the fuckin' car. I mean it was obvious that he was sick so I took him to the vet.

I said, 'Hey doc, there's something wrong with this dog. He's peeing out of his ass. He's not putting any weight on. In fact he's losing weight.'

So he tells me that there's nothing wrong with him.

I'm like, 'There's got to be something wrong with this dog.'

But the doc says no. No worms, no nothing.

Twelve weeks in – I'm a few weeks from graduating – he's skin and bones. He's still peeing out of his ass. This motherfucker, there's something wrong with him. I'm telling them that they need to find out what's wrong with this dog because I can't have this. We're so busy, if he shits in my car, I don't have time to clean it up, because now I have to go somewhere that has a hose and clean shit out of the car. And nine out of ten times, he's got it all over him because he's kicking the shit all over the fucking back of the car.

So I bring in what bit of a stool sample that I can to be tested and they find out that he's got round worm, hock worm and whipworm. I'm like, 'Well, what the fuck!'

Next thing you know, they put him on the medicine and then, within a couple of days, his stool is nice and hard, he's putting on a little bit of weight but he's still shitting ten, twelve times a day. So I'm like, 'He's not eating enough food to be shitting what's coming out.'

He got down to forty-two pounds and I get him out of the car one day and hooked a leash on him. I've got a car that says 'K-9' all over it, I've got a vest on that says 'K-9' all over it and this lady is driving down the road in her car, sees this dog and she suddenly screeches to a halt and she says, 'Oh my! I'm gonna call the SPCA on you!'

I said, 'For what?'

She goes, 'That dog is sick!'

So thinking quickly, I said, 'This isn't my dog!'

She goes, 'What you mean it's not your dog?'

I said, 'This isn't my dog. I found this dog and I'm about ready to go arrest the owner right now and put him in jail for abuse!'

She says, 'Oh, I was about ready to report you for animal cruelty!'

I said, 'Yeah, that's where I'm going right now. To arrest the owner.'

So anyway, I take him back but they say that now there's nothing wrong with him. In the meantime they want him changing vets. So now I've got this dog with sixteen weeks of school and probably another four months later we get a new vet. I take him in and I said, 'Listen, this is what he had, this is what he's doing. I don't care what you have to do to this dog. I've got urine, I've got stool, I want some blood work done, whatever the hell it is that you need to do to find out what's wrong with this dog. If he's got to go back, let's get him the fuck out of here. That way I can have a dog not shitting all over my car.'

The vet says, 'I bet it's Giardia.' Giardia is an intestinal parasite, which basically doesn't allow the food to stay in the intestines to get absorbed and broken down and makes it go right out instead.

Sure enough, it was Giardia. So I get this medicine and within two weeks, just like that, he's blown up, nice and healthy.

He was a monster, man. He didn't look like much – he was so little sitting next to me – but man, he was a beast. And it's funny, because none of the people in the city had ever seen a Malinois before. They always assume a police dog is a German Shepherd. So I'd get him out the car and they'd be like, 'Yo, what kind of dog that is?'

I'd say, 'Man, that's a fox. That ain't no dog.'

'For real?'

'Yeah.'

One time I told them it was an Australian dingo. They believed me.

So anyway, after all that, I worked him for about four more months and then the department lays us off – me and the dog. But I kept the dog. Still have him.

****

My dog wasn't the greatest dog out there but he's found felony amounts of narcotics and he had two apprehensions in the time that I worked him. We didn't do a whole lot of tracking, because, you know, it's urban city, but he had two solid apprehensions.

When he was still a new dog, we had this one guy who had done a burglary. He'd broken into his ex-girlfriend's house four times within twenty-four hours. So I get there and one of the officers on patrol had called for me because the guy was supposed to be in the house. So I go up and they say, 'Yeah, these guys chased him into this vacant house.'

They went inside and they checked the upstairs and the downstairs but they didn't check the basement. The house was vacant. It had no roof, big holes in the floors. Now, the rule of thumb is, wherever my dog goes, I go, and wherever I go, he goes. If it's not safe for me to go, it's not safe for him to go. And if it's not safe for him to go, it's not safe for me to go.

So I figured, let me see if I can bluff this guy out. I get to the top of the steps and we have a K-9 announcement we have to make before we put in the dog. So I make my announcement, I wait. Now, my dog wasn't a barker at all. Put him in the car though, the motherfucker will bark for ten hours non-stop. So I make my first announcement, make my second announcement, I make my third announcement. My leash would double up, so I could open it up and let the dog go a distance. The house had trash on the steps, there was probably about three feet of trash in the basement and as I said, there were holes in the floor. So although I didn't really want to do it, I thought that I could bluff the guy out. So I'm like, 'Fuck it, let's see what he does.'

So I open up the leash and he goes down the steps, down about six feet. He's got his nose in the air – they call it 'casting' – and I'm like, yeah, he's got this guy. So I reel him back in and I unhook him and I say, 'Find him!' Then I shout out to the guy, 'Here he comes, motherfucker!'

So I go walking down the steps and he's sniffing around and

there's just trash everywhere. And there was what looked like a steel cabinet laying over at an angle. My dog comes up and he jumps up on the cabinet, he's got his nose in the air, he goes around and all of a sudden, BOOM! He runs inside this thing and I hear, 'AAAR-RGGGGHHH!'

So I pulled the cabinet back and I'm by myself. Now, I probably shouldn't have done the searches by myself because it's not safe but at the same time if there are other officers there and the dog goes up to them and starts sniffing them or coming in their direction, I have to say, 'It's okay', meaning, that person's alright. But I don't want him thinking. I want him doing his job and reacting to what he's given, so I would do the searches by myself. So anyway, I'm pulling this cabinet back and it takes me three tries and finally I muscle it over and my dog is on the guy. I grab my dog by the collar, he releases and I hook him up. I then tell the guy to start walking out of the building and he falls a couple of times and he almost gets bit again. I load him up in the car and he has to go to hospital because, you know, he has to get checked out.

So we get him to hospital and he had these tiny, black, knit gloves on. It was wintertime, it was cold and he had a great big, giant coat on too. And I'm like, 'Hey man, where did he bite you?'

He said, 'Oh, he bit me on the hand.'

I'm like, 'Fuck, man!' Because I wanted it to be somewhere good, you know, maybe on the leg or something.

So he took his gloves off and he had a bite mark across his hand. Then the doctor comes in and he's checking him out and he's squeezing the bite and the guy's yelping. So I then started laughing because number one, I thought it was funny because the bad guy got bit and number two, I know what it's like, because I've got bit on the hand too. I apologised but I told the guy and the doctor that I had been bitten myself during training and I know what it's like. I was just glad that someone else was feeling my pain for once.

But that incident was like seeing your kid walk for the first time. There were no issues. That dog was out there to work. I had issues with other dogs but this one, well, I trusted him. It's like having a rookie cop – until he's proven, you don't know what to expect out of them. So it was like the greatest day ever. I just wish he'd bitten him somewhere good.

****

We were out on foot – me and my dog – and we see this car go by. It was a four-way stop and this car just goes right through the intersection. I was going to go stop that car but then this other car behind it goes rippin' right through the intersection as I'm getting in to my car to go and stop the first car. So this other officer tells me to go stop the second car, which had a white male driver and a black male passenger.

As I go by this street, I see 'em but I didn't have time to stop, so I had to go one block over and come around and now I'm on a one-way street. By this point, when I pull up, the passenger's gone and the driver is out of the car – I've got my lights on – and he's at the trunk of the car.

So I get on my PA and I'm like, 'Yo, man, get back into your car.'

Then suddenly he takes off running down the street. I didn't get a chance to run the car to see if it was stolen or anything like that because I'm in my car and I'm driving down the street after him.

We get down the block and I guess he must have thought that he could dip in behind a church but it's all fenced, so he stops there and I tell this guy, 'Don't you fuckin' move or I'm going to send in the dog.'

Well, he kind of like… looks at me. I'm getting the dog out and I've got him by his collar when all of a sudden this guy starts running again. I'm running down the street with the dog and now he's getting back into his car. So I let the dog go and the dog is charging after him and he's looking back and he's screaming, 'AAAARRGGHHH!'

He gets the door open, jumps in and slams the door shut, so the dog doesn't get him. As I run up, he's got the key in the ignition and he's starting to turn over the car. I hope that he didn't lock it and I swing the door open – he's putting it in gear at this point – and I get him right before he gets it out of park and drives away.

And I'm like, 'Raider, come!'

Raider was my dogs name; or street name, 'Killer'. I call him Raider because I'm a big Oakland Raiders fan. His name was originally 'Chico' when I got him but half the population in the city was Hispanic, so I didn't want to be yellin', 'Chico, come!' like that, and the next thing you know there're racial discrimination complaints or some shit like that. So I changed his name to Raider.

So anyway, as I'm pulling him out the car, the door's open and Raider comes rippin' around the front of the car, underneath the door – because he was so small – and gets the guy right in the calf. Beautiful! Beautiful bite.

So the guy's like, 'AAAAARRRRGGGHHH!'

I throw him to the ground and I kind of got saved tremendously because he ended up having nine warrants, because other than him running, I didn't have anything.

The K-9's in New Jersey, the way they fell in the force continuum was, if I could spray you, I could bite you. If I could hit you with my baton, I could spray you, I could bite you. But at the same time you had to weigh it out because pepper-spray lasts a few hours – a day maybe – but bites and scars last forever.

But this guy didn't fit the profile, so to speak, of the city. He was a white guy with a black male passenger, so the chances are – and as I found out were correct – number one, he was there to buy drugs and number two, he had nine warrants.

Now, he's got this tattoo on his calf. He leans over and he goes, 'Yo man, you fucked up my tattoo!'

And I just started laughin'. I was like, 'Well, you should have "Raider was here" tattooed on your leg now, as your conversation piece. And then you can say that you got bit by a Camden K-9.'

But this guy didn't care about the warrants. He didn't care that he just got bit by a K-9. His whole thing was, 'Wow! You just fucked up my tattoo.'

****

People hate you in the projects in Baltimore. And the people who do like you are never going to say anything – that's dangerous for them.

People yell, 'Five-O', or they whistle. People stare at you; they hate you. But I have to tell you, my whole career I have been carrying a gun and people might not look at you, they might move away from you, they might give you an evil look or something. You could walk down the street and the reaction was pretty much the same; unless someone was running from you, you'd just get hard stares. Very few people would smile or talk or anything else. But being a K-9 cop, you got that dog out of the car and people were running! Like, running away from you. Crossing to the other side of the street to get away from you. In those neighbourhoods, people feared the dogs. People would run up onto their porches and then they still wouldn't be far enough away and then they'd run into their house to get away from you.

My opinion is, that the concept was that they know you can't just walk down the street and shoot them. They're very aware of the fact that we can't just start taking people randomly off the street by shooting them but they're not exactly sure what you can do with that dog, and when, and what the circumstances have to be.

I think part of that is cultural – with the race riots and dogs being used – people grew up seeing that and they were taught to be afraid of the dogs. And then in other respects, I think with the 'use of force' continuum, they weren't really sure when you could use the dog. So rather than stick around and find out, they would literally vacate the streets. And I'm walking down the street everyday with a gun on my hip and people aren't running away from me. But you get a dog out of the car and walk that dog down the street and people are just losing their minds. It's hysterical.

****

I worked downtown sometimes – when we had special events – and people would let their kids come up and grab my attack-trained German Shepherd. Who in their right mind thinks that that is a good idea?

People would sometimes say, 'Can I pet your dog?'

And I'd say, 'No, you can't. He's a working dog.' But they would do it anyway.

I mean, seriously, what part of 'attack-trained German Shepherd' makes you want to throw your hand in its face?

4

Death

A lmost all of the officers that I spoke to for this book were total
strangers to me; only very, very few had I met before. For this
reason, it was important to gain their trust and to 'warm them up', so to
speak. Asking them to simply start talking about their experiences without
any kind of lead-in could risk officers becoming closed and would certainly
make it harder to get the best out of our meeting. For this reason I would
often start a conversation with a light-hearted subject to get the conversation going. Death, I found, was a great subject to get the antidotes and
hilarity flowing and conversations would more often than not, start like
this: 'So, got any good death stories?'

As odd – and perhaps awful – as it sounds, police officers, for the
most part (but not always), find talking about their experiences to do
with dead bodies an easy subject to open up about. No matter where a
cop works, death will always be part of the job – natural deaths, vehicle
accidents, homicides, suicides, bones in the woods, decomposed, maggot
infested bodies – and usually a cop will always have a story (or many)
to tell about death. So for this reason it was always a great way to break

the ice.

Officers would almost relish trying to shock me with their stories about the rotten body found in the attic or remembering the very first time that their department sent them on a death call. For many officers, it would be the first time in their lives that they saw a dead person and that's something you don't forget, particularly if the brains are dripping off the ceiling and the people around you are expecting you to act like it's the most normal thing in the world.

For most people, there is nothing normal about seeing a dead body, so the very fact that death is an almost daily part of a police officer's life – part of their actual 'job' – makes it perhaps understandable that they want to tell you about it, if only to help them comprehend it themselves, talking about it and sharing the experience being a way of coping. Certainly, there is something peculiar about listening to a person recalling a truly horrific scene of death, whilst they rock back in laughter; but when something like that becomes 'ordinary' and 'routine', it can do strange things to a person. Not all officers were laughing though – some found it distressing or were sombre – they just had their own ways of dealing with it.

The work is kind of surreal. I thought that death was the one thing that would bother me when I came onto the department. I didn't know how I would deal with dead people. I'd only seen one dead person before in my life; it was in a coffin at a viewing. And then after you get on the job, you see a dead person, you do your thing and then go to lunch. You don't even think twice about it.

****

My first dead body on the job was a guy in the Bronx. This guy, he was dead for so long that his body had turned completely black and was five times its normal size. It was the middle of summer, it was hot and this guy was completely bloated and he looked like an aborigine. He had straight white hair, but if you looked at him you would have thought that he was a black guy. I mean, the pictures in the house clearly indicated that he was a white guy but he had been dead for so long. God it was horrible.

It was fucking hot and I just had to sit on him until the fucking ME's [Medical Examiner's] office arrived, put him in a bag and popped him. Literally popped him. They put him in a body bag but they couldn't move him the way he was . . . they fucking had to let the gas out. They fucking popped him with a poker to let the gas out so that he didn't explode. It was really, really hot and that's what happens. It's like when a watermelon gets over ripe and this stuff inside starts to boil because it's really freaking hot and this gas builds up and they explode and their seeds go flying all over the place.

Same thing happens to human bodies if the conditions are right. The gas just keeps building and building and the skin keeps stretching and stretching and then there could be a big explosion or there could be a little explosion.

****

I've seen dead bodies before. In fact some guy once died on my front lawn. He had a heart attack on his bicycle and died on my front lawn. Other than that I had never seen anything gory, although they did take us to the morgue during our training at the police academy. It was so gross. The smell was worse than anything. There were even a couple of bodies that moved on their own and that kind of flipped everybody out. There was a woman – a crackhead – who died from a drug overdose and her body had been opened up in the morgue, you know? She looked like a lobster opened up there. But then her head moved – literally – from left to right on its own. Everybody freaked out.

We were like, 'How did that happen? Oh my God she's alive!'

It's disgusting when you're looking at her, because it's this disgusting crack head. Imagine some druggie from the street – you know how bad they already look – but now they're dead and they're moving! Their parts are actually moving!

****

So, we got a dead body in the alley and we go over there. We're in this alley and it's full of garbage and we're looking for this body. So, here we find it and there's some guy laying on top of the dead guy and we're like, 'What are you doing?'

He's having anal sex with this guy – this dead guy.

He goes, 'He was my friend. We used to do this all the time.' He says, 'I thought he wouldn't mind, one last time.'

And really, you're just like…'What?'

****

The only death that I've ever been on that bothered me was the death of a child and I'm not even sure what happened. I was the second or third unit to show up on a 'child who is deceased' call. Any time that that happens, we have to go to it because people that are young just don't die – so it automatically becomes sort of suspicious.

I remember walking up to the door of the house. You're so used to seeing bags and stuff come out but they have little body bags for children. And I'd never really thought about that before. I remember the coroner, the investigator or whoever it was, bringing out this little body bag. I didn't even see the child but just knowing that it was in this little tiny bag, I mean, that was probably one of the most horrible things I have ever seen. And I don't even know what happened on that call.

I spent all of probably fifteen minutes on that call and just that one moment of him walking out with that little tiny body bag... it just wasn't right.

****

The worst call I've ever been on was a death notification. What sucks about working in a small community is that you kind of know everyone. You watch these kids grow up. You know who they are and you often know who the parents are as well.

We had two kids who got killed a number of years ago, right before their graduation. They were good kids, they were popular kids and I knew the parents. These kids were racing down the road, they'd been drinking on the beach and they'd deflated their car tires down so that they could get out of the sand. The thing is, they never re-inflated them. So now they're driving down the road doing fifty to sixty miles an hour and they were fucking around. One kid went to pass the other one, pulled back into the lane, over corrected and rolled out. Neither one was wearing a seatbelt. They both got ejected with the car on top of them.

I remember getting the call telling me to go to the family home to tell the parents that their son wasn't coming home. And I'd known the father. I was field training that night with a new cop and I told him that we had the worst assignment you could ever get. I told the new cop to take the other kids upstairs so that I could talk to the parents.

I said, 'Hi, can I come in?'

They said, 'Sure. How are you?'

'Can we sit down? I need to talk to you. There's no easy way for me to say this but there's been a car accident tonight. Your son was very badly hurt.'

They were like, 'No, no. That can't be right.'

'It is and actually your son is dead.'

'No, no. That can't be right. I just talked to my son. That can't be right.'

Then you have to watch the different stages of grief kick in.

They say, 'You've got to be mistaken. It's not my son.'

'Yeah, it is and I'm very sorry.'

'No, no. This is a training exercise for you guys, right?'

The reality of the situation kicks in and we spent the next, I don't know, maybe three hours with them, trying to help them find a babysitter so that they could go to the funeral home.

Then they wanted to see the body and I'm saying, 'Let the funeral home have until the morning. You don't want to see your son like this. Let them at least clean him up a little bit and make him presentable.'

I didn't want them to see their son in the state he was in but they were adamant that they wanted to see him and get some closure.

We don't have the physical danger that a city police officer does but the emotional danger of this job is twice as bad in a small community because you know everybody. You're anonymous in a city like New York with ten million people because there are very remote odds that you are going to deal with somebody you know. Down here, everyone you deal with, you know.

I didn't sleep well for a month. It's awful. It's an absolute finality. You're telling a parent that their child is never going to come home again, yet they just saw them forty minutes ago. I watched this kid grow up. He was seventeen when he died and I had watched him since he was two years old. I watched the kid riding around the neighbourhood on a bike, I saw him doing sports, watched him walk to grade school, then high school. And now he's dead, on a slab.

****

On the transit system, we usually average one death every week or two weeks. Sometimes it's accidental but a lot of the time it's suicide. Probably the goriest one that I was at was a fifteen-year-old kid who was on the wrong side of the commuter rail tracks. His mum was picking him up and the kid went across the tracks to meet her. I don't know why he did it but he ended up trying to hop the fence. He didn't make it; there was a train going about 130 miles an hour through the station and it just nailed him. That was probably the goriest one I've been to. Half of his brain was in a different parking lot. It landed like a hundred yards away. People freaked out. When I got there the kids books were all neatly stacked up, so you just knew that somebody flipped out and took this kid's schoolbooks and made them into a nice pile. That's probably one of the grossest I've ever been to.

All the cops go to these calls. In fact, most of the guys *want* to go. Everybody wants to go see the dead body. It sounds disgusting but it's part of the job. We're morbid and we like seeing weird stuff that we don't normally get to see. It sounds really bad but everybody will go to look, usually.

****

We got called once to an odour complaint. It was a house that sat just off State Street. It was a two or three storey home and some of the residents complained about this terrible smell that was coming from the house. I mean, I could stand on State Street and literally smell it and I knew right away that there was a dead guy there because you know what the smell of death is. Once you get that in your nose you never get it out again – you know it right away, anytime you smell it, driving down the street, you know what it is. Especially in the summer and this *was* summer.

So we went up to the person that called and she said, 'Yeah, I've noticed this smell in the house.'

She lived up on the second floor and the smell was overpowering. I don't know how someone can live like that.

She said, 'I noticed it a couple of weeks ago and it wasn't that bad but it's been getting worse and worse.' Then she says, 'There's also a stain up on my ceiling.'

And sure enough there's a brown, reddish, dark coloured stain that was dripping right through her ceiling and down her wall. So we went up into the attic and it turns out that there's a homeless guy there who had somehow gotten access to her attic and he's laying there, dead. His body had basically liquefied. I remember that his eyes were gone and it was like a horror movie - there were maggots crawling out of his eye sockets. And I remember his shirt – he still had his clothes on – he was on his back and his shirt looked like it was moving and it was because his entire body was nothing but maggots. So all of his clothes were just, you know, moving!

I remember I had to help one of the body recovery people pick up his body and put him in a body bag. His scalp was still attached but as soon as we picked him up the scalp and everything fell right off. All his hair was laying there, just a pile of maggots. The smell up there was ungodly bad, just ungodly bad. I think I went outside and actually puked. And that's what the stain was, leaking through her ceiling – it was his body. His body juices were leaking through her ceiling. They all freaked when they found out.

I can't believe no one had smelt that guy before. And there was virtually nothing left of him, so we never found out what had actually killed him. I'm sure it was probably natural causes – he was a homeless guy, there were beer cans all around him up in the attic – but he had been dead for weeks and it was hot. It was probably ninety-something degrees up in that attic. It was nasty.

****

I get called to all kinds of death investigations – suicides, natural death investigations, homicides – so I see dead people a lot. Now it's a matter of routine. Initially when I started, yeah, it would make me sick, it would make me have nightmares. I'd see them in my sleep, I couldn't get it out of my mind but it's routine now, you get used to it. You get kind of callous, it's just another dead body, you know?

The thing that's tough to remember, though, is that whoever that person is, they've got relatives. I mean, you can't come walking into a scene and just go, 'Ah, it's just another dead guy.'

You're always being watched; somebody in that family's watching you. His wife, his girlfriend, his kids – whoever it may be – they're there, watching. And obviously that's the biggest thing that's ever happened in their life – to lose their father or brother or dad or grandpa or whoever it might be. Even if it was natural causes, our way of handling it is something that we have to be really careful about.

****

There was a suicide at the Stratosphere Tower here in Las Vegas, where this guy jumped off the top and I think it's about 110 storeys high. On the video, it was about seven seconds from the time he jumps off until the time he hits the ground.

We kind of have two types of suicidal persons: we have the ones that are dead set on doing it and nobody can stop them. Then we have ones that pretty much don't want to do it but are screaming for help. This guy was the one that was going to do it no matter what.

It kind of stands out to me as it was a very surreal experience. I was coming down Las Vegas Boulevard heading south and I was just about at the intersection of St Louis, which is one block from the Stratosphere. I remember the call came out that there was a person on top of the Stratosphere who was attempting to jump. It was a high priority call and I remember thinking that there's no way I'm gonna be able to make it to the top of the Stratosphere in time to even talk to this guy. Just as I'm pulling up, I see a crowd and cars starting to move out of the way in front of me; there was just chaos. I saw people falling on the ground and I didn't know what was going on. So I got my car up on the sidewalk, hit my lights and sirens and started rolling towards them and just as I'm pulling up, right in front of me was what was left of his body. He had jumped just as I was getting the call. I stepped out of my car and there was nothing left of him. He had basically exploded. I think we found parts of him two hundred and fifty feet away, in the intersection of Baltimore. It was just very graphic.

What was strange, though, was that there were people that were hit by his debris. And because of the sound of him hitting the ground and the velocity that the debris took off at, people would find pieces of him on them and they thought that they had been shot. We had two people that had actually passed out. So I pull up and I have a person laying here and another person laying there, as well as a body. Then a Japanese tour bus passes by and I remember looking up and they're all taking pictures. I mean it was the most surreal experience I have ever seen, all the flashbulbs going off.

So as this happens I'm trying to shut the road off and things like that and there was a guy who got out of his car and he had body matter all over the side of it. He swears, gets in his car and starts driving off.

So the very first officer that arrives, I tell them, 'You've got to go stop him. I don't know what his deal is.'

He pulls over and his thing was that it was a rental car and he was concerned that they were going to charge him for cleaning it, so he was going to find a car wash. This is the mentality of people!

It was absolutely crazy and because of the way traffic was blocked up, I was there, all alone for probably about two minutes or so, although it seemed a lot longer. It was like some strange movie. There was so much going on all at once. And it's hard because your brain – and I don't care who you are or how trained and experienced you are – your brain will automatically have a pre-conceived idea of what you're getting yourself into. I was thinking how I was going to run through the casino to the elevator and take it up to the top. I'm thinking about handling this scene at the top of the Stratosphere and all of a sudden, in a split second, I'm confronted with the scene right here in front of me on the ground and a whole element that I wasn't even ready for.

It was crazy. It was like being in a war zone. It was almost like a bomb had gone off – like a car bomb had got off – and I've got all these victims everywhere but actually I only had one person who was dead. I imagine a suicide bomb would probably have the same look to it.

Later that night we had to walk around with the biohazard bags and haul pieces of him off. We called out a biohazard team – they're private contractors that come out and clean things up; crime scene cleaners – and so to help them out we had to pull parts of this poor guy off of palm trees and we'd have tourists coming up to us and say, 'Hey, I think there's something other here that needs your attention.'

Later that night, as the guy is being cleaned up, there was something white on the ground and the crime scene guy looks at it and he goes, 'Oh my God! You know what that is?' And he goes over to his car and grabs a screwdriver and he starts chiselling at the ground and pops it out.

It was a piece of vertebra that had actually embedded itself into the asphalt. It was 105 degrees that day and so the asphalt's a little soft and a sliver about the size of a domino had embedded itself right into the asphalt. It was the craziest thing in the world.

It didn't bother me a bit though. I guess I looked at it more from a professional standpoint of, 'Well, someone here needs to fix this problem and I guess that's me.'

It wasn't any more graphic than a really serious car wreck where a body has just been shredded apart. I mean, there was a moment of, 'Ooh! That's different!' – but it certainly didn't affect me in any kind of negative way. You have to learn to really compartmentalise in this job. But at the same time you have to learn that there needs to be an outlet for that somewhere – a healthy outlet – because if you keep all that stuff inside, eventually it's going to affect you.

****

People think that cops are pretty peculiar, especially as they come by a gruesome traffic accident and the cop's standing at the side of the road eating a donut, laughing. They must think that we are monsters.

But how else do you deal with it, you know? How else do you deal with it day in, day out? You've got to become indifferent to it. You can't let it get to you every day or you can't do the job. So you've got to ignore it and if somebody tells you a funny story, you're going to laugh about it. You're certainly not laughing at the body but you're like, 'Hey, you should have seen what I was dealing with last night!' It's funny and you laugh and people come by and they see that and they think we're monsters. But you've got to be indifferent to it; you can't let it get to you.

****

I've seen some bad accidents. There's one where I'd love to get hold of the pictures and show them to my kids and say, 'Hey! This is why you wear a seatbelt.'

This guy was driving one of those OJ Broncos. Like an older, bigger style Bronco. You remember when OJ Simpson was driving that white Bronco when he got arrested? It was like that, only bigger. He was coming down some winding road up in North Bend, it's a town out east, in the mountains. It was winter and it was raining and there was maybe some sleet also. It was a pretty steep hill and as he came around the corner he probably went too far into the side of the road and then he must have over-corrected or something because he

69

rolled the Bronco onto its side, although he didn't roll it completely over. He over-corrected and all it did was slide onto its passenger side. But the road was so steep that it just kept going. And this was like four-thirty, five o'clock in the morning, so he was on his way to work. He wasn't drunk or anything like that – just over-corrected and it rolled onto its side.

He obviously wasn't wearing a seatbelt because he got thrown from the driver's seat into the passenger seat. I don't know what it's called but where the top of the door and the roof connect when they're shut, well, it bent back a little bit somehow and his head got stuck outside of it and then it was like a cheese grater all the way down the side of the road. This car probably skid a couple of hundred feet and you could see where his head first started hitting the road because you could find chunks of hair and skull and stuff like that. But that was the only mark he had on him. He was still alive when I got there but he was making those gurgling sounds – I call it the 'death gurgle'.

Literally, if the guy had been wearing a seatbelt, when that car stopped sliding he could have hit the button on his seatbelt and fallen down on the side or braced himself before he undid his belt and crawled out. He probably would have had a sore neck at worst. He couldn't have been going more than twenty-five or thirty miles per hour but since he wasn't wearing a seatbelt he got thrown onto the other side and it just cheese-grated his head all the way down.

He died. He was dead before the ambulance got there. But it's one of those where I want to show the pictures to my kids and say, 'Listen son, listen daughter, this is why you wear a seatbelt.'

If he had been wearing his seatbelt he wouldn't have had a fucking mark on him. He may have spilt his coffee at most, although he might have been able to hold onto that too.

****

I went to this accident and it was one of those where, even if they had been wearing seatbelts, they wouldn't have done anything, they wouldn't have helped. There were four drunk teenagers in a car that came around a corner and hit a giant oak tree that was a foot away from the road – not very far at all. They must have been hauling ass because the oak tree tore the car into several pieces and all four of them went in different directions from the car.

When we got there three of them were dead and one of them was laying there alive – it was a girl. Her guts were hanging out of her and she's holding onto them; it's almost as if she's trying to put them back into her stomach. She's laying there yelling at us to shoot her because she was in so much pain.

She was screaming, 'Just shoot me! Just kill me!'

It was disgusting. Just nasty.

The other officer I was with ended up talking to this girl saying, 'You're going to be fine.' Even though we both know that she's not. She's going to be dead, hopefully sooner rather than later, for her sake.

And you're thinking, 'Why can't I just put her out of her misery?' I'm not a doctor but her guts are hanging out. We all know she's not going to make it. And I hate the fact that she is going to lay here and suffer. I can't be honest with her and say, 'You're fucking dead. Just give up. Just give up.'

But I can remember her very distinctly, screaming, 'Please, just shoot me.'

The ambulance came and they took her but I don't think she even made it to the hospital. Then they just put sheets over the other people and we sat at either end of the road and probably played video games on our computers or something, because when we get accidents like that, we don't even have to write anything. You have to write about a paragraph long sentence that says: I came here, this is what I saw, such-and-such detective took the lead.

So when we got done, we closed the road and the accident team – a speciality unit – came out and did all their diagrams and all the kind of crap they do for those fatality accidents. All we had to do was close the road, basically. It's a simple report for us but it usually takes the accident unit several hours to finish their report – especially with four people.

But I'm sure we sat there and made jokes about it over our Nextel phones and stuff like that. Joking is definitely a coping mechanism for it.

But you've got things to do when you see those types of things, rather than just think about how nasty it is. I don't ever really think about it. At that time I was thinking, 'I've got to get some flares out on the road. I've got shit to do!'

But it was horrible. It was one of those times when I thought, 'why can't we just shoot her?'

I don't want to shoot somebody, you know, but this girl is not going to make it. We'll shoot a deer on the side of the road or something like that but this girl wasn't going to make it so why did she need to lie there and suffer? It wasn't very long until the ambulance showed up but it's not like she stops suffering just because they arrived. I'm sure she suffered right up until she finally died.

****

I was in what they call 'free week'; after you go through the academy you go out to different precincts and ride around to get to know different areas of the county. I was riding with this officer and it was literally my first day. Nothing had happened all day. Nothing was going on. We were up in a ritzy, sleepy part of the county, in a suburb of Seattle. It was a day shift - 6am to 2pm. I don't even remember if we'd gone on a call that day. It was just dead; it was boring, nothing going on.

As we were driving back to the precinct, the tones came on the radio – the tones beep three or four times. Usually it means that something big has just happened – something important or some kind of major incident. So, the tones go off and in that area, the precinct that I'm working in, it's literally hundreds of square miles. It's big. So the call could be fifty miles away from where we're at or, as it turned out, it could literally be the next block.

So, it's my very first day, seven-and-a-half hours into it and we're driving back to the precinct, the tones go off and the dispatcher says, 'A suicide has just occurred at...' and then gave the address.

The guy that I'm riding with goes, 'Oh shit! That's right around the corner!'

And so I'm like, 'Finally! Something's going to happen.'

So then the details start coming in and it's about a guy who had stuck a shotgun in his mouth and pulled the trigger. And his girlfriend saw him do it and she was the one who had called.

My partner hits the lights and sirens and literally, honest to God, it was right around the corner; he made the right and it was the first house on the left. We get out of the car and right before we go through the front door, he puts his hand out and stops me and goes, 'If you don't ever learn anything else from me, if you ever go into one of these calls again, the first thing you need to do is look up.'

And I'm like, 'What the hell does that mean? Why do I have to look up?'

But then we go inside and I look up. There are brains and pieces of this guy's skull and all that kind of crap hanging from the ceiling; it's like, dripping down. And because we were there within two or three minutes of this happening, there was still crap falling from the ceiling – his skull and chunks of his brain and stuff like that. So I remembered never to go into a house and not look up!

Then you look down and here's what's left of this guy's face and he was laying there and I can remember looking and you could see through his mouth. He had put the shotgun in his mouth and then blew the top of his head off. So you could look through his mouth and I can remember looking to where the roof of his mouth should have been and into where his head and brain and all that stuff should be, and there was the wadding packing from the shotgun shell in the centre of his head and his eyeball was lying on top of it. I don't remember a single thing other than that. I don't remember if I had to write any paperwork, I don't remember going home. I just remember that eyeball looking at me.

And the smell! There was this odd smell in the air. I don't know if it was a mixture of gunpowder and brain or whatever, but to me it smelled like a ski-lift ticket. The back of a lift ticket has a sort of glue or something on it and whenever I get a ski-lift ticket it smells exactly the same. Every time I get one of those, I picture that eyeball and the shotgun wadding. That smell makes it come back to me.

But I was thinking, 'I hope this shit happens every day!' I'm kind of gory when it comes to that kind of stuff. The weird thing is, if I'm at home and we've got the Surgery Channel on the television or I'm flipping through the channels and I see someone operating on somebody's eye, I can't watch that shit, that grosses me out. But at work, you've got shit you need to do, you know? There's other stuff to think about besides that eyeball and that shotgun wading looking right back at me.

So yeah, that was day one.

5

SWAT

*W*hen listening back to the recordings I made while speaking to officers from SWAT (Special Weapons and Tactics), I usually had to
turn the volume up, close my eyes and really concentrate in order to hear
what they were telling me. For some reason – and I'm sure this is just a
coincidence – almost all of the interviews I conducted with SWAT officers
took place in bars and involved large amounts of beer. The loud music
and riotous background hum was an almost constant soundtrack to these
SWAT conversations.

When there is something that requires more than just a standard
police response or where the circumstances are so dangerous or require
specialist skills and equipment, SWAT are called in. These are the men
and women whose job it is to go through a door, very often knowing that
there is an almost one hundred per cent chance that on the other side is
someone who is armed with powerful weapons and is not planning to go
quietly, maybe even a lunatic with a death wish. I did wonder if it was the
nature of their extreme job that led so many of them to pull me into a bar
to talk – a kind of work hard / play hard thing. (And play hard we did, so

hard in fact, that on one occasion I missed a very important Thanksgiving event that had been laid on especially for me by an entire precinct. The officer who had arranged it hasn't spoken to me since, understandably.)

The very fact that officers would aspire to take on such a highly skilled yet dangerous job is something that should be admired. They were some of the most friendly, humble, down to earth and welcoming of all the different types of officer I met. And yes, they're also nuts. Perhaps this combination had something to do with their chosen role and the type of personality required to take on a job where you knew that if you were being called upon, it was because the situation was so dangerous that even regular, fully armed police officers were not able to deal with it. They are the best at what they do and so they have nothing to prove.

After speaking with SWAT officers I was left with the impression that their job was extremely dangerous, full of politics but quite often, great fun. I was also left with a killer hangover.

I'll go anywhere in this city, but I have a gun.

****

We had an incident where this guy was walking around and the police notice him because he's wearing a long trench coat and it's summertime. He gets pulled over by these plain-clothes police officers who were just working the street – you know, they got a little hunch.

They're like, 'Let's talk to him.'

So they turn around to go back and they're about to get out of their car when he starts shooting at them. He shoots one guy in the foot. They chase him; they're shooting at him and he's shooting back at them. They run down the street, down an alley and they chase him into a back yard. He's shooting a lot of bullets, to the point where the officers thought he had an automatic weapon, because he would lay down fifteen to twenty rounds, stop and reload.

He had hundreds of rounds on him and several magazines. He'd shoot, reload, shoot a bunch more rounds and that way he kept the police away. But they formed a perimeter and they called us – SWAT – and we had just finished a twelve-hour job on some crazy guy who had barricaded himself in a garage with a knife.

I had just gotten home, ready to jump in the shower, when my friend calls me and he's like, 'Hey, there's a job going on right now.'

And I'm like, 'Get the fuck outta here! You're kidding me?'

He's like, 'No. Turn on the police radio.'

I turn the radio on and could hear the police, with gunshots in the background. I put my clothes back on and start heading down there. I got there and the guy was still shooting. It was half-an-hour, forty-five minutes of him shooting back and forth at the police. And they still thought that he had an automatic rifle simply because of the rapid rate that he was shooting at.

So, we take up the perimeter. We get our 'Bearcat', an armoured personnel carrier, to block the alley and we use that as our cover. We probably had fifteen guys there already and he was stuck in the back yard, underneath this rear porch. There were people in the building that we couldn't get to and they couldn't get out but we managed to evacuate the people in the houses next to them.

We had just gotten that done and as soon as that happened, the guy comes out of the porch, walks down a gangway, probably a hundred feet and then he turns a corner into the alley. He sees the big Bearcat and then he sees the police who are right around the corner of it and he starts shooting. Luckily we had probably about six guys there and they flared out. One guy got shot in the vest, although he didn't realise it. The bullet hit a magazine – like an M4 magazine – and got stopped by the vest. About three or four, or maybe five guys were able to flare out and return fire. We don't know how many times he got shot, because he got shot by one handgun and about four rifles. The coroners said that they stopped counting holes after about forty. Like, forty entrance wounds. The guy literally stood up for about five or ten seconds shooting and he kept taking the rounds until he finally collapsed. Even when he was down, he still had the gun in his hand. But finally he was dead.

He had a bible in one hand, a gun in the other and he still had at least a hundred rounds of nine millimetre and magazines. Just off his rocker. Just walking down the street with a bible in his hand and a gun.

Obviously with the amount of ammunition he had, he was planning to do something, because normally you walk down the street with a handgun in your pocket and maybe one magazine, maybe two at the most. You don't walk around with three hundred rounds of ammo on you.

****

Dogs are fun but they're also a pain in the ass. They cause a lot of problems for police on search warrant. A lot of SWAT teams have issues with dogs. They try everything; we've had teams use fire extinguishers, pepper spray, some use a taser against them, other places immediately shoot them. But here's the problem with shooting them – the bullet may not stop inside the dog. They may go right through them and then you've got to worry about what's behind them, what's below, what's above, what's further out, what's in the back yard. Have you got kids in the back yard or in the next house? You've got to worry about shooting your own guys. If you shot this dog in the sternum and the round ricochets and your guys are over there, you could have a problem.

So we've tried a lot of different things. What we've found is flash-bangs seem to work ninety-five percent of the time. You throw a flash-bang at a dog – even if it's a vicious dog, a biting dog, a fighting dog – it'll run. It'll try to leave this world; it'll try to go through a wall to get away. Seriously, it just freaks them out. One-hundred-and-fifty pound pit bulls – vicious dogs – you'll find them cowering under a bed at the other end of the house. For us it's great, because it allows us to clear the house for bad guys and once we get to that room where that dog is hiding, we'll contain it or noose it, put it in a cage or walk it out. Sometimes we'll just lock it in a bathroom.

I work on point and the ballistic shield a lot on search warrants, at the front of the stick. So usually, if the door opens, I'm the first one in. There've been times where I've had dogs facing me down. I'll call out for a flash-bang, they drop a flash-bang and the dog goes running. We try to avoid shooting them unless we have no choice. Some dogs may be large in size but you know just by the way they're acting that they're not going to bite you. They see the door open and they just want to get out. So we just let them go – just let them run out into the yard.

But some people, for some reason, as soon as they see a dog they'll want to shoot it. I don't know if they get something out of it. Maybe they feel like a bigger man or whatever. Me? I like dogs. It's not the dog's fault he's there. If I can avoid shooting it, I will.

****

We had a hostage rescue, after this guy got into a shootout with the cops. It's three or four in the morning and we're getting ready to go in. He's got a lady held hostage. My buddy's there and I look at him. It's a cool night, it's nice, it's beautiful, but for some reason he's sweating.

I asked him, 'What's up?'

He goes, 'I gotta take a shit!'

I'm like, 'Dude, we're gettin' ready to go in!'

He says, 'I know.'

One of our buddies overhears and says, 'I've got some toilet paper you can have.'

We're in somebody's front yard. He took a shit right there, next to our K-9 dog. And I look over at him after he's finished and there's this shit with a lump of toilet paper right in the middle of it in somebody's front fucking yard!

We go in, we do it – rescue the lady, the whole deal – and I'm laughing because we didn't clean that up. So somebody would have come home and seen that and said, 'There must be fucking werewolves in our fucking neighbourhood because look at the size of this shit in my front yard!'

****

We were doing a raid for the Narcs, our Narcotics Unit. They've got this guy, he's a violent ex-offender. There's also a potential secondary violent suspect inside this house. The Narcs have been going directly to the guy and buying coke right in front of his house; they roll up, the dude comes out to the car and sells them dope.

So they call us to help and we always try to mitigate or minimise our response because the use of SWAT escalates the force. I talked to the team sergeant, because there was a twelve-year-old, another young kid and the wife or girlfriend in the house. We always try to pull them out so we don't have to deal with it, you know? Because if you shock-lock a door – which is a compressed copper round from a shotgun – or you put a stun-stick through a window, there's a chance that you're going to hurt somebody.

It's December and so my other concern is that it's Christmas time, you know what I mean? Dry Christmas trees, decorations and all those things start to come into play. So we're carefully planning how we're going to do this thing.

I talk to the Narcs and ask, 'Is there any way we can call this guy out?'

I already know the answer because the dude never goes anywhere. He doesn't meet them off campus or anywhere; he always meets them right in front of his fucking house.

They go, 'No, he never goes nowhere. We've got to meet him in front of his house.'

I go, 'We were thinking maybe we can hide in a bush and when the dude comes out we'll jump him.'

The problem is, we've got a secondary suspect. If we do that and we start taking rounds, then it's a big problem. So we're ultimately at the point where we have to do a dynamic entry. Also, the problem with dope cases is that you want to catch them with dope – that's how you knock 'em home; solidify the case, you know?

So we plan to use a stun-stick, put it through the window, pop it and go. But I restrict my guys and tell them that they can't do it unless they can clear the window. You've got to break it, clear it and make sure there's nothing there, because my worse fear is that it catches a tree on fire, burns the fucking house down, kills the kids and everybody else involved, right?

So I'm planning this thing with my ATL, my Assistant Team Leader. We've done everything we can to make this the best that we can do. Crossed all the t's, dotted all the i's. So we roll up and it was cold as fuck. I'll never forget it because it was December. I remember riding over there – I was riding the rails on the outside of the van, cold as shit, man. We roll up there, typical breach element up front – you got the entry guy, who's number one, ATL's number two, another guy with the shield is three and I'm four. And then you have another four guys up there doing the breach. You got a guy on shock-lock to pop it and a guy with a hook, to hook the cage on the front door and pull. Then you have a back up shock-lock in case the first guy gets shot.

We have a stun-stick team as well but I remind them, 'You can't use it unless you can clear it.'

Lo and behold the house has plantation shutters – our team can't see in so they can't clear it. Turns out to be a good thing as there was a twelve-year-old girl sitting there at a computer.

So we minimise our response. We go up there, start working it, can't fucking blow the door for shit. We fire six rounds, trying to pop it but we can't get the thing to go. So at that point we realise the ghost is up – we can't do it – so we call out 'tactical' to assist us. One of the things we do when we wait for tactical is, we'd go down on one knee – I don't know why, minimise our size or whatever the case may be. I don't do it anymore, I hide behind the shield instead. But back then

I called tactical and I've already started to go down on my knee and then all of a sudden, POP-POP-POP! Dude starts fucking lighting us up from the inside of the house and I feel this thing on my groin flap – the flap that hangs down from my bullet proof vest – you know what I mean? Didn't think nothing of it at the time though.

Hear one of my guys say, 'I'M HIT! I'M DOWN!'

He drops. The other guys start effecting an 'officer-down' rescue on him. Didn't even know it at the time but another officer then got hit in the thigh and also went down. Another guy picked him up and took him out. So me and my ATL are about the only ones left there and I honestly think, 'This fucking guy's crazy. He's going to come out and shoot us all.' So we roll over to the garage and we're sitting there, my ATL and I, waiting this fucking guy out, sweating beads. He's crazy, he's shooting at us even though he knows who we are because we're yellin' 'POLICE!' Doing everything we can to identify ourselves.

I say to my ATL, 'I think I took one in the nuts, dude. It just bounced off my flap though.'

Later he told me, 'Dude, you were white as a ghost.' I don't know that I've been shot but my body does.

So I'm sitting there and we're looking and the dude doesn't come out. So we get back to the van. One of our guys is back there. He ended up taking one through his thumb and into his thigh rig, where we carry spare magazines. It hit one of his magazines and goes in. He also took one to the chest but his vest stopped it and the doctors were working on him – we have Tac-Docs. The medic from our search and rescue team is there as well and we also have tactical physicians that work with our teams.

As they're working on him I could feel moisture dripping down my leg. So I go to one of my guys and pick my flap up and say, 'Dude, am I bleeding?'

He looks at me and his eyes get big, you know? And he's like, 'Oh yes! Sergeant, you're bleeding!'

I go, 'Ah, motherfucker!'

One of my biggest fears is a femoral artery bleed. So I go, 'Doc, when you get done over there, come check me, make sure it's not a femoral bleed.'

Well, the doc comes over and finally I go, 'I think I've been hit. I think I'm bleeding.'

He says, 'Let me cut your pants off and see.'

So, he comes out with this fucking knife and I go, 'Whoa! Whoa! Doc, hold on.' I reach into my pants, cup my balls and say, 'Okay, cut away.'

He cuts the pants off and says, 'Oh yeah, but it's not the femoral because it would have been squirting if it were.'

So we're sitting there and the ambulance comes around and they load the guys up and one of the other officers comes over and says, 'Hey, you need to go to hospital.'

I go, 'Dude, no. I'm cool. I'm all right. The Ambulance is full. I'm good.'

He's like, 'No, you need to go to the hospital. Doc, tell him!'

And the doc goes, 'Oh yeah. You need to go to the hospital.'

So I go, 'Really doc? I'm all right. I feel okay. I'm good to go.'

But he says, 'No, you need to go to the hospital.'

So I call out, 'ATL, you're in fucking charge. I'm out of here.'

They stacked the three of us up like wood, in the ambulance and fucking rolled us out of there and down to the hospital. At the hospital we're all laughing and joking at each other and making fun of one of the guys for being fat and all this kind of shit.

But I'm stressed about my guys going down – that's my concern. I'm calling their wives, making sure they don't hear about it some other way.

I'm saying, 'Hey, your husband's been shot but he's okay.'

You know, 'blah, blah, blah'. And all of a sudden my phone beeps and it's my wife calling me. And she goes, 'Hey, are you okay?'

And I go, 'What do you mean?'

She says, 'We heard three SWAT guys were shot.'

And I go, 'Yeah, yeah, we're okay. I've been shot. I'm okay sweetheart but I'm on the other line, let me call you back.'

And she's like, 'What!?'

So anyway, all that stress and all that concern is nothing. But low and behold, now homicide – who normally investigate our 'officer involved' shootings – comes out there to investigate this thing, even though we're the only ones who got shot. We purposefully didn't fire back because we knew there were kids in there. We restricted our action – didn't do anything – just rescued our own guys.

A Violent Crime detective comes up to me afterwards and he goes, 'Hey, did any of you guys fire any rounds?'

And I go, 'No.'

The guy in the house was shooting with a 40 cal, so we all got hit with 40 cal. The detective says, 'But we found a 9mm casing at the scene.'

And so I go, 'Dude the only people that had 9's would have been me and my ATL. I guess if anybody had fired a sympathetic discharge, it would have been me, because I got shot. But I didn't know I had been fucking shot. We didn't fire no 9mm rounds. Everybody else had two-two's and two-three's. None of us fired.'

He goes, 'Okay, cool.'

We come out of hospital. When I went down, the bullet grazed my left leg. It hit my groin flap but it was low enough that it pushed the flap up, grazed my left leg and stuck. I've still got the bullet in here, between my femoral and femur, still in my leg. I finally get released that night – we all got released that night – and I'm at home now.

I'm at home and the fucking homicide detective calls me. He says, 'Hey, do you think I can come interview you?'

I go, 'Are you fucking kidding me? Now? I just got home. Okay, if you need to fucking come here, come, but I'll tell you what, I'll meet you outside. I'll come sit in your car. I don't want to concern my kids.'

So he comes and he starts interviewing me about the same thing.

He says, 'Did you guys fire any rounds?'

I say, 'No, nobody on my team fired any rounds into that structure. We restricted our actions. We fucking could have, but we didn't.'

So the investigation, instead of investigating this shit-bag who shot three of us, they fucking glossed right over it and their focus of the investigation is on SWAT who they believed fired back and is lying about it. So now Homicide goes on this big fucking investigation about this spent round.

It turns out that what happened was, when the officer took the round in his low-ride holster with the magazine, it hits one of the bullets, put some burning ember in there which then ignites a round, fires it, pops it out of the mag-holder and hits the other officer in the back. So here was a mission where we did the exact right thing, sucked up bullets, did everything that is right and then we're still fucking being investigated.

Later we end up going to court with a brand new judge who was a thirty-year public defendant. He chastises us on our excessive use of force! Dude, I swear to God! We did everything right! The local news media picks up on it and talks about how excessive we were. They say, 'Imagine being woken up in the middle of the night! This guy's a family man; he's trying to protect his family.'

The truth of the matter was, we had more concern for this guy's kids than he did. He was a fucking dope dealer who was pimping out his own wife!

That's when I realised that this job fucking sucks. I only do this job because of these guys – my guys – you know what I mean? And because of the old adage, 'if not us, than who?'

Right after that, we had a hostage rescue where we rescued a baby. Let me tell you, you come running out with that baby in your arms and it's then that you realise, 'this is what it's about'. It's not about the bullshit.

****

A few years ago on Thanksgiving we get called to a barricade situation. There was a party, couple of guys draw guns, they start shooting at each other, one guy runs out, he runs into somebody else's apartment where a lady lives, locks the door and holds her hostage.

So now the police get called and he starts shooting at them out of the window. A couple of our SWAT guys got called and they get there and he's still shooting at the police. So they call everybody; they call the whole SWAT team. We start heading to the south side and set up on this thing. It lasted thirty hours. We spent the whole night there – all of Thanksgiving – everybody on our team. We froze our asses off because we were outside. The negotiators tried to negotiate with him for hours. They were talking for like, twenty hours, trying to convince the guy to let her go. We tried to figure out that maybe, if he falls asleep, maybe we could do an entry, but he's talking to the negotiators and they seem like they're getting somewhere, like he might give her up. So they keep negotiating; they don't allow us to go in.

After like, thirty hours, we set up a plan to make an entry in case we hear gunshots or he says something like, 'I'm gonna kill her right now.' We make a plan to use distraction devices and hit both the front door and the back door and break the windows trying to get in. But just then we hear a little 'pop'.

The guys are like, 'Did you hear that?'

It might have sounded like a gunshot.

So they try to communicate with the guy. No sound, nothing. No response. So we're ordered to make our entry. We tried to make an entry but it took probably forty-five seconds to get in there. He had already killed her and killed himself. So there were at least two shots. We thought we heard one of them, the other one we didn't even hear – it might have been muffled.

It's hard to say, could you have done something? Maybe you should have gone in there sooner? Then you start second guessing your bosses. Should you go in, instead of negotiating? But there are certain ways things have to go and as long as they feel that they're open to negotiations, they'll try to negotiate rather than try to go in there, assault the building and try to save the hostage.

Well, here's the thing – and at that time and at this point in time, it's still the same – we don't have the benefit of explosive breaching. Our department, it's good, it's a big department, a lot of good things about it, but being progressive? We're not as progressive as let's say, the West Coast departments or some of the Southern departments in our country but especially the West Coast. The West Coast is very progressive. But this is the Midwest and because of the political atmosphere they never allowed our department to train, obtain and use explosive breaching. But a lot of it had to do with maybe getting lucky with certain situations or maybe not running into that type of situation where you absolutely needed explosive breaching.

I think that job – where the girl died who was a totally innocent victim – I think if we were to have had explosive breaching at that point, we could have set them up on both doors, we could have set them up against the walls in the bedroom that they were in – and you know, they do it all over the place – and as soon as it detonates you put a gun in there; within three or four seconds you have a gun in that room.

But we just forced our way in mechanically – ram, sledgehammer – then basically pushed our way in. He had a hallway and he had a door in this hallway and what he did was, he lodged a chair right in there and it fit perfectly. He had so much time that he stacked it up to the ceiling with furniture. That was one door. The other door, he put a refrigerator and stove and a couple of other pieces of furniture against it. So literally, once we beached the lock mechanically, we just had to push our way in; push these refrigerators, stove, cabinet and chairs away to get in. We had guys go in towards the bedroom, we had guys going towards the other way and we weren't a hundred percent sure which room he was in. The guys who went into the bedroom found her, the hostage. She was dead. He was also dead.

The guys that went to the left, went towards the front door and they literally had to pick up a couch and move it for that door to even open. There was no way you could open it without explosive breaching. But it's political; people are afraid of explosives. They're like, 'Explosives! Wow! That's scary! That's dangerous. We don't want to allow that in the city.'

The bosses in the department, they're along with us. They understand now. Five years ago, they weren't. Our own department bosses were totally against having explosive breaching. Now, bosses have changed, they understand that there's a need for explosive breaching but now it's the politicians. You've got to convince the politicians. You've got to give a presentation and explain this is what the explosives are used for; you can defeat doors and walls without injuring anybody on the inside, without injuring anybody on the outside and it should only be used for the worst or the extreme emergencies where you have to get in there, like now.

So it's difficult, bureaucracy. Although now, I think the train is starting to move a little bit but it still takes a lot of work, a lot of convincing and we still don't have it. We're working at it; we're trying to pressure as many of the people that we have to pressure and convince, to get it. But up until now, we still don't have it.

So now, if we had the same situation today and I was in charge or I had something to do with the decision-making, I would recommend strongly that we call another team in, like, let's say, the state police. They use explosives. I would say call them. I would say, let them take over this job. Let them handle it. Let them get in, whatever which way they can or have them come in and let them help us. Because in certain situations, you need explosive breaching and we don't have it yet.

****

Do you know the old adage that 'truth is stranger than fiction'? Well that's so true. I mean we've done things that I would never have imagined. If the department didn't know who else to call, they would call us – SWAT. If it was risky, we would be the ones to go do it, right? So we did lots of shit, undercover stuff, all kinds of things. And every mission's a problem; how do I solve it? How do I go about solving it?

There was a triple homicide, an execution-style slaying that was drug related. They killed these kids over drugs.

The department gets a call from a dude, who goes, 'Hey, that guy who killed those three people, I know where he is.'

So then we get a call from the department, 'Hey, this guy knows where this triple murder suspect is, says he can take you to him. The trouble is, it's out in a wooded, overgrown swamp.'

I'll never forget it because it was the eeriest thing in the world. So we get the word that this dude's supposed to go out and pick this guy up. He's telling us everything about the guy. He tells us, 'He keeps the gun that he did it with, in his waistband.' He's tellin' us all this kind of shit. He goes, 'The trouble is, he lives out in the middle of the swamp. He's expecting me out there tonight, at midnight, to pick him up and take him down to California.'

So we're like, 'Fuck it, we'll do it.'

We roll up and we see this CI – Confidential Informer – and he's about the same size as one of our officers, so we get the officer to dress up in this dude's flannel shirt. We're driving his truck – and he's a carpet layer so he's got carpet in the back of his truck – and we have to drive out in the middle of this swamp. He tells us about this special horn signal: beepbeepbeepbeep – beepbeep, you know? It's split, and that's the signal for the guy to come running out to the truck.

So we put this plan together. I'll never forget it, the officer's got the flannel shirt on, we're driving this old sixties truck with carpet in the back, we threw a sniper with an M16 down under the carpet and I'm laying on the floor of the cab holding a little shotgun with an eleven-inch barrel.

I've got the door on the passenger side cracked open and I'm laying down with my feet against it and I said to the officer who was driving, 'When you see the dude, when he gets right in front of the door, let me know and I'll let him have it with both feet and just fucking try to knock his dick in the dirt. Then the guy in the back will pop up, cover him, we'll jump out and we'll fucking bulldog this guy.'

Dude, it worked like shit, but here's the deal: we roll out there and because of the weather there was this heavy fog – it was the most eerie thing you could imagine. And there's this mound of earth and a dyke that's around this house to keep the water from flowing out, or whatever.

It's the middle of the night and I'll never forget it because we're riding out there and you see the headlights go up through the fog as we go over the earth and dyke and I'm like, 'Oh fuck, this is great!' It was so eerie.

So I'm laying down, I've got a shotgun in my hand, the handle of the doors slipped and it's opened just about an inch so that he can't tell it's open, you know what I mean? Just waiting on him.

So the other officer gives the horn signal and he goes, 'Somebody's coming! Oh yeah, it's him! It's him! He's coming! Alright, get ready, get ready... GET HIM! GET HIM!'

BOOM! I hit him – I knocked his fuckin' dick in the dirt, dude! I jump out, the other officer runs around, the sniper pops up, we grab him, pummel him and cuff him. He's got the gun he killed the three kids with in his waistband. Took him into custody and that was it. Who would have thought that shit would have happened? But I'll never forget it, it was eerie dude, it was eerie. But you know how it is – it was just another mission. But it's so much fun, though. It really is.

****

When I was on the SWAT team, we had a gorilla from the zoo – his name was Little Joe – and he escaped. Little Joe, he escaped from the zoo.

The call came in from a payphone, a 911 call, 'The gorilla from the zoo just escaped. He's out of his cage.'

But it came from a payphone, so they dispatched a patrol unit there. The sergeant said, 'Yeah, have the unit respond but tell them not to kill themselves getting there.' – meaning it was probably a phoney or prank call – 'Still go but don't hurt yourselves by rushing there too fast.'

So it went off my radar until about ten minutes later when the cop on the radio said, 'It's legit! It's legit! He's coming over the fence!'

This huge gorilla was out! So we all responded up there, and the patrol force all had 40 calibre handguns and I wasn't sure – if God forbid, we had to stop him or take him down – I wasn't sure that was going to be enough. So I grabbed my sniper rifle and went up there. I get there and I see him. He's a gorilla! He's out! He's in the park!

You can't believe it. And he was dumping a trash barrel over his own head! And the last thing you want to have to do is shoot this poor gorilla because he doesn't know what he's doing.

So he was just kind of walking around, then he's coming towards us and he's like banging his chest and everything. Then at one point he starts running after us. There had to be probably fifty cops there by now – you know, pistols, rifles, I've got the big rifle and all this stuff – and we all just stated running. Running away. We don't want to shoot him, so we're running and we're kinda laughing too, because it is kinda funny. But it's a gorilla and he's out. He's out on the street.

He was out of the zoo but luckily he stayed in the park and he hadn't crossed the street to where houses and stuff were. And we knew that if he did go any further, we were going to have to stop him. I was going to have to shoot him if he crossed the street. So I'm hoping, 'Please, don't, just don't cross the street,' because the last thing I wanted to do was shoot this gorilla.

So he ended up just staying in the woods and we ended up getting a couple of his trainers up there and they break out the tranquilliser guns. And at one point, one of his trainers – we were going to let them shoot him because we didn't know anything about tranquilliser guns – so at one point one of the trainers has got the gun and she accidentally lets a round off. The thing went flying right through all of us. It didn't hit nobody but we found out it would probably have killed one of us. So we took that stuff from her and we then started shooting him with the darts (I didn't personally shoot him – I still had the lethal coverage, in case we had to use that) and he was ripping the darts out and throwing them back at us.

Finally, it got dark now, but the darts were taking effect, so he went a little more into the woods and we didn't hear him anymore and now we don't see him either, so we had to go into the woods and find him now and I remembered being so scared just thinking that he was going to jump out of a tree at me. One of the things is that he's so unpredictable; this thing would rip you apart.

We ended up finally finding him, passed out and we put him in a net and took him out. I remember seeing his hands and just how big he was. But it was fun. It was one of those calls: when you came on for duty you never thought that you'd be chasing a gorilla around today. You've got to laugh at some of the stuff we have to do – it's the only way to stay sane when this stuff happens – so we joke around a lot.

Little Joe is back at the zoo now. They rebuilt his cage. He was gone for a while but they brought him back.

That was a fun day.

6

Shootings

I expected two things would happen when I decided to speak to officers specifically about shootings. First, that it would be a difficult subject for them to talk about and second, that they would all have been involved in several shootings during their careers. I was wrong on both points.

Despite the fact that hundreds of people are killed by police officers every year in America, in what is termed as 'justifiable homicides', I found very few officers – surprisingly few, I thought – who had ever fired their guns or been fired at. Perhaps it was my diet of American TV cop shows that had led me to believe that all police officers in America are involved in shoot-outs on a daily basis, but it simply isn't like that.

For those officers who have fired their guns, whether at criminals, dogs or even innocent people, there was an unexpected indifference. Talking to me about these incidents was no big deal, it seemed. All officers told me that the last thing any cop wants to do is to actually shoot somebody, but for those that had, I did not find the expected devastation or remorse. It's not that they were cold to what they had done, rather that there certainly seemed to be a lack of sympathy. It was not the cop's fault that they had

had to open fire, after all, and surely it's better that they fired a shot and survived than the other way around.

Although, thinking back to these interviews, the reaction of one officer in particular comes to mind. His face was somewhere between being vacant and being in shock as he told me about the incident he had been involved in and I suspected that the shooting had had a greater effect on him than he was ready to admit, especially as his fellow officers were listening in.

The truth is, most officers have never and will never fire their gun. When I suggested that perhaps there was an argument for some officers in some parts of America to not be armed, they looked at me like I was an idiot. Because even though most will never use their weapon, many officers know someone who has and I guess that's the point: you just never know when you may be that officer.

I've been shot at before. I've had people attack me with knives and stuff. I've just never had the opportunity to shoot people before.

Here in the United States, most departments ask you a question – even before they hire you – 'Are you willing to use deadly force? Are you willing to take a life?'

Of course, if you say 'No', then they say, 'Thanks, but you're not right for this job'. And so everybody – on our department at least – has said yes to that.

But until you're really there, you don't know. And you know, most people question themselves. We use a lot of force. I've got into fights – I've fought over a gun, I've fought with people with knives and stuff – which is not a problem until somebody's actually trying to kill you and you're trying to kill them.

Most people really don't know how they're going to react. So you hope that you're going to react as best you can and you train and you mentally prepare for it and you do your best.

****

I'm going to do whatever it takes to do my job and protect others. Of course, you don't want to shoot people and I don't want to sound like a monster but shooting a person was not that emotional for me.

I had this case where I was out on patrol and I get a call from an officer who says that she'd just heard a gunshot. She was out on a call and there was a gunshot in the complex she was in and she says she's going to investigate it. A bunch of officers are going there to make sure she's okay. She gets on the radio again and says she's found a dead body inside the complex. We don't know if it's from the gunshots or not but we've got gunshots and a dead body, so it's possibly related.

I was on a swing shift at the time and my shift was just ending and as there was a bunch of graveyard units and homicide going I figured that they didn't need me there. So I was just going to go back to the station and finish up my paperwork and go home for the night. I'm waiting to turn at a red light when all of a sudden this car comes the other way through a red light at about a hundred miles an hour – flying through the intersection. I didn't think of it being related to the previous call, I just thought it was some drunk or something. It was very reckless driving and I decided that I couldn't just let it go, so I turned around and tried to catch up with it. By this time it was way down the street. It comes to the next intersection, goes through another red light and almost hits a pedestrian. So I get on the radio and tell them that I'm trying to catch up with this vehicle and giving the best description that I can – as I just saw it in a flash.

They're asking me, 'Are you in pursuit?'

I'm like, 'Well, not really a pursuit yet as I can't get close enough to go to pursuit; I'm just trying to catch up with him.'

I got to about a hundred and thirty miles an hour on the residential streets; kind of dangerous but I knew that if somebody didn't stop him, he was going to end up killing somebody. Ended up finally getting close enough to where I am actually in pursuit and he turns down this street and then tries to take another turn but he's going too fast, misses the intersection and hits the curb and almost goes through a wall. He then continues going down through some residential area with me following him.

Apparently a sergeant called up on the radio and advised that this vehicle may be involved in this earlier shooting. I was kind of involved in my pursuit and I didn't hear it. It hadn't even occurred to me that it might be involved because we've had this kind of thing before and it's usually just some drunk or somebody in a stolen car.

Then all of a sudden he stops, kind of in the middle of the street, kind of sideways in the street and he gets out, takes off running and falls down – trips over. And so I get out of my car and I think, 'Here's my chance to catch him'. So I'm running up towards him and then he starts coming up to one knee and pulls out a handgun and starts shooting at me. I've got bullets coming past me and I pull my gun out and start running back to my car, just shooting at him – BOOM, BOOM, BOOM – just kind of suppressive fire, to get back to my car. Hit him once and he goes down. I hit him a couple of times but I think that first one went in the abdomen area. It put him down and I got back behind my car door. Then he comes up and starts shooting again. So now I'm paying a little more attention and I shoot at him and that time I think I hit him in the chest. It goes in the chest but ricocheted off. It missed his heart but it put him down again. Then he gets up and he starts running towards one of the houses.

Now, I've done a lot of teaching with my Advance Officer Skills Training and I always say, handguns don't kill people; they don't even stop people. They may eventually kill people, because of the blood loss, the trauma. But if you don't take out something major, they're going to keep going and you must be aware of this.

Anyway, he goes running into a house. I go running up and I look at the front door and the front door is open. I'm calling it out on the radio and saying where it is and stuff. All of a sudden an older man comes out.

I order him, 'GET ON THE GROUND! GET ON THE GROUND!'

He's like, 'My son's just been shot!'

And I'm like, 'I know. I just shot him! Get on the ground!'

He's like, 'What's going on?'

I said, 'Just get out here and get down on the ground.'

He says, 'But my wife's inside.'

I wasn't going to go into the house but now I'm thinking, what's his intention? He just tried to kill me and he's acting this way, maybe he was trying to get back to their house to do them harm. I don't know if she's safe in there or not. So I decide I had to go in. I couldn't wait for backup to arrive.

So I go in and she's on the stairs crying and I ask, 'Where is he?

Where is he?'

She says, 'He's in our back bedroom.'

And so I'm like, 'Okay, come out, come out.'

I get her out of the house and then I go back in and I'm looking around trying to find him and I see a gun sitting on the coffee table. I don't know if it's his or not but there's a gun. Then I hear a noise in the back bedroom.

Again, I'm like, 'COME OUT! COME OUT!'

And then he comes into view and I'm ordering him, 'Get on the ground! Get on the ground!'

He turned towards me and he's not armed, so I'm presuming that this was his gun on the coffee table.

But then he charges at me and he says, 'You're never going to take me alive!'

I've got my hands full with the gun, so I kick him in the chest and knock him down. I knelt down on him, put my gun away and handcuff him.

Well, in the mean time, you know, things are a little bit stressful I guess, and I got the numbers on the house wrong. Well, other officers are arriving and they're kicking-in the door next-door. There's this old couple inside their house and the police are beating the door down. It's across the street from where I am but my vehicle is in the middle of the street and I got the numbers wrong. It all got straightened out I the end though.

The dad comes back into the house and I'm saying, 'Get out of here!'

He's like, 'You didn't have to kick my boy.'

I'm like, 'Kick him? I should have shot him again!'

It turns out that this guy had just murdered his girlfriend – the mother of his two-year-old little girl. He had murdered her in that complex and that was what the original shooting was. They found the girlfriend's body in the apartment complex. He then put the little girl in the car – she was in the car the whole time – down below the dashboard on the passenger side. I went past the car and didn't see her in there, but she was in there and she wasn't hurt.

He ended up getting two consecutive life sentences – one for murdering his girlfriend and one for the attempted murder on a police officer. He murdered his girlfriend because of a disagreement, a custody-type thing over the child. They weren't getting along very good, obviously.

****

I can't tell you what it's like in a quiet place but I worked in a place where if everybody wasn't looking out for everybody else, people got hurt. People *would* get hurt. It was a fucking dangerous, dangerous place.

The first week I was there, it was July and we were on the 4pm to 12am shift. We had just turned out of roll call and we're standing on the steps of the precinct when there was a drive-by shooting five hundred yards up the block. A guy drove by with a machine gun and just lit up the whole fucking corner. And the precinct was in the middle of the block! It was a dangerous, dangerous place.

A lot of it has to do with street rep, 'Look what I did. You don't got the balls to do that but I did it! You're not going to fuck with me now.'

They didn't care.

****

Detroit is generally a good city but the criminals are bad criminals. There are good people here and it's not a bad city, there's just a little more despair here, a little more joblessness and a little more poverty than the average city. The criminals here are worse than other criminals but the good people are good people. It's just that the bad are really bad and they overshadow the good.

Let me tell you this, this will show you the recklessness of the criminal with regards to human life. This will also show you the level of respect they – the criminals – have for law enforcement.

It was my first day back from vacation – my partner and I both – our first day back. So we decided that we were just going to take it easy that day, get back in real slow, just patrol and answer some police runs and ease back into the grind slowly. So, we made a traffic stop and gave the gentleman a break on the ticket – we didn't write him a ticket. We said, 'Here's your licence sir, just slow down and you can get on your way.'

He thanked me and he said, 'God is watching you today.'

I said, 'Oh, thank you sir, that's a really nice thing to say.'

He grabbed my arm and he stopped me and he said, 'No, I mean it. God is watching you today.'

So I'm thinking, wow, that was heavy.

So, once we got back into our scout car and made a u-turn, a car speeds by us. I look at my partner, he looks at me and I said, 'Go ahead and get him.'

So we tried to stop him, activated the lights and the car chase is on. I'm thinking, thank God this old man told me that God was looking out for me. So we chase him for a good ten minutes, in and out of the side streets, and we ended up getting on a major thoroughfare.

Then the back passenger leans out from the car with a gun – a big gun – and he starts shooting my car up. I'm five feet from him, maybe ten feet and he's unloading on me. He's in the passenger seat, so he's just firing and I'm ducking, trying to call the chase out whilst my partner's driving. So, all the bullets are coming on my side; he was just tearing us up.

So now the other passenger leans out, so I've got two guns firing at me as I'm calling the chase out. This happened for another few miles, up and down the street, shooting. I'm not shooting anything because I can't. I'm really under fire.

Turns out that they were going to do a robbery; they were going to rob a drug dealer. But we ended up getting the guys after they jumped out of the car and ran.

My car is Swiss cheese, buildings are shot up, but there're no injuries nowhere. It just took me back to that old guy who said, 'Hey, He's looking out for you today.' For him to say that and for me to be that close to gunfire and I didn't get hit, I was like, wow. And it just shows you: we're police, we're totally marked as police and both these guys are shooting at us anyway.

****

I've been involved in one shooting, as far as actually shooting *at* somebody. That night there was a person walking around with a revolver. It was tucked into his front waistband and he had tried to sell it to two thirteen or fourteen-year-old kids.

They want nothing to do with it and they walk over to the pay-phone at Seven Eleven and give us a call and say, 'Hey, there's a guy walking around with a gun that he's trying to sell to people.'

I was probably a good two miles away with another officer at the time. We got dispatched on it. I think it was a Friday night. Real busy night – it was the middle of summer. We happened to be the first ones there. We show up to the Seven Eleven and we talk to one of the kids.

The kid says, 'That's him right there.'

And he was by Luv-it Custard, which is on the other side of the street. So, we pull our guns out and we go across there and confront him. Basically, what we are going to try to do is to prone him out on the ground, pat him down and see if he has a gun. Well, it didn't work out that way. Instead he just turns and faces us.

He says, 'I've got a gun.'

My partner at that time was issuing him verbal commands. The guy lifts up his shirt and shows us the gun.

And it's like, 'Okay, we know you've got a gun, now let's not turn this into a big deal. We're just going to lay you down on the ground.'

So we're trying to prone him down on the ground and I remember looking at my backdrop, which was a gas station with a bunch of people standing around. We have our guns drawn on a guy who's also got a gun, we're in the middle of Las Vegas on a busy Friday night and there're people everywhere. It was not good.

We're trying to tell him to drop the gun and instead of people using common sense and thinking, 'maybe this is something I should back away from', it starts drawing a crowd! And the crowd doesn't realise that they're putting themselves in a dangerous position.

So I had to move around him so that my backdrop was now a wall and I'm warning my partner as I'm coming around, 'Hey, watch behind him. Watch behind him.'

After about thirty seconds of trying to negotiate with him, he reaches down and grabs the gun. But he doesn't do it in a furtive way – he kind of does it in a way that makes me think that maybe he's going to drop it on the ground. So he pulls it out with his finger and thumb and he's holding it up and so we're thinking he's going to drop it.

But then it's becoming clear that he's not going to drop it. He takes it and puts it into a firing type grip down by his side and I'm about to tell my partner that we can't have this go on. I mean, clearly this guy is posing an imminent threat to us and the public. We don't need him to start shooting at us first.

I was about to tell my partner, 'I'm going to drop him.' But just as I'm opening my mouth, the guy starts pulling the gun up. So we shot him. Dropped him. Thank God our backdrop was the wall. I think two or three rounds of the seven or eight that were fired, went errant and they hit the wall. They were all accounted for though. And that was pretty much it. It was over just like that. It's one of those things.

I remember the call that we were on before that one was just some silly civil call where two people couldn't get along, neighbours arguing. And you go from that to all of a sudden, four minutes later, you're in a shooting.

He didn't die fortunately – or unfortunately, however you want to look at it. He got hit three times. He got hit centre mass, hit in the gut and one through the pelvic girdle. Fortunately, we were eight blocks away from the hospital and they say if you make it to trauma alive, you're odds are pretty good that you are going to make it. He made it.

But the worst thing is that now you're off work forever. You're put on administrative leave. And for those of us that like to work, it's like, what do I do? I'm home all by myself, watching all this stuff on TV and of course, you're on the news and things like that. They tell you not to watch the news but how do you not watch the news? Everything that came after was actually more stressful than the shooting itself.

We went to court on him and he got found guilty of resisting a police officer with a firearm and some other things. He ended up going to prison, though I don't know how long he was sentenced for and I don't know if he's still there.

****

The shooting I was involved in was on a major highway between two states. It's a drug corridor. It's the major turnpike between two cities.

Listening to the radio one night, there was an armed carjacking and all of a sudden one of the cops in a neighbouring community says, 'I got the car! I'm behind the car!'

So now the high-speed chase starts. They come into my town and I get into the chase and we go out onto this highway. We're about four miles outside town and we now have five or six agencies involved – state police, several towns police – no one has direct radio communications with one another. The guy comes off the highway and loses it on the exit ramp and rolls the car over.

So with that, the 'blue army' comes screeching to a halt and we're all running around with our guns drawn. A state trooper runs around to the far side of the car and he slipped. He had his finger on the trigger of his gun and as he falls down he blows a round off. But all we see is him going down and the sound of gunshot. So everyone is like, BOOM, BOOM, BOOM, BOOM!

A hundred and some rounds later the guy jumps out the windshield with his hands up. He shit his pants. How he wasn't killed, I'll never know. I was amazed.

****

My first shooting was against a dog and that's definitely the best story. We got a call that there's a fight going on in a parking lot of a bar called The Roadrunner. I'm on the outskirts of town, I respond to it and I get out. There's another officer coming up behind me. We look around but there's no fight. It's dark. We're on the outskirts of town so there's no lighting in the parking lot other than what's coming off the bar. We look around the parking lot and another officer comes by in a patrol vehicle, driving through the parking lot shining a spotlight around. All of a sudden, he lights up this dog – this great big Doberman – on top of a car, trying to eat somebody inside. It's sitting there, biting and scratching on the windshield. The dog looks up and it sees me. I'm probably about sixty feet away from it and it gets to me in about two seconds. By the time it looked up and saw me I was able to drawer my gun and fire three rounds from the hip just before it reached me. Two of them hit it in the chest and the other one missed. The dog turned and ran off and we found it later, down the street under a car, dead. After I shot it, I'm standing around in shock.

The officer behind me is like, 'What just happened?'

He was kind of in shock as well – he was a new officer. Then the other officer, who had spotlighted the dog, got out of his car and starts looking around.

He gets on the radio and says, 'Control, we need homicide out here. We've got a dead body in the car. He's just been shot.'

So I'm thinking, 'Oh no! I just killed somebody!'

I'm thinking that one of my rounds ricocheted off the pavement and killed this innocent person in this truck. I didn't even dare go look. I'm in shock. I just killed somebody. It was not that big a deal shooting the dog but then I just killed an innocent person. So I'm just kind of standing around, you know, thinking, what am I going to do now? I've gotta wait for homicide.

About ten minutes later somebody else gets on the radio and says, 'Disregard it. It's just a 4-0-8.'

A '4-0-8' is a drunk. So he wasn't shot – he was just passed out in his vehicle. But this officer, without checking or anything, just got on the radio and took about twenty years off of my life!

It turned out that it was his dog – his prize breed attack dog. This was his baby. He never went anywhere without it. But he had passed out in his van with the dog in there with him. The dog escaped up though the sky-roof of the van and was then trying to eat people in the parking lot.

Anyway, that was the first time I'd fired my gun in the line of duty.

****

The one on-duty shooting I had to do in defence of myself was of a pit bull. There was an old man and everyday he'd go on a two-mile walk around his neighbourhood, carrying a walking stick. He walked down one street – I don't know if it was his street, but it was one of the streets he usually walks on – and as he was coming down, there were these two pit bull's that were loose and they charged him and attacked him. Neighbours saw it happen and they came out and were giving him aid, then they called the police.

110

I get there and the man's hand is all ripped up where the dogs laid into him and they also bit him just under his crotch on the inside of his leg. So he was ripped up pretty good and he's got this bloody rag holding on his hand, bleeding out of his leg and he was a heavy set old man, probably in his seventies. His walking stick was all chewed up where he was trying to beat them off of him and they were chewing on his walking stick.

The neighbours – when I got there, the whole neighbourhood was outside – they're sayin', 'Those dogs are a nuisance. They've been terrorising this neighbourhood for weeks. Those people have only lived here a few weeks and they let their dogs out all the time and they're terrorising the neighbourhood.'

One lady goes, 'Look at my house! Look at my front door!' And her front door was scratched all to pieces. And she was like, 'That's where those dogs chased me in my house and scratched up my front door!'

A woman who lived next door to this house where the dogs lived – and this is an older woman, she might have been in her sixties or seventies – she said, 'When I hear them barking outside, I don't come out that gate. I stay in my house all day long because I won't come out because of those dogs.'

So I was like, 'What house do these dogs live at?'

And they pointed and said, 'That house right there, where the car's parked. That's where they live.'

So I'm looking and I don't hear anything, don't see anything. So I say, 'That house right there?'

And they say, 'That house right there, yeah.'

I walked back to my car and I get my shotgun and I take my

slugs out and put buckshot in. My shotgun hangs on a tac-sling, so it hangs in front of my body. I walk in the street, in front of the house, then I'm looking around the corner of the house and it's got a privacy fence on one side – a six foot wooden fence that went between the house next door and the edge of the house that the dogs lived at – and then the other side of the house had a car under a carport and a chain-linked fence around the backside, so the backyard was completely fenced in and closed.

So I'm lookin' and I don't see anything and I don't hear anything. So I walked back down to the people and I was like, 'Are you sure it's that house?'

And they're like, 'Yeah, it's that house and look – right there's the dogs!'

So I turn and look and sure enough, right there in the front yard that I just looked at, sit two dogs – a tan pit bull and a black pit bull.

So I say, 'Alright.' And as I turned to walk back up, the dogs disappear. I stay in the street again, then walk up and I don't see 'em. I'm thinking, okay, somehow they're slipping in and out of the back yard. So I walked back down to the far side of the house where the privacy fence was and I walked up that edge of the yard. Then I walked right up against the edge of the house, got up on the porch and I was going to knock on the door because the car was there and I'm thinking that the owners gotta be home; so I'm thinking that they can come out and get their dogs.

So I pull out my baton and when I knocked on the door with the baton, it came down – the baton extended out – so I reached down and I collapsed it onto the ground to close it again. I went to put it back into my holster and as soon as I did that I heard the dogs.

RAWR! RAWR! RAWR! RAWR! They come haulin' around the corner, up the sidewalk, straight towards me and I'm on this little bitty four-by-four front porch; no rails on it, rose bush on each side, so I can't move. It's only about a foot off the ground. As the dogs are running right towards me, I guess instinct, training – I don't know – I screamed, hollered, 'GET BACK!' But dogs aren't going to obey me; they're pit bulls and pit bulls are known for being territorial.

The female was the one at the front and she ran all the way up on the porch – this little bitty porch – and the only thing that stopped her from biting me is the fact I'd swung my shotgun up and it was right in her face and she couldn't get around it. Well, the second I swung it, I pulled the trigger. And nothin' happened. The pucker factor went up considerably because nothin' happened. Well, I realised that I had not taken the safety off – which was a learning experience! So I hit the safety and pulled the trigger and BOOM! And it went right into her right eye socket and never came out. Nine pellet buckshot. She locked up completely, fell over on the porch and the male dog just turned around and ran back behind the house, hid in his doghouse and barked for the next hour. But she just locked up, fell on the porch and just bled out, on the porch.

And it was almost surreal because, you know, when you're on the range and you're shooting, gunshots are loud. You wear your headset but it's still loud. But when I pulled the trigger and it went off there was no ringing in my ears. A shotgun blast is loud – if you ever go out target shooting with your friends and you don't wear earplugs, your ears are ringing after you've fired a shot. But it was almost as though the adrenalin shut part of my body down. It wasn't loud; I could hear the people down the street going, 'Oh my God! Oh my God!' And of course, as soon as the blast went off and that dog fell, I immediately started trackin' the other one but he turned and ran, like I said. So I let him run.

At that point I had to notify my supervisor that shots were fired and I had just had to put down a dog that attempted to attack me after attacking an old man. So my sergeant pulled up maybe thirty seconds later – not even that, probably twenty seconds later – and he said, 'I heard your blast. I heard you shoot it.' He said, 'If you had waited only thirty seconds, I could have shot it and I wouldn't have to do all the paperwork on you because you shot it!'

So they had to call out the supervisors, the field captain, ID, everybody had to come out and they take photographs. They treated it just like I'd shot a person. They had to make me stand on the porch with my shotgun, directed the same way I was and they had to measure how far I was from the street to the nearest residence. If I'd missed, where the pellets would have gone, they measured everything. They took pictures of everything, drew diagrams of the house – where the dog was, where I was. The sergeant had to stand next to me the whole time, had to follow me from the scene straight to the precinct where I had to take a urine test, a drug test and take a breath test. They had to take my shotgun and drive it down to the ID office and they had to test fire it, take it apart, get all of the serial numbers off of it – just like I'd shot a person.

Four months later I had to go to the Chief's 'shoot and review' board to justify why I'd fired my weapon on duty in defence of myself or somebody else. I explained it to 'em – and I was dressed up in my full Class A uniform and tie because you wanna not look like a slouch – and they were like, 'We'll get back to you with our findings once we discuss it. It'll probably be a couple of weeks.'

I walked out and I was talking to another officer when they stepped back out, called my name and called me back in. I'm thinkin', 'Oh great!' Like I'm fixin' to get fired because I shot a dog!

I walked in and they said, 'We talked about it. You're all good.'

But the owners weren't even home when I shot that dog. And they never even called. Animal control came and scooped up the dead dog on the porch, went around back and noosed the other one and took it because it was a nuisance to the neighbourhood. So they took both dogs – one of them bein' dead – and left the blood on the porch. And that blood, by the time we got done, it congealed and swelled up to about two inches thick. It just swelled up on the porch. We don't clean it off – that's their problem. So we left all the blood there and they never called. Never called to ask what happened to their dogs, what all this blood was on their front porch – nothing. Never asked. Probably not the best pet owners.

****

I had maybe a year-and-a-half on the street. I'm in Harlem. I'm in Central Harlem – bad place. Really, really, really bad place. I have a 38 revolver. There was a road – there still is a road – from the 145th Street Bridge at Lenox Avenue up into Washington Heights. Used to be called the Ho Chi Min Trail because so much drugs and money was moved between The Bronx and Manhattan. That's what we called it; we called it the Ho Chi Min Trail. It was an every day occurrence, twenty-four hours a day. Money, drugs and guns were being transported back and forth and they would always use cabs – unmarked livery cabs. They were the only things that operated up there, you know? Yellow cabs wouldn't go above 96th Street back then, or 100th Street, something like that. It was just too dangerous. If you saw a yellow cab up that high, you would follow it because that guy was getting robbed. So these were cabs that you had to call up for – order-a-cab type thing. Or you'd hail it off the street, which was illegal but it was the only cab service that was operating up there. There were no yellow cabs.

So I'm working with a guy who was not my regular partner and you know, cops have instinct and intuition right? When somebody looks at you, you just know. It's the way they look at you, the way they move after they look at you. You just know that there's something wrong. So one of the ways we worked to make arrests would be to follow a cab, because most of the cabs had violations – tail lights were out, drivers would make wacky turns, they wouldn't signal – so you would get your summons quota and maybe you'd get lucky on the car stop, right? Because the minute you flicked your lights on, the guys in the back seat of the car would turn around and look at you and they would do what we called 'The Harlem Dip'. The way that they moved in the back of the cab, you knew that they were stashing something. You just knew. It was such a dramatic movement. You knew that it wasn't normal.

So, we were going westbound and the cab was going eastbound and as we passed each other the two guys in the back seat looked at me and I just knew. I turned around in the middle of the block and we go to stop them on 7th Avenue and 145th Street.

The two guys jump out of the cab and I tell the guy I'm working with, 'You grab the guy who's going towards the bodega and I'll get the other guy.'

A bodega is like a candy store, right? So one guy is like, going into a store on the corner and the other guy is going down the block. No problem. I start to go after the other guy and the next thing I know is, he's pulling out the biggest gun I ever saw in my entire life. It just kept coming; he kept pulling and it kept coming. It was like a 45 or something. It was a huge gun. So he's pulling this gun out and I start to pull my gun out. And I'm a rookie!

What am I thinking? I'm thinking, 'Motherfucker!' I'm thinking that we're going to have a shoot-out right here on the corner, right? So I pull my gun out and I swear to you I was so pumped up and full of adrenalin that I was pulling the trigger before the gun even cleared the holster. I won't lie to you – I'm lucky I didn't blow my leg off, I swear to God. As soon as the gun cleared the holster, I'm sure I was pulling the trigger.

So, clearly I missed with the first shot, right? Because at that point we're facing each other and the guy is still pulling the gun out. Then he turns and starts running down the block. But immediately after I took that first shot, I see in the background that there was this old black guy standing there, right? Shot goes off, black guy hits the ground like a rock – like, BOOM, BOOM!

I'm like, 'Holy shit!'

So I'm already thinking I shot that old man, right? Now I'm chasing this guy on foot down the block and for the first time ever in my life I'm catching him; I'm actually catching up to this guy. He was originally twenty feet ahead of me and I'm now within five or six feet of him. I'm actually catching up and this guy realises it. Like, 'Oh fuck! This short, fat, white cop is going to catch me!'

At that point he had not fired at me. So, I'm within five or six feet of him and all of a sudden he turns around and points the gun at me and I take a second shot at him, which I completely missed and he takes off running again. He's holding the gun under his arm, still pointing it at me and I'm getting closer to him. I'm thinking, 'Fuck! This guy's gonna shoot me. I've missed twice. He's going to shoot me – this fucking guy!'

As we come to a corner, I dip off the sidewalk behind a car and completely lose this guy in a gas station. Gun, perp – gone. Gone! Nobody has a clue where the fuck this guy went.

Next thing I know, over the radio, 'We have a man shot on 145th Street.'

'Fuck, I killed that black guy', that's what I'm thinking. I'm like, 'Motherfucker!'

It turns out it wasn't him, the black man didn't get shot, he just hit the deck. Out of pure instinct he just hit the deck. Turns out it's some other guy halfway down the block who was sitting on some steps. He's sitting on the steps and I shot him in the elbow. I missed the perp and I hit this other guy in the elbow.

So, the whole time I'm thinking to myself, 'Okay. I took two shots. I missed. I shot this guy in the elbow but it's okay because my partner caught the other guy'. Nope. The guy I was working with that day – who I had never worked with before – when the shooting started, he jumped back in the car and hid underneath the fucking steering wheel. Left me swinging in the fucking breeze! That's the God's honest truth. He left me swinging in the fucking breeze. Gun, perp – gone. Second perp – gone. We got nothing. I don't even think the fucking cab was still on the scene. Just an innocent man shot.

Alright, I've got a year-and-a-half on the job, I don't have that much time but it's okay. You know, what's the worst they can do to me? Go to prison? Whatever.

When the detectives come – because now it's a major issue – the detectives come and the first thing the guy that got shot said was, 'I don't know what happened. That cop was chasing that guy with the gun and I got shot.'

Right there I was cleared – because the old man said the guy I was shooting at had a gun in his hand. Nothing happened to me. This man gets shot in the elbow and nothing happened to me. He went to hospital and was saying how he had just hit 'Cop Lotto', because he could have sued the city and got a lot of money. The city laws are that you have to sue within one year and one day. The guy never sued.

Four years later he gets arrested for selling drugs, by two cops. I see him as they're walking him into the station house. I walked over to the two cops and I said, 'Listen, just take the handcuffs off and let him go.'

'What are you talking about?'

'That's the guy I shot in the elbow – he did the right thing. Just let the fucking guy go.'

They were like, 'It's eleven-fifteen, we're just about to make ten hours overtime. We're not letting him go.'

They would have let him go if it was earlier in the day, but they weren't giving up the overtime. I was so fucking mad.

****

These two guys car-jack this girl. Her brother was in the gas station and when he came out they made him get on the ground. He had a CPL – a licence to carry a gun – but they didn't know he had a gun, so when they jumped in the car and took off, he started firing at them so they started firing back at him.

The police see 'em and they ditch the car, jump out, start running and start shooting at the police.

Well, me and my partner hear the call come out and we're like, 'Damn, we're supposed to get off early today! They were letting us go at twelve.' But I was like, 'Fuck it, let's go over there.'

We got over there, they had a perimeter, they had them boxed in and we can still hear them firing at each other.

Then one of them, he came over a fence, pointed his gun at me and I lit his ass up. Knocked him back over the fence. I shot him three times – he didn't die though. I hit him twice in the chest and one in the leg.

He didn't shoot at me – he didn't get a chance to – but he had shot at all these other officers.

Shit, I smoked about two and a half packs of cigarettes after I shot him. But I don't feel no guilt. I didn't feel sorry for him at all. He ended up getting twenty-eight years. I wish I'd killed him.

****

Obviously there is a lot of criticism of police after a shooting. Sure, a person can get shot ten times, but the cops didn't shoot him once or twice and wait until he fell on the ground before walking over to him and shooting him five more times. He was obviously still standing or still coming forward and you're trained to shoot until you stop the threat. So, as long as he's standing and as long as he's moving towards you, you would continue to fire. It's a horrible situation; you don't want to be in it but it happens.

You know, what happens is, especially if there is a gun involved and you know the other guy has a gun, a lot of times, when this thing's happening, you shoot and then your partner shoots, or somebody else starts shooting. Like, where are the shots coming from? You know? It kind of carries on 'til something stops.

I think generally, the perception is, when the dust clears, the true story comes out and that kind of calms things until the next time – until the next shooting.

They had a good program years ago where some of the politicians and outspoken community leaders, who were always moaning about the police and the use of guns and everything else, were taken to a police firing range. They don't understand how split second that decision is to make. They don't understand how quick and how fast you have to make that decision. So they took them to the firearms training centre and they gave them a little lesson on how to handle weapons and whatnot. And they gave them an opportunity to shoot the guns and then they put them into a simulator. They can control the scenario of the simulator and you have either a gun or a can of mace. So, they give you a scenario, you step up to the front of the screen, the scenario plays out and you talk to the screen. And every single one of them – the news people, the church people, the neighbourhood people, everybody who's the first one to be critical of how we act in a shooting – every single one of them, killed every civilian in every scenario, period. The end. They made the wrong choice every single time. It was a little bit eye-opening for them, and it kind of quietened them down for a while.

How do you make that decision when to shoot? Like, how quick do you have to make that decision? Because it does happen quick.

****

The media won't be on your side. They'll say things like, 'The police department murdered an innocent guy today when all he was doing was robbing a bank.' Or, 'Another homicide was committed by offic-ers this weekend and all the guy did was cut his mum's throat with a knife and they shot him.'

If you are not friends with the media, they will say whatever they want to say.

****

I'm not a very religious person but I'll never forget that we had this situation where we had an armed robbery taking place over on Liv-ernois, at this store and the run comes out: 'Armed robbery in pro-gress'.

Officers respond – a male and female team. The female officer, if she wasn't the absolute worst shot in the damn police department, she had to be close. She had as many notes saying 'Does Not Qualify' on her firearms record or 'Did Not Qualify' as she had 'Barely Quali-fied'. If she qualified, she barely qualified. And there were several years when she did not qualify.

So anyway, they pull up and the guy jumps out and shoots her partner – drops his ass. He then takes off running. Livernois is an eight-lane street and he's running across Livernois at top speed. She pulled her firearm, pulled the trigger and beamed his ass right in the fuckin' head! And I – probably as an expert shot for a majority of my career – could have never made that fuckin' shot!

But to me, that was an act of God. No fuckin' question about it. She was probably the worst shot on the department and she beams his ass, right in the fuckin' head.

****

I don't know, maybe it's just me because of my spiritual beliefs but I believe that I have the right to take a life if I need to.

Every time you get involved in a shooting you have to go to the shrink – the psychiatrist. I had to do an interview and write all these things down and then they put it into a computer. So besides him analysing me, I now get analysed by a computer, too. And he showed me the computer printout and everything's down there – there's like a baseline – everything's down below the baseline but there's one that's way high up. I mean, clear to the top.

I'm like, 'What is this? What does this mean?'

'That's the computer saying that you're lying.'

'What do you mean?'

He's like, 'The computer's saying that going through this experience, you should not be all down here so the computer's saying that you're giving false answers.'

I'm like, 'I don't know – this is just the way I feel. I don't feel that I've done anything wrong. I don't feel any shock or trauma or sorrow over this. I was just stopping somebody who was doing bad things and that was my job.'

I have spiritual beliefs and I believe that we're not supposed to take a life but in the defence of ourselves or others, we have the right to do that. If there are bad people out there trying to kill good people, then we have the right to use deadly force in order to stop it. I don't feel any great sorrow or anything that I did my job and shot somebody. I've never killed anybody but I can't see it being that big a difference, in my mind.

Some people can't take it though. I know some officers that have been in shootings and they've left the job because they couldn't deal with it, psychologically. But this is what we do.

7

Vice

I was sitting with a police officer in a harbour-side restaurant, eating excellent crab cakes...they really were very good – big lumps of crab meat, perfectly seasoned... anyway, where was I? Ah yes, Baltimore – and having never seen the TV show 'The Wire' and my only knowledge of Baltimore being 'Hairspray – The Musical', I wasn't ready for where the conversation was going to go. When the officer I was dining with lowered her voice to talk to me about 'blowjobs', I almost stopped eating. Only almost, though, because those crab cakes were amazing.

The funny thing was, even though she had spent part of her career walking the streets of the city, pretending to be a prostitute, she still struggled to use the actual words of the acts she was requested to do by the 'johns'. She was embarrassed. And that's one of the things with vice – there's an awkwardness to it, like sleeping with a new partner for the first time. It's about sex and dirty little secrets and fetishes.

Some officers' though – usually the men – had no problem telling me all about the filthy little situations they found themselves in. Speaking to officers about vice was always eye opening; just when you think you've *heard it all, along comes on officer with a look in their eye of, 'I can't wait to see the expression on your face when I tell you about this'.*

There was a lot of embarrassed (and not so embarrassed) laughter, when these stories were told. And it can be a lot of fun – if dressing up like a prostitute or pretending to be a pervert is your idea of a good time. You get to see and – almost – do all the things that you are about to arrest somebody for, without actually having to physically do whatever they were expecting you to do. I imagined it would be like an actor who always has to play the good guy, suddenly getting offered the part of the villain.

Of course, such a shadowy and bleak world has its dangers and as the officer in Baltimore reminded me, it isn't victimless, despite what people sometimes think. Whether it's the girl prostituting herself out through desperation or the spouse at home, unaware of their partner's secret life, vice can ultimately be devastating for all of the players involved.

We had a guy called 'Bloody Charlie'. He drove up to our undercover officer who was pretending to be a prostitute and goes, 'Are you on your period?'

And she's like, 'What?'

He says, 'Are you on your period?'

She's like, 'No!'

And with that, he drives off. So we can't arrest the guy, as we don't have anything on him. We were all like, 'That was the weirdest thing.'

Later, we were picking up prostitutes – we've got somebody out there patronising the prostitutes, making the deal, then we make the arrest and put them in the van.

So I'm driving and I say, 'You know girls, I want to ask you something. Have you ever had a guy drive up to you and ask you are on your period?'

They were like, 'Oh, yeah, Bloody Charlie.'

We were like, 'Bloody Charlie?'

One of them goes, 'Yeah, all the girls know him. He only likes to fuck girls when they're on their period.'

Is that not nasty? So 'Bloody Charlie' is the guy that drove up to our undercover that day and tried to patronise her. But she wasn't on her period so he didn't want to do it. How disgusting is that?

****

When I came out of the academy they used to put you on the foot squad to make you walk around to try and take all the piss-and-vinegar out of you, so you didn't go out and wreck a car on your first day out there. So I'm in the foot squad for three days, in this horrible little shopping centre where literally no one wants you there – it's not in a good neighbourhood so there are only, like, five stores. They don't want you there. And I'm thinking, 'Did I make a horrible mistake? I can't believe that I just went through six months in the academy to be trapped here. It's June, it's hot and I'm just miserable.'

Then I get a phone call at home – after my miserable three days on the foot squad – and it's the vice sergeant, from the district. He told me who he was and asked me if I was willing to work vice – young female cops like me often get asked that. Remember, I've been on the streets for three days. So I said, 'Sure.' I could either stand in a shopping centre in a hundred degrees, doing absolutely nothing, or I could go out there and lock people up.

So, day four, I'm working vice and I get a little bit of training from the two guys I'm working with, about what I should do, what I should expect, and then they just send me out there. We're locking up people by the wagon-full because the area was known for prostitution. The guys would lock up the prostitutes and I would lock up the johns. In the first three months I got drugs, I got guns, I got wanted felons – you name it. And then, of course, I got the experience, as I had to testify in court almost every single day, because we were locking people up every night.

Being in a courtroom full of people was an experience. I had to say all those things. Some of the stuff I didn't even know what it was. So I literally had to say all those bad words in an open court. If I got lucky, they did a silent reading of the statement and charges, but if they didn't, I had to get up there and testify and say, 'And then he asked me for... this!' Things like, 'half and half'- meaning half sex and half oral sex. Or they would ask you for just oral sex – and you can fill in the term they used for it yourself – or they could ask you just for sex.

The sex in itself was illegal. The oral sex, you had to get a price on. But for me, because I was new at it, I'd get a price for everything. I made them tell me how much they were going to pay me. So yeah, I had to testify in court – hundreds of people in there – to this stuff. I'm twenty-two years old and it was embarrassing. Even the judge once said to me, 'I never saw anyone turn that red in my entire life.' He told me I was hilarious.

I mean, I've done a lot of things in my career but I look back on that and just laugh, because here I am, some girl from the suburbs, and I'm standing out there on North Point, prostituting myself. My parents would be so proud! And I was literally getting the education of my life. It was a very funny moment in my career.

But we didn't have a booking district, so we had to go to the next district along, to book our prisoners and there was a particular sergeant there – a desk sergeant – and you know what these desk sergeants can be like; grouchy, unhappy campers and they'd say all kinds of stuff to you. If you screwed something up, they would let you know.

So I come in one night and I actually had a guy who had offered me five dollars for a particular sex act. I didn't know what I was doing, so I said, 'Sure.' And I locked him up. I didn't care if he offered me five dollars or fifty dollars – it's all the same to me because he's going to jail. So anyway, I get in there and the desk sergeant is reading the charges and he was like, 'Oh, honey, you know if you dressed a little better you'd get more than five dollars!' He was just shaking his head at me.

I thought about it afterwards and I spoke to one of the other girls and asked her what I should have done. She said, 'You should have told him to go to the ATM machine and get more cash!'

But I literally had guys ask me for stuff that I didn't even know what it was. I was twenty-two years old. I didn't know anything about life, let alone the sex trade.

****

A guy once patronised our undercover prostitute with his three-year-old in the back seat. It was three days before Christmas and he told his wife he had to go and get more Christmas lights for the tree and a gallon of milk. But she wanted him to take the baby so that she could take a shower. So he takes the baby, he goes to get the Christmas lights and a gallon of milk and as he's out driving he sees our prostitute – our undercover officer – who happens to have very large boobs. He saw her and he thought, 'The hell with it, I'll get a quick head before I go home.'

He drove up to her and she said, 'But you have a baby in the back seat.'

He says, 'It's three months old. She's not going to know you're giving me head. Come on, let's go, hurry up. I've gotta get home and put the Christmas lights up.'

And all of this is on tape. So we locked this poor bastard up and had the wife come and get the baby.

She's like, 'What did he get arrested for?'

We said to him, 'You tell her.'

He told her, 'I got arrested for a driving suspension.'

She's like, 'How the fuck can your licence be suspended? Your licence is not suspended.'

She arguing with him on the phone and he just tells her that it's suspended, hands me the phone and tells me to hang it up.

He's like, 'Please don't tell her. Please, please. I just had a baby with her, please. You don't understand, for nine months she wouldn't give me sex and then she has the baby and she still doesn't want to have sex. All I wanted was some fucking head. That's all!'

I actually felt bad for the guy.

But our Lieutenant said, 'Fuck him.' After we arrested him, she went up to the car, grabbed the baby and said, 'You're an animal.'

She was so pissed off at this guy for putting the baby's life in jeopardy. Remember, you're picking up women with scabies, HIV, all this stuff, and on top of that, you're in a bad neighbourhood. He literally went there, to that area, to get head, with the baby in the car.

I didn't tell the wife shit but the undercover told her. She said, 'There's no way the wife's not going to know what her husband's doing. He put their daughter's life in jeopardy.'

****

When I worked prostitute detail, they used to have to go lock the girls up before they would let us go stand out on the street. There would be a couple of us and they would have to get the real girls and lock them up first, because if you put us next to them, we would look way too healthy and way too clean. I mean, they used to tell us to go out in the garden all day, get really dirty, don't shower, and then they'd want to black in one of our teeth. But I'm not doing all that, you know? That's just not going to happen. So they would have to take all the unhealthy, really disgusting, open sores girls off the streets and then they could put us out there.

It was an experience men will never have. Obviously they would pick up the girls, so they had their own experiences, but I had a trucker try to pull me through his window one time. Luckily the guys that I was working with were watching me and they saw it. And I was unarmed – back then we had revolvers but there was nowhere to hide a revolver. No radio, either. You just have to trust the guys you work with. They're watching me. But if they're taking a break, that could be a problem.

That was a funny time, but sad too. I think about these guys and most of them are married and they had families and they were going to pick up some nasty junkie and have sex with her and then go home to their wives and their families. People think it's a victimless crime but I don't know. I never saw it that way.

****

We were in what we call the 'P-van' – the prisoner van – and I've got all the arrested johns in the back seat. I was doing the paperwork in this unmarked van, with the prisoners sitting behind me. It had no police markings or anything, so we could pull into an area and not be noticed. We would move up when we made an arrest, cuff the johns and put them in the van. We'd then back the van up and park it in a nondescript area so that we weren't noticed and do the paperwork. So, I'm looking down, writing the arrest reports to get it started, so that when we get back in the office we have less to do, when all of a sudden I hear a bang on the hood of the van. There's a guy getting head from a prostitute on the hood of my van and the prisoners are sitting there watching this. She's blowing the guy on the hood of my van!

And I go, 'What the fuck is this?'

And all the johns – in one voice – from the back of the van go, 'How come he can do it but we can't?'

I hit the siren – WHOOOOP! – and get out of the van.

The prostitute jumps up. She's got a pack of cheese doodles – which are like Cheetos – in one hand and orange cheese doodle shit all over her mouth. She's got cheese doodle all over her lips, she's got cheese doodle on her hands and she's got cheese doodle in her hair. The guy then starts to pull his pants back up and he's got cheese doodle all over his frigging dick.

He says, 'It's not what you think!'

This is the shit you can't make up!

We were like, 'It's exactly what we think!'

****

When I was the undercover john, the signal was that I would take my hat off; that would be the sign that the deal was done, because some-times the radio wasn't working right. The other officers could hear what you were saying but you would always take your hat off because sometimes you'd drive into an area and the radio signal would be lost. You could be making a deal with a prostitute and she might have HIV or something and she's trying to pull your zipper down, and you're like, 'Hello? Is anybody hearing me?', so you would take your hat off to make sure they knew you had made the deal.

Well, I get in the car one day and this frigging real nasty one, she gets into the car and says, 'Kiss me.'

I said, 'Are you out of your mind? Number one, I've never kissed a prostitute, I won't kiss a prostitute. You're here to do one thing, suck my dick and that's it. I ain't kissing shit.'

She says, 'Okay, pull your dick out.'

I'm like, 'What's the matter with you? We haven't even moved yet.'

She goes, 'I want to make sure you're not a cop.'

I'm like, 'I'm not a cop. I wouldn't be putting you in my car if I were a cop. If you're going to get weird then I'm going to think that you're a cop. Just get out of my car.'

She goes, 'No, no. I'm not a cop. I'm not a cop.'

I said, 'You know what? I don't trust you, get out of my car.'

She says, 'No, no, no, no. I'm telling you, I suck a good dick.'

I'm like, 'Well how much do you charge for sucking dick?'

So she goes, 'Twenty bucks.'

I said, 'Alright.'

So I take my hat off – giving the signal – and she starts grabbing my zipper.

I'm waving my hat but little did I know that they're sitting right behind us in the van, laughing their asses off watching me waving my hat with her right in my lap!

I said to her, 'Alright, that's enough! That's enough!'

I got out of the car, took my hat and threw it at them, in the van.

They get out laughing and then she gets out and goes, 'You are a cop!'

I'm like, 'Yeah. I'm a cop.'

She says to the other cops, 'He let me suck his dick!'

My pants are up but she got my zipper open. I'm like, 'Yeah right, you sucked my dick! I don't think so!'

My sergeant goes, 'In three seconds? You know what, I believe her!'

****

Our undercover female officer would have a wire on her and I used to predominately work the wireless tape recorder. We're in a van watching her and we have somebody 'ghosting' her, like a backup that's close to her in case she gets touched or gets into trouble. But we also have the backup cars that move in when she makes the deal.

So this guy drives up and I'm listening to her talk to him and listen to what he's saying to her. He drives up and he says to her, 'How you doing?'

She goes, 'Hey, you looking for a date?'

He says, 'I just want to know, are you clean down there?' And he points at her crotch.

She looks down – I'm listening and watching at the same time – she looks down and she goes, 'Am I clean down here?'

And he says, 'Yeah.'

She says, 'Of course I'm clean down there!'

He says, 'I'll give you forty bucks if you let me eat your pussy.'

She says, 'Wait a second, you want to pay me forty dollars to eat my pussy?'

He says, 'Yeah.'

She makes the deal, we move in and we get him. We get back to the office and I say to her, 'Well, we never had a guy drive up to you and say that before!'

She says, 'Let me tell you what I thought. Remember when I said, "You want to pay me forty dollars to eat my pussy?"'

I said, 'Yeah.'

She said, 'I almost turned the wire off and told him, 'Okay, let's go!"'

****

My partner and I were working a high prostitution area. It was the middle of the night and we see a street girl jump in a car, so we follow them. We see them park up and we give them a little bit of time before we go up on them, suspecting that maybe there'll be an act going on.

We come up on the windows and my partner's like, 'Whoa! What the hell are you doing?'

The girl had a high heeled shoe in her hand and she was hitting the old man's genitals – and he was obviously excited.

We're like, 'What in the world is going on here?!'

And the girl says, 'He pays me to do that. That's all he wants.'

Well, what can you do? You've just got to tell them to knock it off and then conduct your follow up investigation.

That's the dark side – the crazy stuff that the general public would never, ever see.

****

Here in Las Vegas, there are a lot of adult bookstores and these adult bookstores have 'theatres'. Basically, you go in and there'll be all the dirty magazines, all the graphic videos and all the products for sale – you know, dildos and things like that. Well, at the back of these stores they've put in little theatres that might have three or four rows with twenty seats and a large screen showing porn. There're also little arcade booths that you put quarters in and it shows a number of different porn things on them. So a lot of guys will go there.

Well, these areas are high trolling areas for gay men to hook up with other gay men for sex acts in these places, and it's not exclusively gay men – there are couples that have kinky fantasies; husbands will bring their wives there and things of that nature.

The Vice section at that time would bring up fresh faces from patrol or from somewhere else, because a lot of their guys had been there for a while and had been identified or become too well known. Well, one of the things that they would do, they would send you into these little bookstores. You'd go in and observe the different illegal acts. Then they'll throw the lights on in the theatre and you then point them out so they can cite everybody or arrest whoever, depending on the circumstances.

When you first go up – the first time that they send you into the adult bookstore – usually you are horrified. And I certainly was, the first time I went in there, because honestly, I had no idea what went on in these adult bookstores, these little arcades and these little theatres.

I had to go and work with a group of old timers who had been in

Vice forever, and they're giving me advice like, 'Okay, listen, don't sit down in any of the chairs, because obviously you've got a lot of different people coming and going and they're either by themselves or with someone else and they're masturbating or they're engaged in sex acts.'

So the advice to not sit down was easy to figure out. I don't want to sit in somebody else's 'problem' or biohazard or fluids.

And then they tell you, 'Okay, if you stand by the wall, certain people are going to come up to you – because that's like a sign for certain people – and they're going to come up and they might be doing things.'

And I'm like, 'Good grief! What am I getting myself into?'

Obviously we have transmitters on our radios and we're in communication with the outside should something go wrong, but you're essentially in there by yourself.

The particular place I was sent into was one of the larger bookstores, where a lot of activity was known to go on.

They sent me in there and they tell me, 'Observe for a while and remember who's doing what. When you give us the "bust" signal, we'll come in and shut the place down, turn all the lights on and get everybody.'

So I get in there, I pay and I go through into the theatre and I'm just eyes wide open! Unbelievable! It's Sodom and Gomorrah going on in there! Literally. There's guys sitting in seats masturbating, there're two guys on the wall playing with each other, there's one guy giving oral sex to another guy, there's a young gangbanger with a bandana on and a flannel shirt, looking like a tough guy, who was engaged in anal sex with an old man who had a nun's habit on!

And mind you, this is my first time in there, this is early on in my career and I'm the new guy on the squad! It's literally a scene out of Caligula or Sodom and Gomorrah and you're trying to remember each person and what they're doing so that later you're either going to be citing them or arresting them. So, I've got probably fifteen different sex acts on seven or eight different people, you know? They're intermingling and changing around.

I've probably only been in there not even ten minutes and they're telling me on the radio, 'Give it a little time, give it a little time.'

And I'm like, 'No way! This is out of control. You've got to get everybody in here now.'

So I give the bust signal and I'm expecting the lights to come on and everybody to come in. But there's nothing. No response. So I give it again. I wait and I'm starting to get a little nervous and I'm thinking that maybe my equipment's not working. So I'm moving around and literally you have what I would call 'zombies' following you, trying to... you know, because you're the fresh meat or the new person in there that they haven't seen before. They may have their pants down or they're trying to make a motion to you.

The normal reaction of a cop of course is, 'Get the hell away from me! Stay away from me!'

So it had to look kind of funny, like a choreographed dance, where I'm trying to stay away from people but at the same time I've got to get close enough to identify them and see what's going on.

Long story short, Vice not coming in on the bust signal was kind of a joke or rite-of-passage, to make me squirm for a little bit on my first go-around. So I was probably in there ten minutes longer than I had to be, dodging these guys coming at me from all directions. And then they come in and we finally shut the place down and everyone laughs. Ha-ha-ha, you know? But that was just one example of the bookstores, and there are so many more.

8

Gangs

*M*any officers would speak to me about their gang problems but frequently they would state that their gangs were 'not real gangs like you get in LA or Chicago'. When you think about gangs, it is the Bloods, Cripps and Vice-Lords type groups that comes to mind and from what I heard, these types of gangs are better set up in those two cities, with their organised trade in drugs and their well-established neighbourhoods and zones. 'Enterprising' was a word I heard more than once.

In some other cities, officers told me that their gangs were either wannabes or just a bunch of criminally minded kids calling themselves a 'gang' and attempting to emulate those from Chicago and LA. But although these 'wannabes' may be disorganised, they can still be deadly dangerous. Guns, murder and violence characterise all these gangs.

Of all the tours and 'ride-alongs' I have been on over the years, it was without doubt in the gang areas of Chicago where I felt the most vulnerable; feeling that had I stepped out of the police patrol car and wandered down the road alone, I would have been shot dead within minutes. It was seriously frightening. LA wasn't much better – I was once surrounded *by a gang in Compton, South Central and had to be saved by the LAPD. I honestly thought I was going to die.*

In Detroit, a cop told me I would be targeted and attacked very quickly in the 'ghetto' areas of his city but only because the people were poor, desperate and wanted whatever I had. Whereas speaking and riding with officers in Chicago, as well as reading the crime reports, it was clear that in some areas, I would be shot and killed by a gangbanger for literally no reason whatsoever. I read more than one account where an innocent person had been shot but not robbed. Just shot for the hell of it, or perhaps as part of a gang initiation.

Officers who work in these type of environments have a curious relationship with the gangs, as you will read, and I was left with the impression that it was one of feigned regard ('respect' is probably too strong a word, although it was used) whilst always – sometimes metaphorically, sometimes literally – keeping one hand on their gun.

The gangs are basically doing the same thing, but they're doing it differently. The black gangs are all about business, about the money, they're all about selling. They'll do whatever they have to, to maintain their spots. They'll kill you in a minute. Usually – not all the time – but usually if someone gets killed it's because of money. It's because of the drug spot – somebody moving into somebody else's territory.

A lot of times, with the Spanish gangs, it's all about, 'Oh, he looked at my girl', just stupid stuff. They're basically protecting their 'hood'. So if a member of a different gang is going through their neighbourhood and they know he's from another gang, they'll kill him, they'll shoot at him or whatever. And vice-versa, they go back and forth. But it's not about money – it's just about turf. They both sell drugs though, the black and Spanish gangs.

White gangs? They're not too strong in this city. There really aren't a lot of white gangs in Chicago. There are whites in some of the Spanish gangs but very few in some of the black gangs. Usually black gangs are all black. Usually. You may have some Hispanics in there but in the Spanish gangs you'll have a variety. You'll have eighty percent Spanish, ten percent black and ten percent white.

White gangs, they're usually about smoking pot and drinking. They might sell drugs, but they sell inside, they won't be on a corner. It'll just be by word of mouth. You'll go to this house to buy weed, you'll go to that house to buy cocaine. You do it inside.

Spanish and black gangs, they'll have street corner sales, because they do it more. It's a huge business, street corner sales of narcotics, just huge. You'll drive in some neighbourhoods like the Eastside, Westside and Southside, you'll pull up, they'll have look-outs and most of the time they'll look at you, they'll try to figure out if you're the police or not. If they don't think you're police, they'll direct you, 'go to that corner' or 'go to that alley' or 'go to that gang member'. You can either do it on foot or you can do it in your car.

It's crazy. In some neighbourhoods, you'll drive up in your car and you'll get three or four sellers and they're all from the same gang – from the same group or faction – but they're all trying to sell their pack and finish their work. They have one or two packs that they sell. They give the money back to the organisation but they keep a certain amount. So that's their work. So they want to sell and get out of there. So you'll have three or four guys running up to the car trying to sell you the same thing. It's just business. It's business as usual.

Unfortunately, there are a lot of good people in these bad neighbourhoods. A lot of them are held hostage in their neighbourhoods and in their houses because they really don't want to come out, because it's not safe. They go to work, they come home, they lock their doors and they stay in their house. And at night their neighbourhoods turn into little war zones. A lot of shootings. You hear a lot of stories of children getting shot. You know, they're not the intended targets but they're playing in their back yard half a block away and two gangs are fighting each other and the rounds just keep going until they hit something and a lot of times it's a little kid or a woman. It's sad, very sad.

There are a lot of good people in poor neighbourhoods so one thing you've got to remember is, you can't treat people the same. You've got to treat people accordingly. The way I look at it, I treat people the way they treat me. You could be living in the worst neighbourhood but you've got a nine-to-five job, you work hard, you have your little house and a car and if you have an issue with the police, I'll treat you accordingly. If you're a gangbanger and I know you're a gangbanger – because I see you every day and I see you selling and gangbanging – I'll also treat you accordingly.

Sometimes cops get that confused, they think that everybody's an asshole.

****

We're working the Westside, a predominantly black neighbourhood; a lot of gangs, you know what I mean? It's an area where you have to pay respect to the people too. So that's what we did. We worked hard, got into a lot of fights, got into a lot of things but never hit anybody when they were in handcuffs. We never did anything that would be considered wrong.

Well, we were dealing with a guy who was a major crook at the time – a major gangster in this area of town that was all gangs. What happened was, we get a call one night over on the Westside, to a guy with a gun who was shooting, blah, blah, blah. We roll over there and this dude – this major crook – is there. He runs from us and he ends up tossing a handgun – he throws a handgun. We grab him but couldn't find the gun and end up bringing a K-9 unit in. K-9 does a search and they find the gun. Well, one of our guys – he's a good man but he's all this, all mouth – well, he's the one who caught the dude and got him cuffed up.

The dude's going, 'Motherfucker! Fuck you!'

Well, one thing leads to another and this cop ends up slapping the dude whilst he's in cuffs. So the suspect gets majorly pissed off, because it really isn't the right thing to do – to slap the guy. So the dude starts challenging the cop, 'I'm gonna kick your ass when I get out of jail. I'm gonna kick your ass, motherfucker.' After that things started to get heated up in the neighbourhood.

We believe that you have to make your name but you also had to do what was right out on the street too. You earn that respect but you can lose it by doing the wrong thing. Hitting somebody in cuffs was the wrong thing. Times have changed as far as what you can do and what you can't do. Well, the dude gets out and he's running down the department, 'Motherfucking punks! You guys are a bunch of punks!' Then he starts talking about this specific police officer, 'Fuck you, I'll take you one-on-one! One-on-one!'

We all get the word on this. We end up securing a section of town

– a project.

We tell this cop, 'You need to whoop this dude's ass, because he's talking shit about us and we're having to take all these beatings from the gangsters in the neighbourhood. So you need to whoop this guy's ass, dude. Straight up – man-to-man.'

So we have this thing all set up. They show up and this dude's there and we're like, 'Whoop his ass and be done with it. Let's get past it.'

Well, the cop ends up arresting the guy for intimidating a police officer or whatever. We're like, 'Er, no! You need to whoop his ass or he needs to go free.'

We wouldn't let this cop arrest him, so we let the dude go. Well, that just caused open turmoil on the streets, because basically you've got a cop who's backed down.

'You guys are nothing but a bunch of pussies!'

So we're riding it. We we're doing a lot of training at that time, so we we're working out and doing a lot of things – cops like to stay in shape – a lot of karate and a lot of that type of fighting stuff. So, we're driving around in the neighbourhood after that fiasco and we pull over this other gangster who used to drive around town in a bright, Pepto-Bismol pink car. I mean you couldn't miss the dude because he's driving around town with his shit and he was one of the head gangsters. So, we're pulling this dude down for whatever the case may be.

Anyway, one thing led to another and he says, 'I'll fight him.' And all of a sudden he's pointing at me.

It all boiled up from this previous cop having backed down. Now we're nothing but a bunch of punks as far as the gangs were concerned. People were calling us pussies and all this stuff. We lost total street credibility and we lost a lot of respect.

So this gangster is out there pointing at me – he's not an overly huge guy – and he's going, 'I'll fight him.' And he's pointing at me, right?

So my partner's telling me, 'He says he's going to whoop your ass!'

I come out and go, 'You going to whoop my ass motherfucker?'

And he goes, 'You guys ain't nothing but a bunch of punks.'

I go, 'Really?'

One thing led to another and I stripped down to a t-shirt, we went around the corner behind one of the projects and I go, 'All right motherfucker, show me what you've got, let's go.'

So I start throwing a couple of karate kicks, you know? And the dude starts backing up, saying, 'No man, no kicks. Straight up blows man, just straight up blows.'

I go, 'Fuck you! I'm going to kick you on that side of the face and then I'm going to kick you on the other side of the face, motherfucker.'

So I throw a couple more kicks. Now, you've got to realise that we're not the only ones there – everyone from the projects is there. We're surrounded. So basically he ends up backing down and runs away – and this is one of the gangsters, right?

Well, the next day, the same street, my partner and I are riding around together, driving around the neighbourhood and all of a sudden these little kids, five to eight-year-old neighbourhood kids, are riding their bikes by us and they're like, 'Rollers!' – you know, their word for 'cops' – 'Rollers!'

We're sitting there and they go, 'Oh dude! Hey, that's the dude who backed down the gangster, man. You're cool, brother, you're cool!'

So after that and a few other battles, we earned our respect back. You know what I mean? We had tons of fights but never got one complaint.

But all those things we did, it was always straight up, man-to-man. It was a different world back in the day. We'd meet in the parks and do whatever we had to do to gain that respect, but we'd never disrespected anybody, never hit anybody in cuffs. It was always straight up. Like I said, you earned that respect but you didn't disrespect anybody either and that way you never had any problems. We were always fair, we were always firm and we never backed down.

****

The gangs will kill you over a nickel bag of weed. They'll even kill each other in the same faction. They'll have wars within. Like, if somebody gets locked up – a guy who's either middle management or a boss – and has to go to jail, you'll have fighting to figure out who's going to take that person's spot.

A lot of times you'll have three or four little factions fighting for that one spot and they'll start shooting each other – the same gang. They'll walk up or they'll drive up and they'll shoot five people from their own faction, like it was nothing.

****

I'm on 15th and Linden, which is downtown. It's primarily a Hispanic neighbourhood that has some real heavy Hispanic gang ties. I was a training officer and I used to take my trainees down there all the time to try and get them involved in a lot of gang activity. So, this one time there was a group of gang members hanging out at a known apartment complex. There were probably, I don't know, ten or fifteen of them. So I pulled my car up, put the headlights off and everything like that – kind of covertly pulled up – and my trainee and I watch them, discuss some things that gang members do, watch their activity, the way they carry themselves, things like that; see if we can maybe develop some type of reasonable suspicion and go out and stop them.

As we're watching, a truck comes around the corner but didn't see us – and whilst I said that we were trying to be covert, we were in a black and white police car so we're hiding in plain sight. Anyway, truck comes around the corner, pulls right up to them and two guys stand up at the back – on the bed of the truck – with guns and just start firing on the crowd; and we're talking a hundred feet away from us.

And it was like, 'Okay, well, we'd better go do our job.'

My trainee is actually driving and that can be a very stressful thing because now I'm trying to deal with what's going on here but at the same time, putting him in a situation that I don't know if he's really ready for yet. But you've got to trust them.

So I tell him, 'You just drive and follow them and I'll take care of the radio traffic.'

So as soon as the truck sees us, it turned into a vehicle pursuit. The first thing I did was call in the shooting at 15th and Linden. I said that I had no idea if anyone was down but to send some medical that way just in case.

Then the truck takes a right on Bonanza and as he's coming up you can see them standing at the back of the truck, shooting at us as they make the turn. And you could see like… it was kind of like… like sparks flashing on a Bic lighter. You could see it – pop, pop, pop, pop, pop – as they're turning. I don't know if you've ever tried firing from a moving vehicle but it's near impossible.

So they're going around the corner and they just couldn't get us, thank God. But I told my trainee, 'Hey, back off a little bit from them.'

That pursuit went through a residential neighbourhood. They must have been going at least eighty miles an hour. In that part of town, there's these big, huge gutters that cross the road and every time they hit the gutters, the people in the back of the truck would fly up out of the truck and then land back in the truck.

I had to tell my trainee, 'Look, you gotta slow down because first of all we're going to plough into the side of a car that's not going to see us coming. Second of all there's no way we're going to catch up with that truck.'

Our cars aren't like trucks. If we hit those gutters we're going to break our car.

What ended up happening was, they take another turn and just throw all the guns out of the side of the truck. The truck makes a left-hand turn about half a mile down and they hit the last bump so hard that the shooter actually fell out of the truck – the truck's going like fifty miles an hour. And then his partner fell out of the truck too – they both fell out. One of them, he was just road rash, all the way down his body. He was just screwed up. His partner grabbed him and they hid in the back of an abandoned house in this thick grassy area. The only reason we found them was just because there happened to be another truck parked at the side of the road that looked like the original truck but turned out not to be.

So we stopped in that area and said, 'This might be that truck.'

We start looking around and there's blood on the ground that turns out to be from the guy they dragged off. We got the air unit and K-9 unit out there, they set up a perimeter and the air unit found them hiding in the back yard. Then the K-9 unit went in and got them out. There was a lot of luck there and some good police work. That was pretty crazy. It turned out they had actually shot a guy and murdered him right then and there. He was dead right there.

The funniest thing is, the thing that was going through my mind during all this was, 'What training lesson can we get out of this?'

****

We'll have up to a dozen homicides sometimes, on a bad weekend. A dozen homicides! It's just crazy. In the summer, as soon as it starts getting warm, people just flip out and start shooting each other. Wintertime, it starts to slow down a little bit but summertime it's crazy.

And here's the thing, it would be worse – probably twice as bad – if the medicine wasn't as good as it is today. Our hospitals are busy, they're level one trauma. They're the best at fixing guys with gunshots. I actually know the doctor who's head of ER Trauma. The guy's amazing and he's like, 'If you bring me someone with a heartbeat, nine times out of ten I can keep them alive, whether he's been shot ten times or once.'

They're that good because they've had so much practice. They'll have nights when they get five or ten gunshot victims. And now, if you go into a hospital, they'll save you. We'll have guys on the street who are gangbangers and they've been shot two or three different times, on two or three different occasions. Multiple times. They'll show you their scars and say, 'Yeah, I got shot here, I got shot here, I got shot here and I got shot here.'

So if they don't hit a vital organ or artery and they get you to the hospital, they patch you back up and throw you back on the street. So the amount of homicides is a decent indicator but the amount of shootings – they call them aggravated batteries here – the amount of shootings is a better gauge because it'll actually tell you when some gangbanger *tried* to kill someone else and not just when they actually succeeded. The only difference between the two is the bullet going just half an inch over and hitting you in the heart or something.

****

There are different levels of respect. Some gangs respect the police a little bit more than others. Some have no respect at all. Some of them, as a tactic, will act like they respect you to your face. They'll cooperate a lot of times.

You may come to an agreement, you may talk to their shot caller – their boss – and say, 'Don't fuck around any more. Don't fuck around this weekend. You guys put your guns up. Don't do it by this school. Whatever you do, don't do anything by this school.'

And they'll trade you. They'll be, like, 'Okay, we'll cooperate with you here, but when you leave, we'll do whatever we want over there.'

They act like they're cooperating with you, respecting you, but behind your back they don't care.

There are 'unsaid' things. You try to keep them from doing stupid shit but as soon as you leave it's like the mice when the cat's away.

There are certain things that are more critical – little kids, schools, a hospital or whatever. So you try to keep those places as safe as possible.

You'll say, 'When school's out, we don't even want to see you outside your corner. We don't want to see you fuckin' around. We don't want to see you and your gang. Let all the kids go home, whatever, do something over there. Go play Gameboy, go do something. We don't want you to be on the corner and then another gang comes and does a drive-by on you guys but hits all these little kids that are going home from school.'

But the department doesn't want you to trade. They don't want you to do anything anymore, with gangbangers.

So now you try to outsmart them. You try to make them think you're giving them something when you're really not. And the thing is, if you appear weak to them, or you try to trade things with them, then they'll lose respect for you. So you still have to do what you have to do and they understand. I talk to guys' everyday but if they run and they get caught with something, they're going to get locked up. They know.

So I get along with them, mostly. There are only a couple of instances where guys really, really hated me, where I actually thought, 'Man, this guy is crazy enough or bad enough to do something to me.'

There've probably been three of four guys that I've had second thoughts about. Everybody else, they're doing it because either they're too stupid or they're doing it to make money or they're doing it because that's all they know – they're gangbangers. That's their family. So, we understand that it's a game. They do what they do and we do what we do. They play and we try to catch them. I get along with most everybody. I respect them and they respect me – at least to my face, they do. But they know.

****

There have always been stories and rumours about police officers who are gangbangers or used to be gangbangers. You've always got to worry about that. I'm not a betting man but if I was to bet my paycheque, I'd say yeah, out of ten thousand police officers, I'd say there's probably a handful that still have some type of tie or association with gangs.

I think part of the reason they join the police is the intel and the power. They think maybe they can be protected if one of their own is the police.

Some just grew up. They were in a gang, maybe didn't get locked up for any crimes, and they just decided, 'Hey, I'll get this job. It's a paycheque.'

Their heart's not into being a cop and they just look at it as a paycheque. But once they're in the police, unfortunately they can do a lot of bad things.

Like with the military, they have a lot of gangs that send their guys into the military on purpose, to get training. Then they come out and they're trained killers. They're trained with rifles, pistols and tactics. So you figure that they're probably doing the same thing with the police.

There are background checks and investigations but maybe it should be a little more thorough, because some people slip through the cracks and become police when they're just bad. Well, you know what? These guys are not the police. They were never really the police. They just became the police to further their crimes.

****

Maybe once every four or five years you'll hear about an incident where cops go bad. The problem is, you can try to communicate with gangs, you can try to talk to them, but you can't become their buddy.

You can't get too close, because the threat of, 'Well, if you do something for me then I'll do something for you.' You know? Like, 'Ah well, he's my friend, I know him. I've known him for years. Well, not really my friend but I see him every day when I go to work because he's on the same corner selling drugs.'

You can't, because that's where there's a fine line. You go over the fine line and then it goes bad. It happens, not to a lot, but it happens. Guys start getting involved with gangs for whatever reason – greed, power, whatever, you know? They start going over to the other side. Not good.

Like I say, every four or five years you hear about guys getting arrested for stealing drugs and stealing money from drug dealers or gangs – using their police powers to steal. Who knows, maybe they have friends that they grew up with that are now gangbangers. They became the police but they're still friends. They get together for whatever reason. Like I said, money drives that a lot; greed drives that a lot. It's unfortunate, they get together with the gangs – either because they were childhood friends or because they see them every day – and they start getting too close and start making deals. It's bad. It's bad.

We had an incident where one police officer started off protecting a gang's drug sales. He would work with them in that area a lot, while he was on duty. Then another police officer picked one of his guys up and he was 'dirty'.

They say, 'Well, I work for this officer. I'm his informant.'

The officer would say, 'Yeah, he works for me so give him a break.'

So, protecting them like that. Then he started protecting their shipments. When the big shipment of drugs would come in, he would follow the car. Then he would start delivering the stuff to them. Then he started getting paid for this. He got to the point where he was going down to Florida, protecting the shipments. Then he got to the point where he thought, 'Why am I gonna work for these guys when I can do the same thing myself?'

So, he started doing that himself, taking most of the profit. But eventually somebody's going to get locked up for something and the thing is, there's no honour amongst these guys – it's very rare.

So, if 'Joe Blow' gets locked up for something bad and the cops are like, 'Well, what can you give us? We want to solve homicides. Do you know any homicide offenders that you have information on? Do you have any robbery offenders? Anything? Burglary? Anybody? What do you have?'

So they'll say, 'Well, I know this cop who works with this gang. He does stuff. He deals.' Whatever.

So they investigated it and it was true. The guy – the officer – was a piece of shit. After a while he actually started telling the gangs the identity of the undercover police officers – their vehicles, their licence plates, their descriptions. It was just bad.

So that's the problem, you start having people going to the wrong side and now they could really hurt you. They're making money but now they could get somebody killed. They could get a lot of people killed, because in narcotics, undercover officers buy dope. So you pull up to a spot – undercover – and they already know you're the police. And if they think they can get away with it, they'll kill you.

****

There are some black guys having a party. They're all adults, in their early twenties. They're having a rap contest and one of them didn't like the way another one rapped and he said, as an insult to the guy, 'You're weak-ass alphabet soup.'

So the next thing you know, there's a fistfight. The victim in this story is actually a pretty big, strong guy – a pretty muscular guy – and he ends up piss-pounding this other guy in a fistfight. The little guy then goes inside his house and comes back out with his cousin and a gun. They walk up to the guy who just piss-pounded him and they shot him right in the neck and severed his carotid artery. I've never seen anyone live with a severed carotid artery but he dropped right there and he almost bled out but another guy ran over, put pressure on his wound and saved his life.

He then got to the hospital where they did emergency surgery. The doctor said, 'You should have been dead. There's no reason in the world that you should have lived through this.'

But he did live and it was actually the second time that this guy had been shot. He'd been shot once before in the shoulder but this one should have killed him and it didn't.

He had had a lot of problems in his life and he was not a nice, well-respected kid – he was a hardcore gangster. But I made a con-nection with him somehow, because I told him over and over, 'I don't know why, but God saved your life. He saved it for a purpose. Every-body I talked to – the doctors and everybody else – they all said that you should have been dead.'

I'd meet with that kid every week. I'd hook up with him and see how he was doing because I didn't want him to fall back into that same gangster bullshit that he was in with earlier. He had a job at the time and I'd stop in at his work and check up on him. He was a smart kid and he was well respected on the street, probably because of his criminal past and because he was kind of a hardcore guy. We respected each other for who each other were and I had a pretty good relationship with him for a while.

Initially he didn't want to testify against the guys who shot him. In fact he told me whilst he was laying in the hospital bed, 'I know who they are but I'm not going to tell you who they are.' Because that's the way it is on the street; that's the code of the street – not to cooperate with the police.

And that's frustrating for me because here I am with an obligation to make an arrest for an attempted homicide but I can't when he's the victim and he knows darn well who did it and he won't tell me.

My problem is, what happens next time when they shoot someone and kill them? They shot this guy in a playground in a community park. There could have been a kid around who could have been killed. But I worked and worked and worked on that kid and eventually he told me who shot him and we got warrants for them and tracked them down on the East Coast and got them back here, arrested.

He then told me repeatedly, 'I'm not going to testify against them. I'll never go to court and stand up and testify against them. That's not the way the street is. We just don't do that. I'd lose face, I'd lose all credibility if I went and testified against them.'

So again, I worked on him hard for weeks and weeks and weeks just trying to get him to cooperate and eventually he did. He testified wonderfully against them and they both got convicted. I think they're both doing fifteen or so years in prison for it.

But then within a week, this kid went out and committed a rape and a battery. So now he's back in prison. That's very disheartening for me because I put a lot of energy into that kid, trying to get him to see the light, you know? He was finally not being chased by the police and was more or less helping us.

He told me several times, 'It's nice not to be chased. It's nice to actually be on your side.'

I was like, 'Yeah, there's no reason why you can't. You're twenty-two years old, you've got a girlfriend and you have a job – it's time to straighten out your life. I'm here and I will help you. I will do whatever I can to help you stay away from crime.'

And then, within a week, he lands himself back in jail for serious cases.

That's the frustrating part – seeing hope in some of these kids yet they don't see it in themselves. They don't see enough of it in themselves to follow through with anything; that's the world they live in. A majority of them don't look towards the future because they don't think that they're ever going to survive their life. A lot of them don't think that they're going to live to be an adult.

A lot of them just expect that they'll die. They'll say, 'I'm going to get shot or I'm going to end up in prison. That's just the way it is.'

And it's especially true amongst the young black kids in town. I see that all the time. And it's sad. It honestly is sad.

I always ask kids, 'What do you want to do when you grow up?

What is in your future?'

You can't even imagine the number of kids that don't have any idea.

They tell me, 'It doesn't matter because I'm going to be in prison or I'm going to be dead.'

And we're not even a major city. These kids have everything they could possibly want. I can't imagine what it's like in a Chicago or an LA or a New York or somewhere like that, where the kids truly are living on the streets and have nothing in their lives. Part of the problem is that they come up without expecting a future in their lives. They come up with parents who don't give a shit about them. They grow up with parents who aren't talking about college or taking about careers or aren't talking about graduating from high school. There's really no one in their lives to lead them down the path where they should be going. And I think that's why a lot of them get in all this trouble.

But like I said, here's a kid that should have been dead, he had a chance to turn his life around and he had a chance to make things different and I honestly think that God saved him for a purpose and maybe his purpose is down the road. Maybe he'll come out of prison and do great things, I don't know. I think for whatever reason, he was saved that night. But he didn't grab that chance and take advantage of it. Maybe he'll sit in prison for another ten years, get out and think differently. But I don't know.

****

Gangs are moving to smaller, quieter towns and neighbourhoods. It's easier for them to operate as there's less police, less police intelligence and the local cops have fewer assets and resources.

The other thing that's frightening is that gang members are getting into the military and getting training with weapons and tactics. That's just alarming. They go into the marines for a couple of years, they go off to Afghanistan and come back four years later with advanced infantry training in machine guns and assault weapons. Then they're back in a gang. Their training is better than most police officers'.

9

Narcotics

*O*ver the years I have been on a number of raids with the 'Narcs' –
narcotic officers – who specialise in targeting crack houses and the
like. One of the things that always struck me about the houses we raided
was the utter squalor these people operated in. Sure, this was in Detroit,
but even so, there was absolutely no glamour in it. And there was far less
laughter involved when I spoke to officers about narcotics. Although some
did manage to find humour in it occasionally, this was clearly a much
more serious environment and subject.

Over a skillet breakfast in the back corner of an unremarkable diner
in an unremarkable neighbourhood of a Midwestern city, a former undercover narcotics officer told me about his work buying drugs from dealers
and how he had to learn how to bullshit. Dealers were jumpy and buys
were tense, he said. Whether they were an undercover officer or a genuine
user, buyers were always viewed with suspicion and he told me that dealers would often call his bluff. It was an extremely dangerous occupation;
gangs, drugs and cops don't always mix in the way that they should and
even his own colleagues, he whispered, couldn't always be trusted.

We Are The Cops

As the waitress topped up our coffee for the fourth time, the door at the front of the diner opened and in walked a heavy set black guy with a skinny black girl. The officer knew the guy and the guy knew the officer; his days of undercover buys were well behind him but he hadn't been forgotten. We didn't leave and we didn't rush our food but the officer continually raised his eyes to look at the guy and I felt extremely uncomfortable, and not just because the officer refused to let me pay for breakfast. Again, I felt that sense of how different and serious the business of narcotics can be.

Although narcotics may be behind much of the crime we see today ('Take away the drugs and you'll take away 90% of the crime,' I was told repeatedly), operating in that world felt totally separate from regular policing. It all felt very, very dark.

I've seen people alive with their legs completely infested with maggots – heroin addicts, junkies. They get open sores and lesions and they have giant swollen hands. You don't want to touch them and you pray that you don't have to deal with them. You don't even search them.

These open sores would have maggots climbing in and out of them. It's horrible and they don't really care. All they're worried about is their next fix.

Crack just destroys people – it destroys their lives.

****

With street-corner narcotic sales – 'corners' – this is how it works: you'll have your sellers, you'll have your lookouts and you'll have protection – guys who are shooters, who protect the spot. Sometimes they have the gun on them but if the lookouts see us coming, they'll alert them and they'll put it away – they'll put it in a bush, they'll put it underneath a car tyre, in the grass, they'll just hide it somewhere nearby because if another faction – another gang – shows up and wants to do a drive-by, they have to be there to protect the money and the people.

In narcotics we'd run up to them or sneak up from behind and catch guys making a sale or catch a guy with a pack, which is ten or twenty little bundles of cocaine, heroin or whatever they're selling.

But they get smarter, they realise that if they get caught with the whole pack, they're going to do some time. So what they'll do is, they'll stash it somewhere – can be anywhere in a bush, in the grass, underneath the garbage, whatever, in a car, in the house. When that sale comes, they'll get the money, go grab one or two packs – however many they need – and go directly to their car and sell it. So if they get caught off guard, they'll only have one or two or three – that's it.

A lot of times, they'll try to swallow it. A lot of times they'll try to just pitch it and run. They adapt, though. Some of them are dumb, but a lot of them are smart. If something isn't working, they'll change and do it smarter.

So in a lot of ways it's become harder to be the police on the streets now. You have kids working as lookouts on street corners. Kids on the second or third floor of a house, or on the roof, it depends on the terrain. Sometimes they'll have the spot in the middle of the block and they'll have lookouts on each side. If they're really good, they'll have lookouts in the alley, because that's where we used to sneak up and kind of flank 'em, because we knew that they had lookouts on the corner. So they adapt and they change.

Anything from ten years old to sixty years old, I've caught selling. They do it for different reasons. Some of them are kids that join a gang and that's what they have to do when they start. You're going to be a lookout initially, maybe become the server after, with promotion. Later, you may take care of the money and after that you may become the shooter – the security.

You'll have a hype, who's addicted to whatever drug. You ever hear of a hypodermic needle? Well, a 'hype' is somebody who injects – that's why we call them that. You'll have a hype that needs to make money for their addiction, so they'll sell, if the gang trusts them enough. Sometimes they get to the point where they can't trust the hype because he's going to steal their money – even if they're a badass gangbanger – because the hype is controlled by the drug. But if they trust them enough, they'll let the hype sell. So you'll get some fifty, sixty-year-old guy out there who's selling just to make that twenty dollars – for every ten bags he sells, he makes twenty dollars – the rest goes to the organisation.

A lot of times the hypes will see a customer driving down the street and say, 'I'll jump in your car, I'll take you there. But you've got to cut a bit off that rock for me.' So, they'll do that, they'll be like, 'All right, go here, go there.' They'll take you to the drug dealer and then they'll want half of that rock or half of the heroin or whatever, and that's their fee for locating you for that seller.

It's extremely organised. Extremely organised. In narcotics, we've worked up to a year on one group that would sell on two different blocks. They're organised – from the lookouts to the guy who serves, to the guy who does security, the guy who handles the money, the guy who runs that spot, the guy who delivers the product every day, to a guy who picks up the money – and then above all that are the bosses.

Sometimes the bosses, if they're smart, they won't even show up to the spot. They don't need to; they've got somebody doing everything for them. So it's a little harder, you've got to follow them, you've got to find out who's bringing the product to the spot, you've got to find out who's picking up the cash. Some of them are very complicated but some of them are very basic. Sometimes they just sell out of a house. You grab them, you get search warrants for the house, you hit the house.

The problem is the laws and the judges being so lenient on them; you lock them up and they'll be on the street in a few months and they'll start doing the same thing again. There're times when we've hit the same house three or four times. I've heard some teams have hit a house up to five or six times; same house that keeps doing the same thing.

My opinion, if you want somebody to stop doing what they're doing, you've got to make the punishment fit the crime – make it a deterrent. Like homicide; if you don't want people running around killing each other, you have the death penalty and you have judges that sentence. If you don't get the death penalty, at least put them away for fifty years, just to keep them away from civilisation. That's it.

****

One of the attributes of a good undercover officer is the ability to bullshit, talk, make up stories; 'It's not for me – it's for my girlfriend. I don't do this shit'. You know, something like that.

There was an incident where an undercover guy was doing a buy but it wasn't on a street corner; he did it in a bathroom in some bar. It was a one-on-one deal and then two more of their guys came in and threw the undercover guy against the wall and told him, 'You're going to do it right now, right in front of us.'

He was forced to take the drugs otherwise they were going to beat the fuck out of him, kill him, whatever. As soon as he gets out of the bathroom he goes to the other undercover guy, who's with him but was still in the bar, and he's like, 'Call everybody in.'

So everybody just converged and they caught them all. It's all investigated and the undercover goes directly to the hospital and gets his blood drawn, you know? I think he got admitted.

But the department don't want you to do it – take the drugs. They say, 'Avoid it. It's a last resort. If they're going to kill you and you gotta do it, then you gotta do it. Otherwise avoid it.'

When it happens, they have to investigate it but it's very, very rare. Ninety-nine times out of a hundred, you could just walk away from the deal and say, 'Fuck you man, I don't want to deal with your shit. You're not going to tell me what to do.'

But it has happened and the department's always drug testing us. I think when I worked narcotics I set records for them testing me. But they have caught cops using marijuana, cocaine, whatever. Those officers get fired.

****

I bought dope for a little while; I was an undercover officer. I like adrenaline but it definitely doesn't get any easier. The first time was very hard and any time after that you're still on edge – really nervous. But you try to get better, you try to use props, you try to use stories or you try to bullshit with them.

Sometimes they won't even take you. I've walked up to a lot of corners and they're like, 'You're too swol' – meaning swollen – 'You're too big. You're the police.'

They'll know right away and you just get shut down. So I changed my appearance to try and not look like the police. I try to talk to them – talk them into selling. But some places wouldn't and then you'd have to send another undercover officer in and try it with them. I'd probably be successful only half the time.

A lot of gangs, they ask for a resume – like a street resume – literally. A lot of the black gangs on the Southside, they won't sell to anybody that's not black. A lot of them, they won't sell to anybody they don't know from the neighbourhood. They won't sell to you unless somebody that they know brings you; like, someone to vouch for you. So some of the gangs are harder than others to buy from, to infiltrate, to investigate, to lock up.

A lot of places, they'll ask, 'Where are you from? Who do you know? Who told you to come here?'

'Well this guy sent me.'

Then they'll quiz you. 'What colour are our bags? What size are our bags? What's our product called?' They ask that because a lot of times heroin has a street name, so they go, 'What's our shit called?'

So they'll quiz you and if they're not happy, they'll say, 'No, you gotta come back. You gotta come back with somebody. You've got to come back and bring that person.'

So it's very hard and they always think you're the police. They try to figure out if you are or not. Some groups are different; some places will not serve to a white person. They will not sell unless you're black.

Then you have the groups, like on the Westside. The Westside is crazy. Crazy! Almost everyone on the Westside had a drug spot. Some had multiple drug spots. You go to one corner where you could buy heroin, in the middle you could buy marijuana and at the other end you could buy cocaine. It's crazy. And they were a little greedy on the Westside – they would sell to a lot more people. You get a lot of people who would drive in from the suburbs – kids, adults, whatever. Suburbanites would come in and go to a gang and buy their drugs and then get right back on the highway and leave. That's where you'd see three, four, five guys run up to a car and try to make that sale.

But if you're a little greedier and you want to sell more, the chances are you're going to get caught.

****

I worked on this organisation run by two guys when I was with drug enforcement, and they were basically robbing other drug dealers to get both money and drugs. Drug dealers robbing other drug dealers. And they were dressing up as police, to do it. They were torturing their victims; they were brutal.

It was a group up in northwest Baltimore, they were second generation drug dealers and they had an entire organisation, which they ruled through fear; they shot their own people, stabbed their own people, basically to keep them in line. If their people messed up money, they would hurt them. And part of their enterprise was robbing other drug dealers. They dressed up like the police, put masks on and just robbed them. So they were enterprising in that way. Then they started robbing businesses and they would plan these elaborate heists.

So these guys were really an entire crime wave. One guy even shot his own brother-in-law. He was basically without a conscience – both of them were. They owned a legitimate business – a barbershop – but it was really just a hangout for drug dealers and people in the trade. After all, everybody has to get their hair cut.

But yeah, they would dress up like police. It wasn't a uniform so much as they got BDU's – Battle Dress Uniform; you know, pants, police style jackets – and they wore balaclavas over their faces. They just tried to make themselves appear to be police. I don't necessarily think that people really thought that they were police but if somebody is chasing you down the street and they look like they might be the police, maybe your first inclination is to think that they are.

So they would break into people's houses, rob them and torture them if they didn't tell them where their drugs were. They would cut them, beat them, whatever they had to do to get the information.

Those kind of guys are real Baltimore boys. But we got lucky with them because they left such a trail of mayhem. Even their own people turned against them, because they were brutal. Their people were going to jail and they weren't necessarily helping them out. They had a good run, though. But they pleaded guilty and got fifty years federal time, which means you don't get any time off for good behaviour. Fifty years. They decided not to go to trial, which was smart of them, because I don't think they would have fared too well at trial. And we couldn't even prove everything that we knew that they did – although we proved everything that we could.

There were some other elements to it too. A couple of female police officers in this department were actually dating some of these guys and having children with them. It was a travesty. We couldn't even go pull our own police records, because at central records there was a girl working there – a police officer – who actually had a baby with one of these guys.

Some people call Baltimore, Bodymore, or instead of the Charm City, the Harm City. But do you know what else they call it? Small-timore. It's a small world in Baltimore; everybody knows everybody. Those female cops knew what their boyfriends were doing.

But that's not even the worst of it. I actually put handcuffs on three cops and I've never even worked in Internal Investigations. It was all drug related. It was all females. It was all their boyfriends. The worst one, she milled the drug deal for her boyfriend – she facilitated a drug deal, with heroin – for her boyfriend, and there was a murder.

But when you take that oath as a cop, some of your family members are no longer going to be people that you can hang out with and some of your friends are not going to be people you can be with. You probably shouldn't start dating drug dealers. Or having children with them. But it happens in Smalltimore because some of these girls grew up with these guys and they have known each other their whole lives.

****

The most ingenious guys I've ever worked with in my life were these two uniform guys. One is real tall and the other guy is... I wouldn't say short but he's not real tall either.

It was Halloween and this crew are selling drugs like mad, out of this one building. I mean, there'd be a line of people all day going in and out of there. So, what these two cops did is, they bought two white sheets. They put holes in them to make eyes and then put the sheets over themselves - like they were ghosts. Then they just went and stood in line. Just standing in line with all these crack heads.

So they walked up to the dealer when it was their turn to get served and the dealer goes, 'Yeah, what you want nigger? Yo man, what's this ghost shit, man? What you want?'

The two cops just pulled off their sheets and they had their guns out. They go, 'We don't want anything.' And then they just grabbed them. Ingenious.

****

We'd do what we called 'reversals', where we'd roll in, we'd hit a dude up, do a buy, get a warrant, go bang the door.

We hit this one place, a motel. There were these three gangsters from LA that were there and they'd been selling dope, stealing shit and all that stuff. So we end up getting a couple of buys into it. Now, you have to pretty much picture just a regular motel room: you walk in, the door's there, immediately to your right is the bathroom, past that's the one bedroom and then the bed, right? So we roll in there, we bang the place, take the three guys into custody and they've got literally bags of shit from Nike and all these outlet stores, that they've stolen. So no sooner do we get in there and get them secured before there's somebody at the door knocking – a customer looking to buy dope. I took this 'triple X' Nike black t-shirt and I put it on over my rig and my gear. I've got a low-ride holster, black boots, green BDUs – my SWAT gear. But I put the Nike shirt on and the dude knocking at the door couldn't see any of that.

So I go, 'Yeah, what do you need, man?'

And they'd go, 'Give me a rock.' Or whatever.

All right, I get the rock and say, 'Come on in.'

They come in, I give them the rock and I'd go, 'Bad news, I'm a police officer. You're under arrest.'

So we'd take them into custody, right? We'd just swing them around in the corner of the room by the bed. Dude, before we even got them put away, there's another knock at the door. These guys are rollin' in the dope. It's so funny because now there are six to eight people in there with handcuffs, stuck in the corner or the room, right? When the door was knocked, we'd be saying to the prisoners, 'Hey, shhh! Shhh! Be quiet, you guys. Be quiet. Let us do our thing.'

So now these freaking suspects, all handcuffed – six to eight of them – they're all going, 'Shhh. Be quite. Be quite!' Like they're enjoying it. Like it's a game.

So I do the thing and give the tagline, 'By the way, I'm a police officer. You're under arrest.'

And the other prisoners would turn to this new suspect go, 'Oh you stupid motherfucker! Are you stupid?'

I'm looking at them and I go, 'What are you talking about? You're in cuffs too!'

But once you roll, you just had to keep rollin'. We ended up walking out of there with fourteen people. Took em' all to jail.

****

I went on hundreds and hundreds of drug raids. There were gangs, well, crews – that's what we called them, crews. They were selling crack by the colour of the caps. The top of the vial, they're colour coded and each crew would have their own different colours. So you'd get the red tops, the blue tops, the green tops, the purple tops.

The crews weren't organised, though, and when they were first starting out the boss would give a dealer a bag of five hundred rocks and say, 'Here, go sit in this abandoned apartment and pass the stuff through the hole in the wall.'

171

But when the dealer gets arrested, all the crack gets seized, so the bosses started giving them out in little packs of ten. That way, if they got hit by the police, they didn't lose so much so fast.

Then the dealers started to buy these walkie-talkies; they thought that they were pretty smart. They had their own little walkie-talkies or whatnot but every once in a while we'd get hold of one of their lookouts when they weren't paying attention. You would just take the radio off them and send them on their way. Then you'd listen to the radio and find out what was going on.

There was this one crew and it was really hard to get to these guys – really, really hard – because they were pretty ingenious. They'd have a hole in the wall and they'd get the local handyman to come and fill the hole in the wall up and re-enforce it – a nice re-enforcement job – so you couldn't get in without bashing down the walls and by the time you did get it, the dealer would be gone; he'd be away through a maze of abandoned buildings.

So what we did is, we got hold of one of their lookouts and just spoke like they did, over the walkie-talkie we'd taken.

We'd go, 'Yo! Yo! Come on nigger! They be coming! They be Five O! Bring that shit with you!'

We would have the place surrounded and the dealer would come running out with his bag of crack and shit. We'd get him with all the drugs, the fucking scales, all the money, everything.

****

Christmas in Harlem is a sad time. You know, you're making money, you're living a good life. I have a nice family, always had everything I wanted, didn't really need much, and then you see people who have nothing. They know that on Christmas morning they're

172

getting nothing.

There was this one case: the woman worked and the husband sometimes worked but he has a drug problem. The day before Christmas – it was the 24th or the evening of the 24th – she took the kids out to do something and when she got home, all the presents were gone. Everything was gone. And he was gone too, off on a crack binge. He'd sold all this stuff for next to nothing, for crack.

The two cops that went there, they came back, ran around and we did a quick collection – everybody put in ten or twenty bucks – and they got this guy to open up a store and went in there and bought Christmas presents and a bike and all sorts of stuff for the kids, because at the end of the day, these kids didn't do anything to deserve what their father did. It was terrible, but it was a nice story where something good happened in the end.

But it's a sad time of the year. You know that you're going home at the end of the shift – if you have to work the holiday – and you know when you go home that you're going to have a nice place and a tree and this and that.

But you go into these apartments and you're like, Jesus Christ! One wall was covered with roaches. There was no light – they didn't have electricity, they shut the power off – and if you do put a flashlight on, the whole wall would move, because it was nothing but cockroaches.

10

Homicide

A contact in Washington State led me into a tall, grey building, where we stepped into a lift and he pressed a button for one of the higher-up floors. I had asked to speak with a homicide detective and he had one in mind.

Every now and then I would speak to specific officers because I already knew the story they had to tell and I wanted to record it. But more often than not, I never knew what I was going to get when I talked to someone. This homicide detective in Washington was just such a person. He spoke slowly and softly and I stared out of the window and watched as the rain dribbled lazily down the panes of darkened glass, whilst the detective's mellow voice began to hypnotise me. Just as I was in danger of drifting off, he said, 'Let me tell you about the Seattle police officer who became a murderer.' And just like that, I sat up, leant forward and double-checked that my recorder was running.

This was often how meetings went; me, unsure of what I was going to be told and worrying that the meeting would be unproductive when suddenly the officer I was speaking to would say something completely *unexpected. And a cop turned murderer was unexpected.*

When a murder occurs, everything else seems less important. In busy areas, after the initial response, where every cop and his K-9 attends, homicide detectives may simply work in pairs or even alone and have case after case after case to investigate. Every day will deliver them a new body. They will deal with the victims, the suspects, the families, the evidence, the paperwork, the media, their bosses, not to mention their own wives or husbands or families and demons.

The thing that always struck me about the homicide detectives that I spoke to, was just how exhausted they always seemed. It is a fascinating area of policing – particularly when there is a 'good homicide' to investigate – but it's also utterly relentless and it's no wonder that not everyone is cut out for this type of work. 'Tenacious' would be a good word to describe homicide detectives. However, I got the impression that – somewhat ironically – being a homicide detective can send you to an early grave.

We had a saying in the murder squad: Our day begins when your day ends.

****

Horrific acts occur daily and we tend to have a stoic face on it but inside you've gotta be affected. Having said that, I have a friend who was a homicide detective for years and he's one of the funniest human beings I ever met. He could sit and eat a plate full of spaghetti whilst he was on a decomposed body. He's just one of those people who are able to separate it.

Here in the desert, a lot of bodies fill with gases as they're decomposing. There are funny stories of homicide detectives having to stand at a distance and throw rocks at the body to try and pop it, so that the gases are released.

On the flip side, you hear about detectives arriving at a scene and just as they start to do the preliminary investigation, the body pops all over them. Just imagine how horrible that would be!

****

In New York we call police stations 'houses'. Houses are rated A, B, C. A Houses are extremely busy, B Houses are obviously less busy and C Houses are country clubs. My first station was an A House in Central Harlem in the mid-80s. It was the killing fields back then – literally the killing fields.

Now, although there are still homicides, there are nowhere near as many and it's actually a neighbourhood that's being gentrified. This was a neighbourhood where the only time white people came there was to buy drugs. Now white people live there.

It's still classed as an A House – definitely – but it's not busy like it was. The precinct was less than a square mile and it handled about ninety homicides a year for probably the first four or five years that I was there.

****

Any homicide that you can't solve is a terrible burden. Because as a cop, it's your responsibility to investigate the case and if you don't solve it, the stress alone takes a terrible, terrible toll on your personal life. I've seen it on a couple of detectives that I've worked with.

There've been a variety of problems, such as divorce, that have happened over someone throwing years of work into a case that they can never solve.

****

I don't like to be around death. I don't really have an explanation for it – and I've been around a lot of different scenes – I just don't like the surreal nature of a dead body.

I remember the first time it really had an impact on me, I was a graveyard-shift officer and I was asked to respond to a housing area that was under construction, as somebody had seen someone running from the area. I got there and checked the house and there was a body under the stairwell. It was one of the most gruesome things that I've ever seen in my life. It was just so gruesome and so surreal and uncomfortable and I had to stay there by myself and wait while other units responded.

So I was there with this dead body that had just been mercilessly beaten to death. A female. It was essentially a sexual assault where a woman was kidnapped and taken up to this construction site and raped and beaten to death with implements – two-by-fours and nails and things of that nature. It was just such an uncomfortable thing, that it affected me, not in a psychological way so that I couldn't continue to do my job, but it was just like, 'Wow! I don't think I could do this every night and deal with horrific crime scenes and the dark side of the investigations.' It was just so grotesque and it disturbed me.

It kept me from wanting to really delve into the investigations behind murder and homicide. And knowing the impact that this career has on you, I never wanted to pile on more. I was exposed to so much as it was.

****

I've seen more dead bodies and homicides than most people can even imagine. I remember distinctly – and this is no bullshit – handling three homicides in a single night. One upon turnout, one in the middle of the shift and one at the end of the shift.

Back then it was the crack wars. It was the early 90s and it was the crack wars. People getting killed was no big fucking thing. And back then two detectives would respond to the scene. Initially there would be a big response, but only from within the command. Maybe you'd get two radio cars, a sergeant and the detectives. You secured the scene, canvas the area and do whatever else it was that you did. Then you were taken out of the chart for twenty-four hours to handle the homicide and then it was business as usual. Now a hundred people will show up. Everybody and his brother shows up.

But the clearance rate back then was much better than it is now because most of the homicides were all fucking related. 'Well, I killed him because he killed Johnny and he killed Johnny because he killed whoever.' You know what I'm saying?

So you would catch one guy and you'd be able to clear five homicides. You'll still get your occasional homicides related to a robbery or drugs or whatever, but most of the homicides now are more domestic related.

But back in the early 90s there was so much money to be made out of crack. There are still a lot of drug homicides but it's not like it was.

****

I've been on homicide scenes where we'd have crime scene tape stretched out all over; cops all over the place and police cars with lights flashing. And then here comes this guy, walking down the sidewalk, lifts up the crime scene tape, walks right under it and just about steps on or over the body which is covered in a white sheet.

And when you stop them and you say, 'You didn't see the crime scene tape?'

They'll say, 'Oh, I'm just going to my cousin's house and he lives right over there.'

It's like they don't give a shit about anything. It's like they're on a mission to go 'here' and it doesn't matter that we've just had a shooting where someone died.

At another scene, same thing; there was a shooting, the person was dead, we had the crime scene tape up, my car was just about blocking the centre of the road and here comes this car, right down the street, right through the crime scene and it just about ran the body over that was laying in the middle of the road.

The lady said, 'Well, I didn't know what was going on.'

My car was just about blocking the entire street; she just about hit my car in order to get through and the crime scene tape was right there – CAUTION! DO NOT CROSS! POLICE.

Are you fucking kidding me?

****

We had this case where a real estate agent was murdered in 2001 whilst he was showing a house to a man. I think it was January 3rd. They looked at a number of houses and then the guy called him back on the 4th and said he wanted to look at a couple more. They didn't go into the first house but the second house they went to, this guy attacked the real estate agent and stabbed him to death. He dragged his body into the bathroom and put him in the bathtub and turned on the shower.

It's really kind of a bizarre case. There was no apparent motive for it. There was an immediate description of the suspect based on what the agent had told his wife the day before. So we put that description out. But then what happened was, the suspect took the agent's car and drove back to where he was originally picked up, which was a shopping centre in Kirkland. The car was later found there and the description went out for this older man with a cane and sure enough there was an older guy with a cane that frequented the area, so he was an immediate suspect. Turned out he was a real character, with a past. He claimed to be mafia, organised crime from the east coast. So he looked really good as a suspect and there was all this focus on this guy.

Anyway, what happened was, during the altercation – during the murder – our victim got a little bit of the killer under his fingernails, so we had DNA from the beginning. But the DNA didn't match this one suspect we had and the case just kind of went cold for a long time. Then in 2010 we got a hit on the DNA. Turned out to be a man who was a former Seattle police officer. He had retired on a mental disability. He had been involved in a couple of deaths whilst he had been on the police department; he shot one guy and chocked another guy out but they were both justifiable. He retired in 1980. By 1984 he was robbing banks – he robbed a bunch of banks over the course of a couple of years and then he got arrested. He was sent to prison probably for about seven or eight years. He got out in the mid-nineties – '93 or '94, something like that. He had a gambling problem, real strange guy. Then this murder occurred in 2001.

So we got a DNA hit on this guy and we started looking for him. We find out that about six months before we got the DNA hit, he and another fella had attempted a residential robbery of a doctor, down on the waterfront on Lake Washington. But this robbery didn't work out too well – the doctor fought back and they took off on foot.

Now, this waterfront area where the doctor lived, is down a real steep hill and these guys were somehow down there on foot. We suspected they originally planned on taking the doctor's car for a getaway but when they had to take off on foot, they ran down the street where they found a dock with a boat on it. They launched this boat – like a rowboat. They started rowing it, trying to row away, across the lake. Well, what they didn't know was, was that the owner – because it was the middle of winter – had taken the plug out of the back of the boat, so that when it rained the water would drain out. So unfortunately as these two fat old guys started rowing across the lake, the boat started filling up with water. They must have got about half way across before it sank. So both were dead – drowned. They were down in that lake for six or seven months.

It was about a week or so after we get the DNA hit that our killer pops back up in the lake. You see, the body is decomposing, it's building up gases and stuff and so they float back up.

Anyway, the investigation proceeded and we started talking to this guy's wife. She, over the period of several interviews, eventually gave up the fact that this guy had been involved in four other murders over the years. Maybe one or two of the murders even occurred when he was a cop. All the murders that she knew of – that he had told her he had done – were done either for revenge or for a friend. One of them, he had actually killed another former Seattle police officer. In another case he and another fella had apparently killed a guy that had dated the other fella's wife, before they got married.

Then they killed a guy who was the head of a local labour union who was going to fire a friend of our killer. So, our killer went and killed the guy so he couldn't fire his friend. And the last one was a bizarre thing, after our killer retired from the police department, he got into real estate and I think he had his own office for a while. Somehow there was some kind of a debt over this real estate business and he owed thousands of dollars. The bank had given the case to some local attorney to collect the money and this attorney had been calling the house and bugging people, particularly calling his wife. You didn't mess with his wife! So, they made an appointment with him late one night and went in and killed him – shot him a bunch of times and stabbed him a bunch of times.

I think these people are a creation of the Vietnam War. They seemed to be total psychopaths. He's dead, but the guy that was involved in some of these other cases is still alive but we can't prove anything because all of our information is what they call 'hearsay'. So it was a really bizarre case. It's still under investigation.

The murder of the real estate agent – the guy who got the whole thing started – we strongly suspect that it was a contract murder. We say that because it was the only murder that he didn't tell his wife about. All the other ones had a justification – if you can justify killing somebody. He seemed to have that justification, at least in his own mind; guy was screwing my friend's wife; this guy had screwed my other friend's wife; this guy was calling and bugging my wife over a debt; another guy, he killed him so he couldn't fire his friend – those are the 'justifications' for those murders. He was very loyal to his friends! But there doesn't seem to be a connection to the real estate agent. So we strongly suspect it was a contract killing. That's probably why he never told his wife about it, because he couldn't be as proud of it or was more ashamed of it. She might think less of him.

We've got five murders we know he did or was involved in – and that's just the ones we know about.

****

I know there's nothing funny about death, but it is pretty funny. This thing happened in a really nice part of our area, which is hard to believe but there is one or two blocks in Harlem that are really nice – very rich people live in them – and there's this one building that is really nice.

Now, a majority of the time when you get somebody dead in an apartment, you just sit outside; you're not going in there. Once everything is done, you're waiting for them to come get the body, so you've got to stay on the door because you don't want nobody else going in there or anything happening. So somebody – an officer – gets left with the body. So ninety-nine percent of the time you're literally standing in a hallway; you don't ever see the body because you don't want to sit on anything in the apartment. But there was this really nice building and in this apartment somebody had chopped up a body – it was chopped up into piece and put in the bathtub. So it's a big crime scene and this officer is left behind to wait for the guys to come and remove the body.

So, he's in there – with the cable TV and nice furniture – sitting around watching TV and he thinks, 'Oh, this is pretty cool, I like this.' And then he thinks, 'I wonder if they've got anything to drink? Maybe I'll get a beer.'

So he opens the refrigerator and goes, 'Oh fuck!' He gets on the radio and says, 'Yeah, erm... Are the detectives still around? Yeah, erm... could you come back?'

'Why? What's the matter?'

He goes, 'Yeah, one of you guys forgot some of your equipment.

You'll need to come back.'

He didn't want to say it over the radio but when he opened the refrigerator, there was a leg – from the knee down with the sock still on it. Two legs, in fact. Then he opened the freezer and there was the head with icicles sticking off it. It was almost surreal.

So obviously there was another body that was chopped up that nobody found. Well, originally the whole crime scene appeared to be in the bathroom, so why would you be looking in the freezer? The kitchen was perfectly clean. There was no reason to look for anything; nobody else was missing. So it turns out there were two bodies.

But the best thing about the crime scene pictures was seeing the socks – the leg from the knee down with the sock still on.

****

Last year, an officer calls me, 'Commander, we've got a body in the river.'

That happens. People jump in the river, so okay, whatever. It's six o'clock in the morning and I'm on my way into work.

So I get to work and I said, 'So, what have you got?'

And they go, 'Well, it's not a body; it's a torso.'

'A torso? Why didn't you tell me?'

'I thought we told you.'

'No. There's no head?'

'No.'

'No arms? No legs?'

'No, just a torso.'

So I say, 'Let's go take a look.'

But then he gets a phone call and he says, 'Oh my God. There's a second torso.'

I said, 'Stop messing with me.'

'No Commander, it's a second torso. A female.'

So we go down to the river and the border patrol is out there and they get the bodies. Then the news media shows up, and being a smart Commander, I said, 'No, no, no. Stay away from the crime scene. Move over there. This is a crime scene. I know what I'm doing, you go over there.'

They bring these two bodies – these two torsos – ashore. Then some fisherman comes walking up. He says to the guys from the news crew, 'What's going on?'

They tell him, 'They found two bodies over there.'

He says, 'Oh my God. That's terrible. So why are you over here?'

'Well, the Commander told us to stay away from the crime scene.'

'Oh, sorry, that really sucks.'

The guy goes fishing and he throws out his line and looks down and all the body parts are in the water. So we didn't know it but I'd sent them to the crime scene. The water was clear that day – it's usually murky – they look down, a suitcase had popped open and there was one of those battery-powered saws and he had cut off their heads, their hands and their legs and stuff and put them in the suitcase. I'd sent the news crew to the crime scene.

Then they call me and say, 'Hey!'

I'm like, 'What?'

'Come over here.'

'What?'

'We think we found your crime scene.'

'Why?'

'Look!'

So it's shit like that, you think, what else can go wrong? I'd followed the book but it still didn't work out.

Anyway, they caught the guy who did it. He was a jilted boyfriend from years ago who had asked these women, 'Hey, can I stay with you a little bit? I'm down on my luck.' They said, 'Yeah.' I think it was around Christmas time or New Year's. But then he didn't want to move out so he killed them both.

****

The Green River murders; that was a case that started in '82. July of '82 was the first victim. The guy was killing prostitutes. The first five that were found, were found in the Green River. The Green River runs through the Kent valley in Washington State and eventually dumps into Puget Sound.

The first victim was actually in the city of Kent. The second one was outside the city of Kent, not too far away and the third, fourth and fifth were found all at the same time, again, outside the city of Kent.

The murders were originally investigated by David Reichert, who at the time was a detective but later became the sheriff of King County. He was the sheriff when we finally solved it. He worked on the case from '82 to '84 with only a little bit of help. Then in '84 he got a lot of help and they formed a taskforce, because by then there were fourteen known victims and probably another six or seven suspected victims – people who were missing – who were all prostitutes. So we started this taskforce in '84 and over the next year we probably found another twenty-five victims. By the end, the count was up to nearly fifty or something like that.

The prostitutes – the victims – were picked up on either Pacific

Highway South, which is Highway 99, or in Downtown Seattle. Some of them were on Aurora Avenue, which is an extension of Highway 99. Highway 99 runs through Seattle but north of town it's called Aurora Avenue. Before they built freeways, it was the main road that ran north and south from Washington to California, so there were a lot of motels along it that catered to the travellers back in the day. But once they built the freeway, these motels ended up becoming sleazy. They weren't frequented as much, they didn't look after them but they were still there, so they were used a lot by prostitutes.

I think Gary Ridgway came to the attention of the taskforce two or three times over the years but never popped to the top until about '87. There was enough evidence at that time to get some search warrants so we searched his house. All we had to look for were some fibres and hopefully some evidence that might link him to one of the victims, but nothing ever came up. But at the time, they got a cheek swab from him or a gauze chew or whatever and then a couple of years later DNA started coming into its own, although it took a lot of sample in order to get anything. We had a couple of victims that had sperm observed in their vaginal fluids, that were collected after they were found but that was just the first five. After the first five victims, almost everything that we found was skeletal. There was only one other victim that was not skeletal and we did eventually get DNA out of her too. So we tried some DNA work in '88, '89 but it didn't work out. Everything was said to be too degraded – our samples had been sitting there, in the freezer, for seven years. So the samples went back in the freezer and stayed there. We were kind of waiting for the technology to get better. We didn't know how much sample they had used up, so we didn't know how much was left.

I think we started looking into it again in late 1999 or early 2000. There were lots of new techniques that had come into play in the development of DNA, particularly with some of the degraded stuff. So we submitted the gauze chew they had got from Gary Ridgway in '87 to the crime lab along with some blood from a couple of other suspects. And we submitted the vaginal fluids that we had tested previously and a couple of others where sperm wasn't necessarily observed but we wanted to give it a try and see what we could come up with anyway. And then – I think it was September of 2001 – we got word that they had matched a sample from one of the river victims with Gary Ridgway. It was from one of the three victims that were found at the same place all at the same time. It was a pretty good match and at the same time we had a partial profile that also couldn't be excluded. So with that, we started a new task force.

They processed another one of the victims – an intact body – and they got a full hit. A full hit! You know, smack-dab! So now we had him on two cases and a partial on the other one. So we linked him to two different scenes and we were getting ready to arrest him, as we now know that we've got the right guy.

If it had just been one hit, he could have said, 'Yeah, I do prostitutes all the time, and I had sex with her but I can't help it if someone killed her later.' But now we've got two hits with fresh samples from him. And then later on, one of the scientists that had been working on one of the cases – one from the river which was real weak – got a lab slide on which they had mounted a pubic hair. She took that, washed it and found one sperm on the hair. Then she processed that and she got a full hit. So now we've got three full hits – three positive matches on the guy.

We made the arrest and proceeded as if we were going to go to trial and it was a big production because he had quite a large defence team. And we had a pretty good size prosecution team with our task force. We had five lawyers – that's five prosecutors working with us. We had a pretty good team. We moved the whole operation out to a building by King County airport. We were about fifteen months or thereabouts into it, preparing for trial. But we had also submitted some evidence to a microscope trace evidence guy who specialised in paint. You see, Ridgway was a truck painter – he worked for a company which makes these big trucks. He was in the paint shop and when you spray paint, the paint that hits the truck goes 'splat' and sticks, but the paint that doesn't hit anything, as it travels through the air it gets hard and it forms itself into a really little ball, so it ends up basically being dust. So Gary Ridgway was, on a daily basis, carrying these dust balls around with him, everywhere he went – little paintballs, paint spheres – and so everywhere he went and everything he touched ended up having these paint spheres on it. We ended up submitting all of our victims' clothing and I think it was early 2003, we got word that this microscope expert had positively identified the paint. The paint was unique; the truck paint was a particular brand of paint with a certain molecular structure. The expert positively identified the paint that he had recovered from some of the victims' clothes, as being a positive match to the paint used by the company where Ridgway worked on these trucks. So with that, we then charged Ridgway with three more murders.

Before, we only had three DNA matches and another victim at one of the scenes who was just going along for the ride – because her body was there, he had to have done that one also. So we only had four charged cases, although we had some forty-odd victims, but we charged him with three more homicides based on this paint evidence. I think the defence thought they could attack the DNA evidence but now, with the paint, there was a totally separate physical evidence field – physical evidence that positively linked him to additional victims – and I think they felt that if he wanted to make a deal, now was the time. Somebody over there convinced him – or he decided – that it was in his best interest to plead guilty if they would forgo the death penalty.

It was a controversial thing because after he got charged with these murders, the prosecutor said, 'I will not make a deal on the death penalty. There'll be no plea bargaining with the death penalty.'

But as it turned out, although we had seven charges, he was willing to plead guilty and confess to forty-eight or forty-nine. It seemed like the trade-off was certainly worth it and it would save millions of dollars in trial costs. It wasn't done for the money though; basically we got answers for forty-two more families than we would have if we had just gone to trial.

We were going to interview him, so we had to try and figure out where to do it and we looked at all the options. It had to be a secret. He had to totally cooperate. If he didn't totally cooperate, the deal was off and we'd go back to where we were. So the pressure was kind of on him but he was also a psychopath and a dumb shit. He had an IQ of something like 85. So the whole thing had to be done in total secrecy; the world couldn't know we were doing it, in case the deal fell through and we had to go back to prosecuting him. It could taint the jury pool and then we would have a real tough time prosecuting him.

So what do we do? We can't check him out of the jail every day, because somebody would eventually notice that. We really had to take him some place where nobody would see us, so we figured that the best place would be to just put him in our office. He agreed to do it, so we took him out of the jail, Friday the 13th June, I think. 2003. We had him in our office for a hundred and eighty-eight days.

So we had this building, we were on the lower floor of it and we had a room that was about ten-by-ten, I think. We fixed it so he couldn't escape. Basically they taped up all the outlets and we put a mattress on the floor and gave him a sleeping bag. Then we put a table in the doorway - a round table. We stuffed it into the doorway so he could sit at the table and he could do anything that he wanted - writing or stuff - and outside the doorway there were always three people standing there. We didn't allow guns in there so all three of those guys had tasers, in case he tried anything. He was very mellow and I don't think he would ever have tried to escape. We rigged up a shower in the bathroom and we would talk to him every day. We had a room set up with video and audio and we'd go in and interview him.

Then about once a week, we'd get up really early and go out in this caravan of cars and he would take us to the dump sites, where he left the victims, one after another. Most of them we already knew about but it was up to him to show us and prove to us that he knew where they were. As it turned out, it was one of the few things that he could do to establish that he actually had done these things. There were so many of them, that he couldn't give you specifics as to what happened with any one particular woman and half of them he couldn't recognise from the pictures that we had of them.

There were so many of them and he did them all the same way.

191

As I say, he was dumb as a stump but he found a way to kill women – at least prostitutes – that was fool proof and that was part of his success. His trick was – and the girls were always in a hurry so it worked well – to say, 'Well you know what? If I could go at you from behind, I'll get it over with faster.' And when he was done, he'd suddenly say, 'What's that?' The girl would then lift her head up, look around and he'd throttle them – strangle them to death – usually with his arm. There were a couple of them that were obviously done with rope – with a ligature – but most of the time the ligature was put on later just to make sure that they stayed dead; he may have had some problems with some of them popping back up alive or something.

So, we interviewed him for a hundred and eighty-eight days and eventually he went to court and pleaded guilty to forty-eight murders and went to prison.

I think about a year or so ago – two years ago maybe – we found the remains of another victim that he had admitted killing and had actually taken us to the spot where we found one victim but we didn't find the second one. We brought him back out from prison, charged him with the forty-ninth murder and that's where we stand now – forty-nine. We didn't charge him with any that we hadn't found. He was charged with four murders of women that we don't know who they are – or didn't at the time. We recently identified one of them. So we still have three unidentified sets of remains, but he was charged with their murders.

There were several more that he acknowledges that he had killed and he showed us where he dumped them, but the site had been developed into parking lots and industrial areas; their remains will probably never be found. But he wasn't charged with cases where we didn't find anything. He took us to several spots; he dumped the girls in a lot of different types of places. There was the river but he couldn't go back there after they found the bodies – it was too exposed – so he started taking them into the woods.

He was also into necrophilia, at least early on. He was going back, visiting the bodies again for three, four or five days. That's why I think there was so much sample available to us with the DNA, because he was, you know, going back to them. He wasn't using any condoms or anything. He said that later on, he didn't want to do that anymore so he started dumping them further out, on the I-90, fifteen to twenty miles out of town.

One of the areas he took us – it's highway 410 – it's kind of a route over the mountains. I'm not even sure if it's open all year long. But it goes up quite a ways and he took us to a number of spots along this road, which is quite remote, logging area type stuff, probably some big cats, cougars, maybe bears, but certainly lots of big animals. He said he dumped a bunch there. He took us to lots of spots but we could never find anything. I think the animals took them. The reason I say that is because one of the places he took us was only about fifty or sixty yards from a place where the highway department would throw road kill. Sometimes these dead animals would get dragged off and probably the only thing that could do that would be a big cat or something.

I don't know if the Green River case affected me. I guess we'll find that out some day. I don't feel affected, although it was obviously an emotional experience. It was traumatic I guess, to some extent, but I don't feel affected by it. I guess it could drive you nuts talking to a nut-job like that for as long as we did but we all seemed to survive, mainly because it wasn't like talking to Hannibal Lecter. It was more like talking to your ten-year-old kid and trying to get him to admit to breaking the window, only he had actually broken a hundred windows and was trying to remember which ones he broke and when, and whether he used a rock or a stick. That's the kind of thing we were trying to deal with.

We were expecting a lot more detail than what we got from him. I mean, he told us a lot of stories but he could never tell you which victim it was he did 'this' to, or 'that' with. Sometimes it was like pulling teeth.

I don't look at it as if I did anything special and I don't make a big deal over it. The guy was already a suspect. The lab is what did the work.

In the end, he got forty-nine life sentences, without parole.

****

The thing about homicides – and I hope I don't sound insensitive when I say this – is it's just criminals killing criminals, for the most part.

11

The Negatives

*A*s I sat in a quiet office on the fourteenth floor of a tower block overlooking a grey, rainy, West Coast city, talking to a police detective, I quickly – perhaps too quickly – changed the subject from our initial 'get-to-know-you' conversation to the negatives of police work. The officer stood up, slowly walked to the office door, shut it carefully, closed the blinds, calmly sat back down and then began to shake. Police work had taken its toll on him, and even though he had never met me before, and even though we had been talking for just a few minutes, he opened up and told me how his job had affected him. His experiences were of divorce, depression and suicidal thoughts. It was important, he felt, that anyone wanting to become a cop knew that the risks were not just those you faced on the streets. There were also the risks you took with your home life and your mental wellbeing. 'Being a police officer can damage your health,' he told me.

Most of the time, I never knew what a cop was going to say to me when I spoke to them. But I always went in with a set of topics I wanted to discuss and one of these was the negative side of police work. Perhaps *naively, I didn't initially take into account just how distressing the subject could be for some of the cops I was speaking to and I often came away from these interviews feeling exhausted and saddened, but also extraordinarily grateful that the officers had been so honest and willing to speak to me about something so private.*

The officer I mentioned above was the first one to do so and I learnt not to be so blasé in my questioning when I brought the subject up with other officers in future. Voices would be lowered, the tone would soften and I vowed never to push the officers for anything more than they were willing to give. But then I didn't have to, because – as I found – they were willing to give me everything, which I felt was brave, generous and extraordinary.

You can ask me what you want. It doesn't matter. You ask me and I'll tell you straight. I don't powder stuff. I shoot from the hip. Some people don't like it but that's reality. That's the way I handle it.

****

I had a point where I burnt out mentally and I needed to recover and get healthy again. The thing is, out on the street, your daily diet is people who hate you, people you've got to fight all the time or people you've got to chase all the time. You see nothing but bad. It affects you and I was affected by it; I went into periods of depression.

Part of becoming healthy again was getting out of the field. That really helped, getting out of that environment and taking on new challenges. And I saw it in other people – I'd see the same thing that was on me, on other people.

I'd give them some advice. I'd say, 'Hey, get out of here, get a new assignment. Don't stay here too long.'

It affected my marriage and it affected my family. It was a tough time for me because I was heavily invested in my job. I was heavily invested in *me*. I was trying to get the job done – going out there with an ideal and a purpose. And you take a lot of things personally. If it's a job failure or you did something wrong, you take it too hard. It's sometimes hard to keep perspective. I had to relearn some things, get friendly with people again, do obligations again – go to their parties, go to their get-togethers, which I didn't want to do before. The big thing was to wait for the next cop party or something. I needed to get healthy, which included seeing my old friends and doing some activities.

Being a police officer can damage your health. I think I knew it – I had a sense that this could wreck me. The depression scared me. I was so dark and so heavy. And here's a scary thought: I understood why people killed themselves, because I could relate to it. If you're in this dark, heavy depression you can see why people would want to kill themselves. And that was a warning light for me.

The other part of it was the medication angle – I didn't want to have to take meds to get up and to live. I was afraid to go on medication. I didn't want to do it or even have to do it. But I didn't want to stay in this dark hole either. I needed to take care of myself, get rest, get out and be active with people, be social. Do things outside of the job. And I was able to say that I recovered. But it wasn't easy.

I would say that police suicides are not that common but I think what we see is lots of acting out in all kinds of other ways – drinking, or for some people, drugs. Some guys want to womanise, they want to do lots of things that really damage their personal lives, because they just don't know how to cope.

Even though I spent a good few years in administration, I saw a lot of fast and furious action in a good chunk of my career where it put me in this depression, so I'm very careful now. I do not want to go there again. And my wife reminds me, she warns me about that.

I even have to be careful with the stories that I tell. When I was teaching at the academy I said, 'Do you know what could happen to you? Let me tell you…' And you go through your stories, reliving them because you want to deposit in the deputies and recruits, enough of your own experiences to keep them safe. So when I taught at the academy, I was as tense as when I was on the road.

****

We've got a poster hanging up in the precinct. It's a hand with a pistol in it, kinda pointing out and says something about, 'all too often officers end their careers by taking their own life', or something like that. 'If you need help, call…', you know, that kind of thing; just trying to prevent suicides or whatever.

That's not really anything that ever crossed my mind but for about a year – between June of last year and June of this year –I went the full year without wearing my bullet-proof vest. I know for a fact that I went for a year without wearing my vest because I was depressed after my marriage broke down. Apparently my wife didn't respect the sanctity of marriage and decided that she was going to have multiple affairs behind my back with multiple officers that I have to work with. She works for the police department too – she's a civilian employee.

I found out about them as they were going on. I found out about the first one and that was three months into our marriage. The second was last year, with a guy who I considered a friend. And then four months later with another guy who works with the sheriff's department.

I wasn't trying to hurt myself by not wearing my vest but to be honest there were times when I really didn't care what happened. There are a lot of officers who think that vests are a false sense of security. You know? People think that they're bullet-proof just because they're wearing a vest, which isn't the case. But I think it made me a better officer because I was more vigilant. I paid more attention to what was going on around me because I didn't have this vest on that can protect me from everything that could hurt me. I found the difference between concealment-and-cover as opposed to standing behind a trashcan thinking it's going to stop bullets, you know? I'd put my body behind something that was heavier and thicker and could actually stop rounds if they came my way. Because I wasn't wearing a vest, it actually made me more tactical, it made me think about things more. I didn't put myself in positions where I could be hurt.

But there were a lot of people who knew that I didn't wear a vest. Some would ask why, some didn't care, some would just beg me to put it back on. And eventually I got to the point where I did – I put it back on.

I think part of me had a death wish at that point. When you are at the bottom, you don't see that there is a way out. But there's a difference between being suicidal and just letting things happen the way they do.

There were days when I came to work and I was happy to come to work. I love my job. It's great to come out here. It's great to interact with different people. And there were days when I came to work and I thought, 'Maybe today is the day that some idiot is going to end it for me and I don't have to worry anymore about going home to an empty house, to two children who I only see four days out of a month.' But eventually you realise that that's no way to live – it's not living. One day something just clicked. So I come to work every day, I put my vest on and I enjoy my job.

****

I can deal with death because I've learnt to care less. And that's honestly the way it is. I used to care a lot more about it when I was younger and newer. I'd think about it more, let it get to me. Now, when I leave work at night I try to leave everything at the office. I don't even think about work when I get home. It's unfortunate.

You try to disassociate yourself from it. That's what you do. It's sad but I think that's where a lot of cops get into a lot of trouble and I had problems with alcohol and everything for a while because I got too stressed out. I quit drinking years ago but for a long time, that was my outlet. I think a lot of cops fall back on alcohol but it causes personal problems, family problems.

Being a cop is a stressful, stressful job. You've got to see things that most people don't ever want to see – things that they see on TV and don't believe are real. But a lot of stuff you see on TV *is* real.

****

It's an enormous struggle to be a law enforcement officer in Detroit – in the most violent city in America. For forty years Detroit has been consistently 1, 2 or 3 – but mostly 1 – in the overall violent crimes statistics of all major cities in the United States. For forty years!

Just take a look at the amount of mayhem you see as a law enforcement officer. Some guy comes out of school, he gets recruited and becomes a police officer and the next thing you know, he's looking at shit you don't see on combat fields. You know what I mean? I mean, people blown up.

Some of the things that happen to people in automobile accidents are bad enough. When you see somebody run over somebody else, drunk, and then drag their ass for half a mile and half the body has literally been sanded away, but they're still alive, that's tough enough to look at, right? But to see some guy who's had the lower portion of his face blow off with a sawn-off shotgun and he's still alive and he's trying to tell you what happened... and he's sitting there conscious, with the bottom part of his face missing, trying to tell you who shot him – it becomes almost like a fuckin' Creature Feature! You know what I mean? And then you're expected to go home and go to sleep like a normal fucking person – 'Oh yeah, I'll just go sleep this off.' Really?

I mean you have no idea how big the emotional closet has to be for some of these officers when they hide this stuff, just the shit that they see every day. Like last night, we got some twenty-three-year-old kid finds out that he's got some girl pregnant – she's six months pregnant – and now she wants to move in and now he sees his whole life crushed and crumbling down around him because he's now got a twenty-year commitment. He's in a life-long commitment with this broad when he just thought it was a one-night thing. Well let me tell you what happened: he pulled out a gun and blew his fucking brains out, right there. Blew his own fucking brains out right there. Like, 'Fuck this, I'd rather see what's on the other side, bitch, than spend the rest of my life with you!' For real? Holy shit! You know what I mean?

We grew up watching John Wayne movies, you know what I'm saying? That's the kind of shit that John Wayne would do. John Wayne and Jimmy Cagney, that kind of thing. Tom Cruise and them, they don't do that kind of shit, man. Boy, this kid's got the balls to do that? It just blew my mind. I was like, 'Wow!'

****

I'd say a majority of cops I work with are divorced. I think the job has a lot to do with it – crappy hours, working weekends. Like I said, seeing a lot of crap that normal people shouldn't have to see – that's what we get stuck dealing with and cleaning up. Every time someone dies, every time they blow their head off, every time they commit suicide, the cops have gotta be there. It's just death and death and death and death. Eventually it eats you up.

It's also people lying to you. It's the lying, the death, everything. You're not dealing with the average Joe Blow citizen for the most part, you know, someone with a good job and a good family and a nice life. For the most part you're dealing with the dregs of society – the liars, the cheaters, the scumbags, the rapists, the murderers, the people that no one else wants to deal with. Those are the ones we deal with.

****

You're here to do two things: do your job and live your life. I really believe in the service to the community, in that there's a certain trust they put in us to be here, and we owe it to them, whilst we're here, to give them that service and trust. But when you look at it from sort of a personal objective standpoint, this job is also here so that you can live your personal life. Your personal and private life is not there so you can just be a cop and only ever work and I think a lot of time that line really starts to get blurred and you see these guys that are just 'cop, cop, cop' all the time. They go home to their family and everything is police work and when they hang out, they hang out with their police friends. Their whole life becomes this police thing and I think a lot of them realise too late that maybe they should have concentrated on other things when they weren't at work – because it destroys families.

I lost a marriage to it. I was young. I had just started in this business – this job. My wife was young as well. We had just moved to Las Vegas. Nobody had ever really just sat down and talked to me about family and even if they had, I'm not sure I would have understood at the time because of the maturity level – I was twenty-three or twenty-four years old and our marriage just dissolved.

I realised when I looked back on it a few years later, it was really kind of my fault and I didn't realise it at the time but it was because I was bringing all this stuff home, from work. I was used to being the alpha dog everywhere I went at work, because everywhere you go you have to be the alpha dog, not only with bad guys but people you work with, so you get used to your interpersonal relationships being all about competition and contest. If I'm not always asserting myself or showing my manhood – or womanhood, whatever the case may be – over people that I work with, then I'm failing. Well, I got so used to that in my interpersonal connections at work, I brought that home with me and so my wife and I would argue all the time. There were all kinds of problems.

Eventually she just left. I didn't realise why. Of course I blamed her at the time. I blamed life and everything else and I didn't realise until about two or three years later that maybe I need to take a serious look at myself to see why that happened. Then I realised it was just me.

I've slowly tried to make provisions to fix that and I think I've done a pretty good job. Now I'm trying to bring this knowledge into the academy when I'm up there as an instructor. My role at the academy is kind of like a drill instructor, like a troop handler. When I have time with my recruits I emphasise police work but I also try to emphasise the interpersonal things that happen off duty, that are far more important than your work, and that's your family. I learnt the hard way.

****

I'm on my third wife. Part of it is the hours, working holidays, the things you see; you tend to bring it home with you, you don't mean to but you do. Death. I worked in 9/11. I was there when the second building came down. I was a brand new sergeant and was put on the morgue detail. I was assigned and I was there for two days straight. Never went home. You see that death and you come home – and it's good to be home – but you tend to take out your emotions on the person that is closest to you all the time, whether you mean to or not.

Also, cops have this stigma of being womanisers. There are women who like the uniform, so I think inevitably my wife's friends filled her head at the time too, with, you know, 'What is he doing that late, working all those hours? How come he's in the bar again?'

We work these very odd hours. I would get off at two o'clock in the morning and when you would get off work you didn't want to go home; you were so riled up at what happened during the tour. We were doing prostitution units or we were doing drug buys. After that you're so riled up and now your tour's over, it's three o'clock in the morning because you got an hour's overtime, so you don't want to go home and sit in the dark alone because your wife's asleep. You're just sitting there, wound up, so you walk across the street to the bar with the guys and talk and converse about what happened and everything. So you end up being in a bar for a couple of hours, 'til five o'clock in the morning. It's just something you did to get it out of your system and then when you went home and you try and explain to her, she didn't want to hear it.

My new wife now is a cop. We understand each other but it also works against me. My wife is surrounded by men 24/7 and you know what cops are like. So what I was just talking about reverts in the other direction. I never thought I would marry a cop. I never thought I would date a cop. Now I have to deal with what my ex-wife was dealing with. She's beautiful, my wife. She got a great body and like I said, you know what cops are like. Cops are the worst. Firemen too.

****

We pretty much see the same thing every day: dope dealers killing each other, traffic fatalities and low-income people beating the snot out of their kids.

We try not to remember most of it because if you do it'll drive you nuts. You take it off when you take your boots off.

When you see the kids, those are the ones that are the worst, you know? Because we all have kids. When I didn't have kids, it didn't bother me. I mean, I saw a kid stuck to a telephone pole one time at a traffic wreck – didn't think anything about it. But then I got one of my own and when you're standing there looking at this little kid, taking pictures of it, you're like, 'Man, that could be my kid.' But of course it wouldn't be my kid because we're intelligent enough to know not to beat the snot out of our kids. But it happens every day.

But somebody has to do this job. Somebody has to. And we're crazy enough to do it. If we sat down for therapy, it would put the doctor into counselling.

****

Unfortunately a lot of cops drink too much and they don't talk about their feelings. I think we as a profession have got better about it now but when I first came on they said, 'Whatever you do, don't go see a mental health professional or they'll put you on the rubber gun squad. You'll lose your job. They'll take your gun and put you on a desk. They'll take your job away from you.'

I think the fire service was always more progressive because they realised that seeing people burnt up in a fire is one of the most horrific things you could ever see. If they have a critical incident, they have a critical incident stress debriefing. They bring people in, they sit everybody down and everybody talks about what they saw – their feelings – then they're debriefed one on one with a mental health professional. They don't have the burn out that cops do.

But cops have got better about that. It's still not good but it's gotten better.

****

You go into work and you're hyper-vigilant for eight hours, ten hours, twelve hours. You're always looking around, sizing people up. Then when you get home, the mind has to reset, so your body will crash. I don't know what you do when you get home but for the first four hours, I'm watching television and switching channels with the remote.

People that I'm dating are like, 'How you doing?'

'Fine.'

'What do you want to do?'

'I don't know.'

You're like, catatonic. You're not capable of having an intelligent conversation. You need seven or eight hours to reset. 'Go into town? Are you insane? I've just come from town!'

We don't explain it to people enough. If your body does this, it needs time to sleep and reset. You need to tell your wife, girlfriend, boyfriend – whatever – that that's normal. 'I want to be with you right now and I want to spend time with you, I'm just not capable of it, so give me a few hours and then we can do our thing.'

****

We've all got our little ways to release. I sit down to Razerblade and Death Metal music. I sit down to my Scandinavian Black Metal music and reload bullets. I listen to Enya too. And Sonny and Cher. And Elvis. Beethoven sometimes. Anything except for that rap, although I'm kinda switched because I've recently discovered Gangstagrass. It's bluegrass rap. So I'm kinda into that now.

So yeah, we're weird. If we weren't weird we wouldn't do this for a living.

****

The thing is, once you leave, once you retire, what are you? Suddenly, overnight, you are no longer anyone of importance. You don't matter to your community. You no longer know what's happening, whereas the day before you knew about everything and everyone. It's a real shock to the system.

12

Officer Down

*O*ne *of the final interviews I conducted was with an officer in Boston, Massachusetts. A friend from another force had arranged for me to speak to this cop as he felt that the officer had a good tale to tell. My problem was that I had a flight to catch back to the UK and I had just a couple of hours spare so didn't believe I had enough time left. And, if I am being completely honest, I was exhausted after a long, demanding trip and simply wanted to get one last lobster roll and a pint before heading to Logan International. But on my friend's insistence, I met with the officer. He picked me up in his car outside South Station in downtown Boston and as soon as I jumped into the front passenger seat I noticed a large amount of scaring – almost like burn scars – around the lower portion of his face and around his neck. With my schedule so tight, I didn't feel there was time for the usual pleasantries and 'getting-to-know-you' chat, so I took a risk and leapt straight in, asking about the scars. The officer's story was simply amazing and if I had needed to miss my flight home to hear how he had survived being shot multiple times, I would have seriously considered it.*

Although this courageous Boston cop – and he is still a cop – was happy to tell me about the incident that had come extraordinarily close to taking his life, this chapter was still a challenging one to write. Speaking to officers about their careers and encouraging them to recall their funny stories is one thing, but to bring up so sensitive a subject as one involving the injury or death of police officers was, to say the least, difficult. Officers weren't always talking about themselves; often they were telling me about their colleagues who had been lost or seriously injured in horrific circumstances. In fact, I found that officers were far more comfortable talking about their own injuries than talking about their fellow officers and friends. Tears were shed. Even after I had returned home – as you will read – tragedy continued to play itself out in devastating ways.

I have received many gifts from officers during my visits to America – department patches and mugs, for example – but I have also acquired a number of t-shirts. These t-shirts are printed with the name of a slain officer. The shirts have become a way for a department or unit to remember and honour officers as well as a way of raising funds for the families left behind. For a long time I felt uncomfortable wearing these tops. It seemed like a strange thing to do, to wear the name of a murdered police officer on your clothing, but I now feel very differently and when I wear one of these t-shirts (I am wearing one as I write this) I realise that the officer is being remembered on the other side of the world, by someone who never knew them. And to me, that seems like a good thing.

The dedication at the start of this book came about because of the accounts I recorded for this chapter and the shirts I continue to be given.

It was the coldest day of the year, six degrees out. It was January 16th. I can remember the date. We were going to serve an arrest warrant in the town of Quincy, which borders the southern part of Boston. It was for a guy wanted on warrant in Boston; he'd shot at his brother-in-law or something like that.

So we were going to arrest him on this warrant and seeing how it wasn't in the city, the plan was that after we surrounded the house we were going to knock on the door and pretty much just call him out. So we set up the perimeter and we knocked on the door and called him out but we got no response for several minutes. Whilst this is going on, we're waiting outside, waiting to go in, and it is really cold out. In our minds, we just want to go in to get out of the cold.

So finally, we say that we are going to make entry and breach the door but as soon as we are lined up to breach the door, the door opened up – the guy had lived there with his wife and his girlfriend and several of their children – so they all came out and said that he wasn't there.

Despite what they told us, after we got them out, we went and started to clear the building, to look for him. We cleared the first two floors and the basement. And then we went to clear the crawl space in the attic, and me being the small guy, I volunteered to go up there. It's not that it's dangerous – I've done it before, I've done it since – but on this one we had cameras up there and we were able to clear a vast majority of the attic by sight. But there was one corner where I couldn't really see. It was about a fifteen-degree arc that I was concerned about. So I was focusing on that arc and the guy coming up behind me was going to clear the rest.

So I just put my head and shoulders into the attic, clearing that and it turns out that the guy was under the insulation, between two of the joists, so you couldn't see him. Then he popped up from about ten feet away and fired. I don't really know how many rounds he fired at me but I was hit twice in my arm, once in my jaw and then one into my neck. I don't remember any sounds – no sounds at all – but I remember the lights and the flashes and then I remember being at the bottom of the ladder. I was looking back up, clutching my arm, looking at my hand, which is all covered in blood. I was looking in disbelief, thinking this doesn't happen to me, it's always the other guy who gets shot. It's never you, you know? This probably all happened in half a second – time just kind of slows down.

But I was able to tell the guys, 'He's not over there, he's over that way.'

Luckily we had an ambulance waiting for us. One of the other officers helped walk me down and I get into the ambulance. I can feel everything so I'm thinking, 'Okay, this is good.' Well, obviously it's bad but I can walk and I can talk. It hurts really bad but that's a good thing, because feeling pain means everything is working. But I could feel the bullet in my neck; I could tell that something was not right. I could feel that there was something in my neck, so I was concerned about that.

My arm hurt the most, though, because it shattered the bone. But also my jaw got shattered and everything was just burning and I could feel the bullet in my neck. So I was just kinda clutching my arm but I was only concerned about the bullet in my neck. I was trying not to move my neck, and I could feel the bullet, it's hot and it's sitting in my neck. That was my biggest concern. But again, I was walking, talking, it hurt really bad but I was in the Marine Corps and we were always taught, if that happened, it's a good thing, it means everything is working.

The EMT was asking which hospital I wanted to go to – because we were in Quincy – and I told him the Boston Medical Center, which was not far away but I had been to that hospital for work numerous times with shooting victims. That's where most of the shooting victims from the city are sent to, so that's the place to go, so they took me there. I spent nine days in the hospital, I think. I healed but I've still got some nerve damage in my face – it hurts to shave – and I'm missing a little piece of my jaw. My arm has nerve damage and it's kind of sensitive but it's normal to me now, so it is what it is.

The guy shot me with 9mm bullets. The EMT's and paramedics of this city are awesome. And the hospitals are too. I've seen so many people get shot and live that I knew that once I got into the ambulance and with the paramedics and the EMTs and the hospitals, I'd be fine. I wasn't really worried. I knew obviously that there'd be some damage but there was no question that I wasn't going to make it. So I just calmed down and once I got to the ambulance – aside from them putting the IV in me – everything else was good. By the time we got to the hospital, they'd given me morphine.

I have a thing – not a phobia – but I hate IVs and stuff. You know, people shooting up heroin and going into your veins or giving blood, I hate doing that. It's not the needle – it's just anything going into your veins. So I was in the ambulance and they had to give me an IV and all my attention went to that, like, 'Whoa! Whoa! What are you doing?' And then when I was in the hospital I kept lying when they went to put the IV in and I'd say, 'Oh, they did that this morning.' So they caught on and started writing the date and stuff onto the IV.

So anyway, now I've got a metal rod in my arm and there're some little fragments from the bullets left here and there. There's a little bit left in my chin but I can't really feel it. And I think I've got nine screws in my arm. I've got a little plate to hold in my voice box – it's tiny, though – it holds my voice box together because when the bullet went in, luckily it didn't really hit anything although obviously it broke my jaw, went in, landed and cracked my voice box. So they put in a tiny, little metal plate, to hold it together. But I was lucky, it could have gone different.

I can still do push-ups but it's hard so I have to come up on my knuckles and just once in a while, I'll hit it the wrong way and it'll hurt. Like I said, there's some nerve damage but it's just normal for me now, but it's obviously not a hundred percent. But I can still do everything fine, not as good as I could before but still good enough to pass all the qualifications and all that stuff with no problems.

I probably could have retired from this job and I probably would have made more money because I'd get one hundred percent pay and every raise. But you know, I came back. It was never an issue – I never, ever thought to leave. It's mainly because of the people I work with. I always wanted to do this job and if I left, I've lost. It's not an 'us-versus-them' thing - but me personally, I didn't want to quit. This is something that I always wanted to do and I'm not gonna let this get in my way. So I came back. There are times when I'm like, you know, 'I should have just left!' But a vast majority of the time, I'm glad I came back. I've got a lot of friends in the job and I like doing the job. I know it sounds like a cliché to say, 'oh, you like helping people', but you do. I like helping people a lot. Even little things like helping people who are locked out of their cars.

I was engaged at the time of the shooting and we got married later on. The good part about this story too, is this: we had got engaged and I had to start working a lot to pay for the wedding. But once I got injured I couldn't work. I still got paid by the police department but I was planning to work a lot of overtime, road details and things like that, to pay for the wedding. But obviously, once I got shot, I couldn't do that. So all the guys at work – the whole department – and a lot of people from the community, had a fund-raiser for me. It pretty much paid for my wedding. We had a big wedding, rented out a function hall, everybody showed up. I couldn't even talk during it because I was so emotional. And that's part of the reason you come back – all these people that do this stuff for you.

My wife knew that I wasn't going to leave. All my friends and everyone who knew me, knew that I wouldn't leave. Right off the bat they said, 'He's not going to leave; he's going to come back.' So she knew. She was fine when I went to K-9 and when I made sergeant but she got worried when I went back on the SWAT team. But I think in reality, the most dangerous part of this job is just being out on patrol, because you never know what you're walking into on that. She also didn't like me riding the department motorcycle. I'm not the best at it. I'm one of the worst riders the department has and that's one of the most dangerous jobs. She was more concerned about me riding the bike than getting shot. So I do K-9 and SWAT now. My mother thinks I'm just on the dogs. She doesn't know that I now do both. She doesn't know that I went back to SWAT.

We had a dog with us on that warrant but we didn't use him. You don't want to send a dog up to their death, either. You'd rather send a dog than a person but you're not going to just throw them to their death. I found that a lot of the time, if you just get the dog barking, it gets a lot of reaction from people. But we're not just going to sacrifice a dog. So to get the guy who shot me, they just turned the heat off. It was the coldest day of the year, so they turned the heat off and froze him out.

So anyway, the guy pleaded insanity. It went to trial and it was a hung jury. A couple of the jurors thought that he had mental issues, so we had to go for a retrial. But once they set the date, he pled out. In the initial trial they found him guilty on the gun and the bullets. But a couple of the jurors couldn't decide on his mental condition in regards to shooting me. So the judge gave him the maximum he could have given him – four years. Two years for the gun and then two more years for the bullets. Then he ended up taking a plea deal for another twelve to sixteen years on top of that. So it could be anywhere between sixteen to twenty years or twelve to sixteen years, so not as much time as he should have got.

I've arrested people who had guns but didn't shoot at me and they got charged federally, took plea deals and got nineteen years. It's weird that we have a guy who actually shot me and he gets less time than someone who did have a gun on them but who didn't use it on me.

Since the incident, I now talk to recruit classes and stuff like that. I tell them that it could happen to any one of us. My biggest thing at the time was just the disbelief – the feeling that this just doesn't happen; it's always the other guy. And I tell them, 'Always wear your vest,' because a lot of people take their vest off. They think, 'It's never going to happen to me', until it does.

****

I was working patrol section in a busy and rough part of Detroit with my partner. It was a rainy day and we ended up answering runs here, there and everywhere. Right before five o'clock we got an alarm to a regular business. We checked it out and then we decided to just go get something to drink. I was the driver and as we pulled up at a heavy narcotics location, we see three guys walking right in front of an area where we had had complaints of loitering and crack sales, right there. We went up to talk to these guys and as I pulled up, one of the guys automatically took off running. My partner stayed with the other two guys whilst I chased the third guy. As I tackled him, I was on top of him, ready to effect the arrest and handcuff him and I could feel his hand down near his pocket area and what I sensed – that he was attempting to pull a gun – became reality, and he pulled a snub-nosed 38. Well, we wrestled briefly over that weapon and he was able to get one shot off where I was struck in the butt area.

I was immediately aware that I had been shot and it came to a point where I had to decide whether to continue fighting over this gun or do I pull my weapon also. I was on top of him and I could see the gun coming so I started fighting him for it. I held his arm and thought I had shielded it enough to get my gun and that's when I got shot in the butt – because he was able to come across my back area and it struck me.

I returned fire and fatally killed him right there. I shot him in the chest and heart area. He was shot twice. Two shots and then I deemed that it was enough.

It was a ripping pain when I got shot. Whatever the velocity of the bullet was, it just ripped through, because, you know, when you think of a butt compared to any other part or your body, it's all tissue.

All I remember was that it was hot. Hot and tearing. So, not knowing at the time if it was the butt area or the back area, my mind started to wonder. I knew I had been shot because I could feel the warm blood coming out but also the cold air – it was February – and just blood running down my leg. So I knew I had been shot. At that time I had been around fifty to seventy-five shootings in three years. But I was thinking, did it hit my back? Did it hit something internally? I just knew it was in that area and after speaking to a doctor later on, he was like, 'Yeah, there's a major artery that it could have hit and you could be dead.' But of course it became a teasing point among officers – once they knew I was all right – that I had been shot in the butt.

I didn't know the other guy's condition at the time but he was fatally wounded. My partner was two blocks over with the original stop and he had taken those other two into custody, not knowing where I was at. He just radioed that he had heard shots fired and then he pulled up – it felt like minutes but I'm sure it was seconds – and that's when I told him that I had been shot and that the suspect had been shot. The code – blue or red, or whatever – goes through the entire city and all the Detroit cars and all the precincts are on alert and then you have probably fifty police cars converging on that area, as well as the state police, and we're probably talking minutes. And the protocol when you have a police officer shot is that the first car on scene, it's 'load and go'. So I remember two officers pulling up and them taking me a quick, direct route to hospital, but I'm laying on my side, knowing I had been shot and there's the panic in the head because, you know, it's not like I can look down. I just knew I had been shot but where did it hit? Then I remember getting to the hospital and the cutting and the x-rays and everything going on.

That was eerie. Eerie because someone's life was taken. Some officers would say, 'Well, he deserved it.' But I never took a point where I thought that the suspect deserved it. It just went back to, 'I have to survive. I know I've been shot.' So I returned fire and fortunately his wounds were fatal. It would have been different or I might have had a different outlook of it if it had been a kid with a toy guy – or it *had* been a toy gun – but the fact that I know that I've been shot and returned fire, it was different. At that point I had to do what I had to do.

My brother is a police officer with the department also and he came to the hospital within minutes. I remembered him coming into the emergency room and my only thought was for my mother. I remember looking up at the clock and let's say it was 5.20 and I knew that my mother was still working and she was already frantic about us being police officers, so he had to call her before 5.30, because the first thing that was going to hit the news was that a police officer from the tenth precinct had been shot and she would straight away think it was one of us. I didn't want to send her into a heart attack and luckily he was able to get hold of her.

Later I sat down with her and I sat down with the girl I was dating at the time and my brother, and told them that I was a career policeman and that there was nothing in my mind that ever doubted that I was going to return to work. But my partner never returned to work. That was the final incident for him. He had previously been stabbed from his wrist up to his elbow and pretty much lost all control of everything as it had hit a lot of nerves. I think he should have took more time off after that stabbing. I don't think he took enough time off, and then he comes into this! He wasn't my regular partner and he pretty much went off on stress leave and never, ever came back.

But the next psychological part is that whilst I'm in the hospital, I still have homicide detectives and the prosecutor waiting on the case. The body still goes for an autopsy and the autopsy reads 'homicide'. Luckily this was a justified homicide. But from February until July – upwards of six months – the case just sat in the prosecutor's office.

The way a police shooting goes – or if you're involved in a fatal police shooting – you're released from the hospital the next day and then with my attorney or the attorney provided by the union, you go down and the investigators want to talk to you. You're read your Miranda rights. You are a suspect. You are a suspect in this investigation. It's tough because you're the police but they're reading you your rights for the death of somebody. I know what I did was right but just the fact that it can linger for six months before it's even reviewed, can affect you. I eventually got a letter saying it had been reviewed and was a justified homicide and I'd been cleared. Six months later! That was troubling. I guess they put it on a shelf and said, 'We'll get to it when we get to it.'

But you just jump back into work and I remember it was probably one of my first nights back on midnights and I was working with a familiar partner and we get a run to go and arrest a mental guy, and he went to grab for my gun and I immediately went back to my training. So I think that it takes a special breed to do the job where you can just kick back into your training. Granted, some people can't just bounce back into it but I was just fortunate that I was able to bounce back in and I've had no lasting effects.

But it's an inherent danger and we sign up for it – not that I signed up to be killed, but I know that at any time in this career, when we go out on these runs, it can happen. But it's needed. Without us – the police – it would be complete chaos. We'd be no better than a third world country. So that's just a sacrifice that I've made. But there's still that drive in me to come into work. I still have that fire. I still want to help and be out there, even with the shooting.

****

There's a lot of small aircraft up here in Alaska. You've got the little Cessnas and the Beaver airplanes, so as a state trooper it's pretty common to deal with and respond to these plane crashes. That's not an uncommon thing. If you look up the 'line of duty' deaths for our state troopers, a lot of the troopers that died in the line of duty are actually from aircraft crashes.

There are a lot of pilots out there that have a job to do as far as trying to deliver freight or whatever it is. And people fly so frequently just to get to places and deliver freight and deliver mail to some of these smaller places that I guess it's one of those things – like driving a car on a highway down on the Lower 48. We have probably a lot more air traffic up here and unfortunately we have a lot of bad weather too.

I worked a search-and-rescue team out of Sitka one year and there was a small commercial aircraft that had left Sitka airport and they were on their way to a lodge. A second aircraft was leaving the lodge and coming back to the airport so at some point on this flight path that this company used, the planes would have passed each other and been in close contact. But the pilot who left the lodge, coming back to the airport, got to the part where he has to fly through this pass and he radioed to warn the other pilot that he was coming through this pass and to be careful. That's when the other aircraft should have been around the same sort of area but he ended up not having any radio communications with the second pilot.

We found out that that plane had several passengers on board and we launched an operation to find the aircraft but we never found it or anyone from it. It was interesting. We contacted the Coastguard and they assisted us with the search. We contacted some Sitka mountain rescue group and had them assist us with the search as well and a lot of man hours were put into that search but we never found any sign of that aircraft. It was a smaller aircraft with five or six passengers.

No one has any idea what happened to that plane. It's one of those ones where we were never able to figure why that aircraft went down or what the circumstances were. No emergency locator beacon on that aircraft went off so there was no indication of where they might have went down. The Coastguard wasn't able to find any sign of, or any clue of, any aircraft skimming over trees and damaging any trees, like they would have if they went down in a certain area or anything like that. So it was just one of those cases where it was unfortunate for the families of the pilot and the passengers on board because they never received any closure of what might have happened to their loved ones. I don't know how many times that happens – where we don't find the plane – but I know it does happen.

I've started to get more concerned about the safety aspect of flying – especially while I was in Juneau – because much of the travel is by those little aircraft to these smaller communities. A lot of times, we're flying in bad weather because someone in that community absolutely needs our assistance and we have to go. There's been times where the weather has been so bad where we can't fly or the weather was just marginal enough where the pilot felt it was safe enough for us to go up in the air, but those pilots are sometimes pushing the limits of their flying abilities and the limits of the aircraft.

There were a few times where I'd fly up to Haines and have to do work up there and then try to get back. I remember getting on the airplane one time and it was snowing and it was blowing sideways and I said to the pilot, 'Are we gonna make it out of here?'

And he's like, 'Oh yeah, we've got it. We should be fine.'

But we got up into the air and there was a moment where visibility was zero and he was flying by instruments. That was an interesting flight. The pilot just goes, 'Well, that was a close one!'

We ended up losing our Trooper helicopter this year with the pilot and one of our troopers on board. They were on a search and rescue. Our trooper helicopter got called out to find a person that was in need of aid so they went out – it was in the Talkeetna area – and the helicopter went out and picked up our trooper and they went out to find the person who needed help. My understanding is, they found the person and were able to pick him up and they were supposed to radio when they got back but they never radioed.

They then ended up having to launch a search for the trooper helicopter. They sent out our wildlife troopers on some other aircraft, and they located them. They located the trooper helicopter.

There were no survivors on board.

****

It's just devastating when a friend gets shot. It could have been you, you know?

This one guy who got shot, the night he got shot, he and his partner had come back early after giving evidence at court and he's like, 'Can I just borrow the car real quick? We're going to run around and see if we can make another arrest and get some overtime.'

I said, 'Yeah, give it an hour.' And I got on and did some paperwork back at the house – the police station.

So they take the car and they're not out ten minutes before they grab some guy with a big bag of drugs – a big bag of crack. So they bring him back and they said, 'Here, throw him in the cell, we're going to keep going.' They're gonna try to get another arrest because now one cop's got an arrest, the other cop's wants to try and get an arrest also.

So, this cop's sitting in my seat – in my car – and they pull over a cab and they walk up to the back of the cab and they just kind of look in to see if everything is alright. But the passenger looked a little funny, so the cop just opened the door and said, 'Hey, is everything alright?' And as he opened the door the passenger shot him.

He took one shot but it happened quick and there was a struggle. They get the gun, they get the guy and one cop says, 'Holy shit, I think you just got shot!'

And he goes, 'Yeah, I think I did!'

So he picks up his shirt and right about at his belt line, he has a little hole. He's this real thin guy and as he pushes on his stomach with his hand, the slug – the bullet – falls out into his hand! He was wearing two belts – he had a regular black leather belt on and then he had his gun belt over the top of that. He was in jeans and plain clothes and what happened is, the angle that the bullet hit, it hit the two belts, which slowed the bullet down. It went inside of him but didn't go too far.

So anyway, with this, the radio heats up and they're screaming that an officer has been shot, 'Officer shot! Officer shot!'

So we're like, 'Holy Jesus!' And then you became aware of who the guy was that got shot.

They brought the bad guy in and when he got to the front steps, it was like, well, his feet never hit the ground until he was in the back room. He just went flying to the back.

In a case like that you have to be so careful. Because, of course, you really want to hurt the guy – that would be the right thing to do – but it's going to come under a great deal of scrutiny and if this guy turned up in court all beat up and bloodied, that would not be good for the case. So he got off relatively easy, other than going to prison for quite a few years.

As for the officer who got shot, fortunately they did more damage poking around, making sure it didn't nick an artery when he got shot, than the actual bullet itself.

So yeah, that was funny.

****

A young lady had been kidnapped – no one could find her – and this guy was abusing her sexually. He had her handcuffed to either the sink or the bathtub. So one day he took off and she managed to escape. She was totally naked and she escaped. It was in the middle of winter and she ran to the house next-door, completely naked with handcuffs hanging down and told them that she had been molested and all the rest of it. They called the police.

Now this guy is coming back home and he sees all the police around his house. He thinks, 'Shit! They got me.'

So he drives up here to the police station – into the Northwest

District building in Detroit – on a Sunday afternoon, walks in with a shotgun, walks right through the front door and starts shooting, right here in the lobby. There are still remnants of the gun blasts in the walls. That's why we have a person checking you at the door now. That's why. We never had that before; it's a police building. You walk into the station and you make a report. But after that incident we instituted an officer at the front door with the metal detector.

So, this guy walks in with a shotgun. One officer, who'd been shot before – and his wife was thrilled that he was on a desk because now she thinks he'll never be shot again – he got shot in the head. He wasn't armed, because he was behind a desk and he had his gun in the drawer. There was also a female officer sitting at the front desk but the chair was too tight and bulky, so she had her gun under the drawer. The sergeant was standing there, not really paying attention, because some guy just walks in, and the guy unloaded. The sergeant got hit in the ear with the wad of the shotgun blast. So the gun goes off, one guy gets shot in the head and the wad hits the sergeant hard enough where he started bleeding.

There was another officer sitting at the desk and after the first officer was shot, everybody goes for cover but this officer actually goes to the ground, reaches up and starts shooting. People start coming out of the other rooms and the guy looks down the hallway and BOOM! – he fires another shot. A female sergeant just happens to be standing sideways and the round went through her shirt and tie and grazed her vest. She had no clue what the hell was going on.

Two other sergeants come out and they see what's going on and BOOM, BOOM, BOOM! So now the guy – the shooter – dives over the front desk because he's taking fire from down the hallway. In the meantime, we had a Commander also standing at the front desk who just happened to be here on his off day. He didn't have his gun but he had an ankle holster and he was checking some paperwork. Anyway, this guy walks in and BOOM, BOOM, BOOM! So they hit the ground.

The sergeant, who has been hit, hits the ground. The Commander falls on top of the sergeant. We're trained to always go for your gun – we never train to go for your ankle, because you just don't train that way – so naturally, the training kicked it and the Commander grabbed the gun off the sergeant who he was laying on top of and starts shooting. They're shooting for a minute and a half. BAM, BAM, BAM, BAM, BAM! Point blank range – I mean, right across the desk. BAM, BAM, BAM! He shot the guy a couple of times. The Commander got shot a couple of times also and the guy's gun finally clicked and he just collapsed.

You need to YouTube that. That happened here. It had never happened before.

I was on duty and I got the call. 'What's going on?'

They're saying, 'The Commander's been shot!'

'Where?'

'Northwest District.'

'I know, but where?'

'Northwest District.'

'I KNOW! Where?'

'In the lobby.'

I'm then thinking, 'The fricking police building?'

I got here real quick. I come in here and there was smoke everywhere. This whole room – the whole lobby – was filled with smoke.

226

All the officers were standing there with their hands on their guns because they're in shock. They didn't wait for EMS. They took two cars and hauled ass and took everyone to hospital, which is five minutes away. 'Stupid' died, behind the counter, but it was suicide by police. He knew he was going to jail for raping that woman so he came in here to take police officers with him.

The Commander had run down the hallway saying, 'I'm shot! I'm shot!' He ran into the office and collapsed into a chair and they just wheeled him out of here.

The only person who died was the asshole. One officer went critical that night through loss of blood. He got hit in the side and it blew off some of his hand and fingers. Another officer took – through the grace of God, it must have been either buckshot or something smaller like a twenty gauge – he took one point blank to the head, right into the face. I just remember him sitting there saying, 'Hey, I'm shot. Can anybody help me? Can anybody help me?'

That was bad. It was unreal. Most of those officers never returned to work after that.

****

I was in the Eastern District and we had one officer killed and four others shot in the same incident. One fatal and four wounded.

What happened was, a run came out on a B and E in progress – Breaking and Entering – a home invasion in progress. Two rookie officers got the run. But two veteran officers were closer, so they said that they were going to make it to the scene too. So the two veteran officers show up and they see movement in the house and the next thing you know, shots are fired. The guy comes out, guns a-blazing, onto the porch. He's running out – BAM, BAM, BAM, BAM, BAM,

BAM, BAM!

It was two-thirty in the morning or three-thirty in the morning, I think. Everyone starts responding – you know, 'officer in trouble' – and the sergeant gets there and there's cops laying on the front lawn, shot. One was shot in the arm, one was shot in the leg, one was shot in the groin; I can't remember where the other one was shot.

So he takes the first one to the hospital and EMS come and they're taking them as well but they can't find the fifth officer. He was the first one shot and no one knew it. He died instantly on the front porch. He walked up to the front porch to open the door and the guy lit him up. Unfortunately we didn't know that at the time.

When they called me, 'Commander, Commander, we got four officers shot!' I get in the car and started going there and then I get a phone call, 'Commander, we found a fifth officer. It doesn't look good.'

He was a big guy, a huge guy. Unfortunately in all the pandemonium no one had seen that he was the first one down.

Now, the bad guy was shot one time and the ironic part is – and thank God no one else got shot – the bad guy got shot and they tackled him and they cuffed him to a fence. They tell another guy to sit on him, to watch this guy. Unbeknownst to us, the guy still had the gun – he just couldn't get to it. But he had the gun close enough that he could have shot another officer.

That was the worst incident as far as total officers shot. We've had several incidents through the years where two officers have been killed at one scene but that's the first time we had five officers shot at one time and that messed up a lot of people. It was a bad thing. It was very traumatic for the department. He was a big guy, this officer.

He was like a mountain man. He was huge. Always smiling. That was unfortunate.

But I thought at the time that it brought the department together, like they always do, a little bit.

****

This officer was four or five years out of the academy. This was his first police job. I worked with him for three or four years on midnight shift.

It was a Sunday night and he made a traffic stop of a car with a broken taillight. He pulled it over and it was a fifteen-year-old kid without a driver's licence. He decided to cut the kid a break and he directed him to park his car at a gas station and lock it up and he was going to give him a ride home. The kid gave him the address of an apartment complex nearby. So the officer drove him there and I think the kid thought that he was just going to let him out but the officer walked him to the door because he wanted to speak to the parents. Well it turns out that it was the kid's girlfriend's house. So then he asked him to get a parent on the phone. So the kid got some woman on the phone and the officer realised after talking to her for a little bit that it was the kid's sister – it wasn't his mum.

So the cop had enough and he probably informed the kid that he was under arrest. But then the kid took off up the stairs. They were cement steps, about twenty steps up to a landing and then it goes down twenty steps to the other side of the apartments. Based on what I saw at the scene and the reports, it sounded like they either scuffled on the landing or coming down the stairs on the other side and they tumbled all the way down the twenty steps. And it appears that the officer hit his head and got knocked unconscious. The witnesses who were in the hallway said that the kid then reached down, pulled the officer's gun out of his holster and just shot him in the head. Executed him. Shot him right in the side of the head whilst he was just laying there. Killed him instantly. And then the kid took off, running.

After he fled he got picked up by somebody. His dad took him to a hotel a few miles away where they holed up overnight. We knew who it was, because reviewing the officer's in-car video, there was the plate. He also ran the kid's name to the dispatcher, so they knew who he was. The Detroit Fugitive Apprehension Team actually came up and helped our department. They worked with the kid's family pastor to convince him to turn himself in. I was actually there the next morning when they brought him in. He was convicted. He got life in prison.

He was fifteen at the time and the Michigan Supreme Court recently passed a law where they've ruled that it's unlawful to sentence juveniles to life sentences regardless of the crime and they've made it retroactive. So there's a chance that he will not have to serve out this life sentence. So all of the police unions in the state are working hard to get that overturned.

This kid was a turd. He was a local gangbanger – a thug. He posted pictures on Facebook prior to this – guns and drugs and money. He'd been pulled over one month earlier by another police department in the same car and was actually arrested. But before the cop took him to the station, he decided to cut him a break and let him go. And so this is how he repays the police a month later, by shooting one of them in the head – a cop who was trying to do him the same favour.

He was the first officer on our department to be killed since 1976.

It was terrible. I got the call from the station, probably ten minutes after it happened. I live a two-minute drive from the hospital where they took him to. So I drove straight to the hospital and I ran into the Emergency Room and they were still working on him, still trying to revive him. They actually had me hold the bandages on the sides of his head whilst they we working on him.

There were two officers who just happened to be two apartment buildings over from where this happened, on an unrelated incident, in that same complex. They heard the shot and they were able to get there pretty quickly. They were both in the Emergency Room, just in shock. One of them was actually walking around the hallway in circles. The other one that was in the Emergency Room was leaning against the wall, just staring. It was pretty traumatic and obviously throughout the course of the night, other officers started showing up.

I had to work the next morning. This happened at around midnight and I was at the hospital until five-thirty, went home, slept for about half an hour, showered and I had to be back at work at seven. They ended up bringing the kid in around noon. So I had to book him – you know, here's this guy that just killed one of my officers and I've got to take his fingerprints. I've got to ask him all these questions. I've got to take him into the holding cell and then we had to take him over to the court. That stuff's tough.

But then I was fortunate enough that I was actually working back on midnight shift when his trial happened, so I was able to go up to his trial every day. I was there – front row – and other officers filtered in on their days off and stuff. But I was able to be there pretty much for the entire trial, which, you know, helps you see that justice is being done at least.

It's not that we – the officers on the department – are psychopaths or anything but most of us can shake stuff off pretty quickly. I mean, we still honour him – his picture is still on top of the refrigerator at the station. We had a wake for him at a local pub. I'm familiar with what a wake is supposed to be so I took his composite photo and had it blown up to eight by ten and bought a frame and a stand and took it so that we could put it on a pool table with other mementoes of him. Well, that picture is still at the station. It floats around, pops up in different places and right now it's on top of the refrigerator. It's always around. And we do a charity golf outing every year that raises money for officers killed, and it's in his name.

The thing about his death though – as tragic as it was – it was completely preventable. There were about seven or eight mistakes that he made, that had he not made even just one of those, had he made six mistakes and not the seventh, this never would have happened. The first one was, he didn't handcuff the kid when he put him in the back of the car, so the kid was able to use his cell phone and call his girlfriend and say, 'This cop's bringing me home, pretend that you're my sister.' That was the first ruse – she was supposed to pretend to be his sister and their parents weren't home. Had he not been able to do that, they would have just shown up at the girlfriends house and she wouldn't have known to pretend to be the sister and maybe the ruse would have been caught earlier and something would have gone different.

Second thing was, you don't ever transport anybody without another officer following. That's just safety. Protocol. He didn't do that. He also didn't call where he was going with him. I think there was some radio traffic with this other incident – it was a malicious destruction of property – that was going on a couple of buildings over. I think he just didn't want to get in the middle of that radio traffic so he thought, 'I'll just throw this kid in the car and take him home.' So he didn't call up where he was going. So when he did call, his last transmission was asking for assistance – I think that's right before they scuffled. When he asked for assistance, we knew where he was, not that anybody could have got there in time, though.

The third thing is, I don't think he needed to arrest the kid. He was the type of officer who if you lied to him a few times, he'd get upset and I think he let that get to him. I think if he had given the kid one more chance, it might have gone differently – who knows? But the other thing that we can't understand is – I mean, I know it's in our DNA to chase – when someone runs from us, we chase. That's what we do, but why did he chase him? It's a fifteen year-old kid. He knows who he is. You don't need to catch up to him. We'll get a warrant for him later. It's just bad practice to chase somebody on your own, because things can go sideways. So that was another thing.

So just a litany of things that had one of them just gone different. Like, he had a taser. When he was running from him or when he was scuffling, why didn't he just taser him? Just a variety of things.

It was a lesson to all of us. A sad lesson – this is how you don't do it, this is why this happened. It wasn't one of those things where he was just sitting in his patrol car and someone came up and killed him – stuff you can't stop – this was preventable.

****

I have friends that have been shot on the job. I've had friends who have been killed on the job. I've known other guys who have been killed in car accidents and helicopter crashes. You know, there are a

233

lot of ways to die on this job. Being shot, of course, is probably the worst of all of them. But the fact of life is, it's part of the job, although you never go in wanting to be that person or know that person.

But as well as the officers who get killed, we also get a lot of people injured on this job and they don't always come back. I don't know if we do enough for them. We have guys who have been beaten with a hammer and they're brain damaged. There are officers who have been involved in horrific shootings and they'll never be right again.

I've been to a lot of police funerals and they're really sad and tragic and I really feel for the families afterwards but these guys that are shot in the line of duty – or are maimed or hurt – and they live, you know, their names don't go on a wall anywhere. Their families are left coping with their injuries and their lives have been altered completely and that to me is just as tragic, but you don't get the big hoopla. You have a big police funeral when a police officer dies – and it's horrible and it's sad and it's tragic and somebody has been ripped out of their family's lives – but then we have people walking around who have suffered devastating injuries and their families are caring for them and they're not working any more and that's a sad situation all the way around. I feel for both groups but I don't know who I feel worse for. They're both pretty devastating.

I've certainly known a lot of people that have been killed in the line of duty – if not personally, I know who they are or I know of them – but I know a lot more people who were hurt in the line of duty who are going to walk around with those issues forever.

We have a guy who teaches at our academy who was shot point blank in the head. If you've ever read the book *Homicide* by David Simon – the one they based the show, 'The Wire', on – well, he's in the book. His name is Gene Cassidy, he works at the academy; he teaches law. Basically a guy was wanted on warrant, Gene was by himself and the guy just pulled out a gun and shot him. Someone from the neighbourhood called it in, actually. Gene never had the opportunity to call for help himself.

Gene's blind now – completely blind – and he has no sense of taste or smell. He's not a police officer any more; he's retired but he's a contractual employee. He's had two children that he's never seen and he almost died again last year. When they saved his life back in 1987, one of the blood transfusions he had, he contracted hepatitis from. They never knew about it because they weren't checking for hepatitis back then. He didn't know about it until he was so sick that he almost died. He had to have a liver transplant. Gene's a fighter. He's an amazing guy. He doesn't let it stop him at all. But he almost died twice from the same incident – once from the gunshot wound and once because of the transfusion that they gave him to save his life, which almost killed him twenty-something years later.

But he never complained about what he can't do; he went back to school and got his masters in teaching, whilst blind. He's raised two kids and his wife is amazing, obviously. She's had to shoulder a lot of that burden. But he's never lost the desire to be a part of the police department. He worked really hard to get and to keep that job at the academy. That job isn't promised or guaranteed to him – you'd like to think it would be but we're not always so conscious of the people who have been hurt rather than killed.

So those are the kinds of guys who are fighting. They're fighting every day. I've worked with a couple of guys over the years who have been hurt so badly, they'll never have a normal life. They keep moving and they keep going and you know, existing – sometimes on a feeding tube – and that's really the tragedy that nobody talks about: how many people get hurt in the line of duty that don't die but who will never be the same.

You know, we're great for a big funeral but when somebody is hurt in the line of duty and they can't function any more, how do we treat them? Do people still come around? Do they still see them? That's almost worse, I think. I don't know; I don't want to go out either way. I don't want anyone I know or care about to have to face either one of those things. But the truth is we have a lot of wounded warriors of our own.

****

These officers were in plain clothes and they were chasing this guy. They were like, fugitive hunters and this guy was wanted for murder. Unfortunately they boxed him in and he came out shooting, and so they came out shooting too. I can't remember what kind of gun he had but everyone came out with the heavy artillery, firing back and forth. One sergeant got shot in the leg.

Then this one officer, unfortunately, came up and he was in a car behind the suspect's car. One of our other cars came from the front and started shooting and the officer who was behind the suspect's car, got shot. He got hit in the head. I think it was just a fragment but it got him in the brain. They think it could have been friendly fire. He's been permanently handicapped and on life support ever since.

He'll never come back to work. He'll never get out of rehab, probably ever. He'll probably never walk again. He's not responding to any treatment. He's almost like a vegetable and he's only thirty-seven years old. He's got four little kids. He's like a vegetable. He's on a vent and he's not coming back.

Author's note:
A few weeks after returning home I received an email from the officer who told me about the above incident. Six months after being hit, the police officer had died. Here is a slightly edited version of what he wrote in the email:

We buried him [the officer] today. It was determined to be friendly fire. Shot April 2nd, died last Saturday. Officer responsible is a mess. All have seen a shrink, but it still hurts. Can't even begin to understand the anguish he feels. It was a fragment from a shotgun blast that struck the top of the perp's vehicle. The sergeant that was shot in the leg during the same confrontation is back at work.

13

Politics

*P*olitics is everywhere in policing, whether it's city politics, the public's politics or the media's, office politics, departmental politics, bosses' politics or even the politics between officers themselves. Policing has many frustrations and most of it comes down to politics of one kind or another.

When politics was brought up during these interviews, I heard strong opinions, thoughtful comments and also some anger. In an office in downtown Manhattan, I sank further and further back into my plastic chair and listened as an experienced detective unloaded a couple of decades' worth of deep dissatisfaction on me. What started off as a cosy chat turned into a full-blown rant about the changes he had seen, including the poor attitudes – in his eyes – of the new recruits and the current trend for officers to align themselves with specific religious and racial groups.

Other officers were also struggling to understand the attitude of the younger cops, especially their views of how more experienced colleagues approached dealing with members of the public. One officer explained it by telling me how the new, younger generation of cops had been brought *up watching news reports of alleged police brutality (something that could possibly be timelined from the 1991 Rodney King incident in Los Angeles). He thought attitudes to policing were changing and there was a far more liberal generation of cops joining the force than before, one that had a different view on how the police should police.*

Personally, I feel that social media is having a dramatic effect on the police and how the police are being perceived. With the advent of camera phones and the Internet, the police are being observed and scrutinised like never before. Social media can be such a powerful force – as witnessed during the 'Arab Spring', for example – and it is giving people a voice, an audience, anonymity and a soapbox; all this regardless of whether what they have to say is correct or not, right or wrong. People – including cops – can be tried and convicted around the world over a 30 second video clip filmed on someone's phone. Social media has opened up a whole new dawn in how communities, political groups and individuals challenge authority and speak out. It's not all bad but it's not all good either. Exposing wrongdoing is a good thing but there needs to be some balance and sometimes I feel that the police need to catch up – and quickly. They need to be ready to defend their departments and their officers' actions where appropriate. And there were other issues that surprised me, when they were brought up – a black officer's opinion on racism, for example. Surprising because he wasn't talking about white officers being racist towards blacks but rather how he himself – a black officer – could be racist. Or the police officer who told me that he didn't like cops (something I actually heard a number of times). And then there were the allegations of crime statistics being massaged, political correctness and bosses who had forgotten where they had come from.

Not everyone is happy about the past and not everyone is happy about the future, and there are those who aren't happy about the present, either, but just like the public and the media, cops too have a lot to say and their experienced and educated opinions are certainly worth hearing. And hear them I did.

You are your police; your police department should represent your community. I'm not saying that if you had more black officers, crime would be less, but with a department this size and our city being probably fifty per cent black, I think we only have six black officers out of forty-five. We're still behind the curve and I'm talking about different races; I'm talking about Lebanese, I'm talking about Iraqi, Hispanic, whatever. When you can start counting on your fingers how many you have, I think that there needs to be a bigger drive.

But we've gone out to colleges and wherever we know there are more African-American – or minorities – and attempted to recruit them. So as long as you're attempting to recruit them, that's a good thing. And I think you get departments now that are attempting to do that, and the same with recruiting females.

But even in a city where you had a majority or at least half a police department that's African-American, like Detroit, the citizens don't respect the police any more than before. They won't speak to a white officer but if they have information, they won't speak to a black officer either; it just goes with the general face of police work.

Me – as a black officer – I'm considered an 'Uncle Tom', a sell-out. If I go to lock up somebody, they'll say, 'Oh, you're acting just like a white officer.' No, I'm just enforcing the law and if that has to do with whatever colour you put on it, well, it's an easy way out to say that you're just doing this because you work for the government or a police department.

With more black officers in departments, you'd think that you'd have less police brutality cases among African-Americans or any other minority or you'd think that you'd have less stereotyped pretext stops but I don't think you do, because police are still police. I think you do stereotype at some point. It's one thing to be racist and go out and do your job based on colour, but on the flip side of it if I'm in a predominantly black neighbourhood and I see a white guy walking down the street at six or seven in the morning, I will stereotype, because I see that white guy and I think, 'He's going to buy drugs' or 'What is he doing here?' It's weird when you look at it that way but stereotyping is in all police officers – black and white.

I had a truck, a nice Chevy, with some nice rims on it and between white and black officers in Detroit I was stopped equally. If I was stopped six times in that truck, it was three times by white officers and three times by black officers. And the six times I got stopped in that truck, it had nothing to do with a traffic violation; it was just a pretext stop based on my colour. They didn't know I was police and whatever reason they gave for stopping me, I can tell you that it was baloney.

So you have to be careful when you say someone is stereotyping or someone is racist, because you can still be racist and you can still stereotype among your own people. Even as a black officer, I can still stereotype against a black person. And that's what's swept under the rug, whereas it stands out if you're white and you're pulling me over because I'm black, or whatever. But on the same thing, it doesn't give me a pass just because I'm a black officer and I pull over a black person when I don't have probable cause or reason. That is something that is definitely under-reported, because, 'I'm black; I can't stereo-type.' Yes, you can and people forget about that.

****

I have to thank my partner for this. There had been a robbery and at roll-call we were given the location and description of the vehicle. They'd robbed several people of their jewellery and they thought it might be drug-related. The vehicle had a Maryland registration plate and we had to be on the lookout for it.

So when we turned out to go on patrol, my partner kept saying, 'Come on, let's go look for this vehicle.'

I was like, 'Are you serious? What are the chances of us finding this vehicle?'

Let me go back. Prior to that roll-call, three days previously, we actually pulled over that vehicle. We did a car stop and it was during a controversial time where officers had taken some guys out of a vehicle and were being charged for it – it was in the media that the officers had racially profiled them. Well, when we had pulled this vehicle over it was for turning without a signal.

After we walked back from the car, my partner said to me, 'There's something dirty about these guys.'

I said, 'Well, what are we going to do?'

And he said, 'A few days ago I would have pulled them all out of the car and searched them because there's something not right. They're acting strange.'

I said, 'I agree with you but what are we going to do?'

They were two male Hispanics and one black male. But we were concerned because of this recent thing in the media about racial profiling, so we didn't want to take the chance. They had Maryland plates on the car, we issued them a ticket and just let them go. Two days later at roll-call, we hear that the same car and the same guys were committing robberies with a firearm – two firearms, actually.

So we went out and that's when my partner said to me, 'We need to go back to that area.'

And I said, 'What are the chances of finding this car now? Are you serious? These guys aren't going to be driving around.'

He kept breaking my chops about it so we went down there and took a drive. We literally drove down the block, drove into the sector area and drove right by them.

So he starts screaming, 'There's the car! There's the car!'

We pulled the car over, we called backup to help us and as the back-up patrol car was pulling up, it was coming towards us, head on. We had the car stopped and we were behind the car.

The passenger of the police car – one of our partners – got out of the car and said, 'He's reaching for the gun!'

We hadn't even gotten to the window, the guy had the gun in his hand and we thought that he was going to try to shoot us, so we all pulled out our guns. He dropped his gun on the floor of the car and just put his hands out and we ended up arresting them all for robbery. They were wearing the jewellery that they had robbed. It ended up being a good arrest.

The thing is, we could have had them three days prior to this but we walked away. If we had pulled out our guns and arrested them, we might have stopped three more people from getting robbed. But because we were afraid of being seen to be racially profiling, we didn't stop them. It had nothing to do with them being Hispanic or black; it was their actions in the car that were making us feel suspicious. But the public, when you take a male black, a male Hispanic out of their car and put them on the hood of the vehicle, the public perception is, 'oh, he's doing that because he's black' or 'because he's Hispanic' – the two 'white cops', you know?

So we effectively didn't do our job because of racial profiling. Because it was in the media at that particular time and we were afraid that we would be the next ones in the media and end up losing our jobs or be brought up on charges and questioned by internal affairs.

****

I think crime is slightly on the rise. However, the figures are definitely fiddled and they've been fiddled since the early 90's with the creation of CompStat – Comparative Statistics – which is a brutal freaking interrogation by the bosses downtown asking precinct commanders why they've had a rise in crime in their precinct. And that rise in crime could be by just one case.

The cops on the street would take a report, which would then come into the command. But before we detectives even got to look at it, somebody else would be reclassifying it as a lower crime. We would battle with them because according to police department guidelines there are only two people who are allowed to reclassify a crime – one is the precinct commander and one is the squad commander. They are the only two people allowed to reclassify a crime but suddenly you had civilians doing it.

What would happen is, we would get the complaint or report in the morning and we would hand them out to whoever would catch the case. The case detective would then call up the complainant and ask, 'Can you tell me what happened?'

And the complainant would say, 'Yeah, but I already spoke to someone.'

'You spoke to who? And what did they say?'

We've already put it on our sheets saying that it's a robbery and you'd go downstairs and you would talk to this civilian who'd say, 'Oh, no, no. We've already reclassified it to a grand larceny – a theft.'

'But I spoke to the victim. It's clearly a robbery.'

'No, it's a grand larceny now.'

So robberies became grand larcenies. Grand larcenies became petty larcenies. Like, you've got to be shitting me.

Every police department is the same.

****

Talk about discretion. I used to tell my guys, 'Look, a street officer has the most discretion of anybody on the police department. The higher you go up in the ranks, the less discretion you have – because you don't have that freedom of decision making that you do on the bottom level. You're the one that's out there; you're the one collecting the information; you're the one that has to make the decision.'

Now, obviously the officers are going to get into situations where they're going to say, 'Sarge, I need your input.' And then maybe the sergeant is going to say, 'I need the lieutenant down here.' But that doesn't happen very often. Mostly the officer on the street makes his own decisions.

So when you come right down to it, the patrol officer on the beat has the most discretion of anybody in the chain of command. Even the Chief doesn't have as much discretion as the patrol officer does! The Chief answers to the Mayor's office and every reporter that's standing outside his office wanting a statement from him about this or that or one thing and another. And it just goes down the chain like that, from the Mayor to the Chief, then the Assistant Chief – they're all worried about their asses, in case some newspaper reporter writes some bad story about them. But not the patrol officer – he doesn't have those worries or concerns.

****

The NYPD really believes in the separation of worker and rank. Most bosses, as they go up the ranks, they forget where they came from. They forget what they did to get where they are. And that's probably the truth. Whether they forget or not, they just change. The higher you go up, in order to really succeed you have to become a company man. It's all 'do as I say and not as I do'.

Not everyone is like that, though. I've worked for some real lunatics – I mean some complete lunatics! And they were great lunatics.

****

I've been with this department for my entire career; started as a patrolman and now I'm the Chief.

I won't lie to you, it can make it uncomfortable when you have to administer discipline or you have to assert your authority and let your guys know that they screwed up and then discipline them. It's not fun but it's something that I won't hesitate to do. More times than not, they understand my position – as long as you're fair about it. You can't do things one way for one set of people or friends and then all of a sudden you're coming down extra hard on others – because you can lose respect and the faith of your men that way. They may not like it at the time and there may be a little bit of sour grapes but I think, over time, they realise that you have been fair and they come right back in line.

And you can't worry about it. Not everyone that you supervise is going to like you. They're not going to carry you out of here on their shoulders when it's time to retire and say, 'All hail to the Chief!' You hope that they would but I am sure there are some that won't like you for whatever reasons, if they felt that they didn't get promoted and they got passed over or you had favouritism or they just didn't like your philosophies on how you wanted things done. Those are certain issues that you have to deal with and you have to accept.

One of the other things you have to be real cognitive of is how you try to sell something to your guys and gals, or how you try to get them to behave or conduct business in a certain manner. They're looking at you – they're like your kids. You tell them not to do something but if you're doing exactly what you're telling them not to do – or not doing what you're telling them to do – they pick up on that.

They'll be the first ones to call you out and call you a hypocrite or say, 'I remember when…' You know? 'I remember when you were out here riding around and we used to do this and that and now you're in this position of authority, you're telling me not to do it.'

So that's something that you have to be careful and mindful of as you're coming up through the ranks. Some of them may have thought that you were a marginal-at-best, type employee and yet you're telling them to be this super-cop. So that's something that can take away or diminish the respect of the people that you supervise.

But when it's done and over, if you've done everything according to the best of your ability and in a respectable manner, then you should be able to go home and sleep well at night.

****

There was a point where I made a decision to stop taking promotion exams because being a sergeant was great. I enjoyed being a sergeant. I was a first line supervisor so I was out there with my troops – with the guys. I could respond to calls and be as involved as they were. So I loved being a first line supervisor. Then I looked at the lieutenants and as far as I'm concerned they're the most worthless level on the police department. They're like fish out of water. It's like being in limbo. You have the captain who's in charge of the precinct, you have the lieutenants who supposedly supervise the sergeants and then the sergeants supervise the guys on the street. So the sergeants are the ones that really run the show. Lieutenants don't know what the hell to do with themselves. They're usually totally lost.

I have always had a belief that the so-called military chain of command that police departments have is a dysfunctional organisational structure, because you have all these chains and all these levels of command and at least two levels are totally useless. You could get along without them and nobody would miss them.

****

We would never write anything down. You're supposed to do 'stop, question and frisk reports'. We would never do them. The only thing the bosses cared about was how many summonses you wrote in thirty days – like moving violations, traffic and so on. You had to give a book of summonses a month. The rule of thumb was – to stay out of trouble – you had to give a book of summonses and make at least two collars (arrests) in a month. But I decided I'm not giving any summonses and I would just collar everybody. I made a lot of collars.

Regular police officers have to write a book a month. It's a quota. You have to. If you don't, they deny you days off, they fuck with you. They'll deny that there's a quota but there absolutely is a quota.

****

If you didn't live in Detroit, you'd think it was absurd that people have as many shootouts with police as they do here. Working here, your mindset has to be that it's commonplace, so you have to accept it. Because if you didn't, you'd be sitting here for hours, worrying, 'Why are they shooting at us?' If your mind couldn't grasp it, it'd drive you nuts.

But working here, well, it's a wild city; the criminals are wild. This block here is very nice but two blocks over the whole street is crazy. And it's like that – one good, one bad, one good.

When you hear that there are more good people than bad, that's an accurate statement but the bad definitely outweighs the good. It's survival of the fittest. People aren't working and they're trying to survive. If they see you out there by yourself, whatever you got, they're going to take it.

Being a cop in Detroit, you have to accept that you can get into anything, not just specifically gunfights. You have to accept that you're going to have to get physical at work. You have to accept that. You may not come back alive. You have to accept that. When you accept that, it helps you clear your mind so that you can do your job.

Do I get frightened? No. Do I get scared? Yeah. But doing your job supersedes you being scared; you'll be scared after it's over. You can't retreat – I'm not sure if that is the right word to use, retreat – but that's not even in your mind. Your mind is, 'I've got to get this guy and not get shot.'

So scared? Yeah. Scared is good. Frightened? No. Here's the difference: Frightened is cowering behind a desk not doing anything. Being scared means you're going to be cautious whilst you're trying to deal with whatever it is.

But these guys here – the police officers – in Detroit, they've been taken advantage of for so long. The officers here make less money and get less benefits but they still come into work and do the job. That's the hard part. That stuff makes me wonder, 'Wow, they must really like this job.' To do what they do, even after they've had their pay taken, getting their medical benefits taken, getting their pensions and stuff touched on, they still come to work and they still put their lives on the line for people that don't appreciate it. I mean, some people do appreciate it, but there's a lot of people who don't. They're always ratting on police, but these guys still do their job. That shows you how special they are.

But working in Detroit is one thing – I don't live here and that's for obvious reasons. But if we didn't police, who would? If we all just walked away, where would we be? That's the reason I still work in Detroit. I know people who still live here and can't move out. If they don't have me, who do they have? If they call me, they know I'm going to come. If I'm not here to do that, who's going to come?

****

This incident I'm going to tell you about is one where I get made fun of at my work because 'it's not what cops do'. You may find it strange that I get made fun of for this but these are the types of people that I work with. They're very selfish and self-absorbed. This is just a city that they work in and that's it. And the people we encounter are 'turds', and that's it. It's hard to work there sometimes.

Anyway, there was this kid, he had a BB gun and he went up to a kid at high school and robbed him of his Cartier glasses. Took the Cartier glasses down to Detroit and sold them. Well, this knucklehead is on video at the high school, doing it. I showed the video to the school security and they identified him immediately. Well, this was a kid who went to an inner city Detroit school and he was running track down there. That school's track coach ended up taking a job at another school as their track coach and he brought some of his kids with him – because it's all schools of choice; you can go to school where you want. Well, this kid runs the 400 meters in like, 42 seconds. He has Olympic scouts looking at him. He was a senior at the time when he did this robbery. He had a full-ride scholarship to a college for track.

So I'm interviewing this kid and he's polite – 'yes, sir', 'no, sir' and all this kind of stuff. I told him that I knew he had done the robbery. I showed him the picture from the surveillance.

I said, 'I know you did it but I don't get it. You're full-ride track scholarship to college, you're doing well at the school. I don't get it.'

He starts crying. Then I come to find out that this is his story: he lives in one of those houses that you think is abandoned in Detroit, but it's not. It just looks like it is. There's no power. They have gas – it's the only utility they can afford to keep on – and they heat the house but the furnace is broken, so they heat the house with the oven, by leaving its door open. They borrow water from the neighbour and boil it to wash with. The entitlement benefit card that underprivileged people in Michigan get – it's called a Bridge Card because there's a picture of the Mackanow Bridge on it – is for your food benefits. The only person in the family who was able to get the benefits was his sister. So they were all living off the sister's Bridge Card for food. The dad had some horrible disability so he wasn't able to work. This kid hadn't gotten any new clothes or shoes for two years. He was wearing clothes that didn't fit, dirty shoes where the ends were blown out because his feet were too big for them. Now, you know as well as I do that at high school, if you show up like that, what's going to happen to you? Peer pressure's a bitch, right?

He stole the glasses, sold them for two-hundred bucks and went to a resale clothing shop and bought a pair of tennis shoes, two pairs of jeans and a couple of t-shirts so that he could go to school in clothes that fit him and were clean. You don't have a soul if that doesn't break your heart. Did the kid just commit an armed robbery? Yeah. But did he do it because he's a thug, a turd, a sociopath? Would I like to have heard that he took the two hundred dollars and used it to turn on the electric service or buy food? That would have been better, right? But to an eighteen-year-old kid, having clothes and shoes to wear to school is just as important as those things. I'm not so callous that I don't understand that.

Unfortunately for the kid, I had to send the case to the prosecutor's office – it's an armed robbery – and they come back with the warrant for armed robbery. I had several phone calls with the prosecutor, wrote two letters to the judge urging them not to give this kid a felony conviction. He was going to confess. Oh, and I petitioned for them to release him on a personal bond with a tether, which his unheard of in felony cases but I was able to convince the judge so that he was able to go back to school and run track. My next hope was that they give him a 'high misdemeanour' – where he doesn't do any jail time and no felony so he can stay out of jail and keep running track. This was a kid whose life was at a fork – one way was felony conviction, prison, lose scholarship, come out of school, go back to abandoned crack house in Detroit and end up back in prison. The other way was get a misdemeanour, get my ass back in school, I learn my lesson, go to college in Ohio with my track scholarship, I become something. I wrote two letters to the judge and pleaded with the prosecutor but unfortunately my prosecutor's office didn't see it that way – or the judge didn't – and he got a one-year felony conviction.

But I caught so much shit at work for fighting for this kid. But here's the thing, I don't do this for everybody. In my time in the detective bureau, I've probably dealt with four hundred 'in-custody' arrests. Probably two-thirds of those were fifteen to twenty-year-old black males. Maybe four or five of them I've fought for. Like I really didn't think they were bad guys; I really thought that they deserved a second chance, that the reason they did what they did was more societal and due to where they were growing up and their circumstances, not who they were as people. So it's not like I'm trying to set everybody free and give everybody a break. There're a few that I'll fight for but, as with that kid I'm talking about, it can be disheartening.

****

I know that the women before me, who were on the job a long time, were tortured every day. It was just impossible to be a woman on the job before. It's definitely much easier now because we have diversity and all these lawsuits and things like that, so everyone walks on eggshells around the woman on the job now.

You definitely have your guys who are, you know, they push the envelope. You've also got the public; nobody wants to listen to a woman. That's never going to change. There are things that are just never going to change but it's probably a lot easier than before.

Most of the guys on my job are very good. There are a handful of guys that will, you know, every time they address you, they're addressing you as, 'Hey baby.' Oh my God, I want to punch them in the face! Or like, they just say inappropriate things. They say lots of vulgar things that a man should never say to a woman. But there are only a few guys – maybe two or three – that are even remotely inappropriate like that. I just tell them that they are disgusting pigs and then move on.

****

I requested to go to the graveyard squad, because that's where I'm comfortable; I like working graveyards. Everyone out there had just got off field training and that's where they send them – they send them to these graveyard squads – you work from ten at night to eight in the morning. As soon as they get off probation or field training they go to one of these graveyard squads because they've got no seniority and older guys don't want to work it.

So I'm the old guy at that point – been on fourteen, fifteen years – and these other kids that have been on a year-and-a-half , they don't what to go and ask their sergeant anything, so now I'm the fricking guy they all come to.

So I'm making a car stop and I pull this guy over – a meth cook. His girlfriend's a prostitute – a documented prostitute – who's got a small warrant. So I'm standing there by the window getting ready to do my business with this guy and this kid comes up and he's doing the cop cover thing. I talked to this guy a little bit and he had a shitty attitude – he was being a little prick – this customer we had.

And I said, 'Look, asshole, if you tell me where the dope is, I won't take your whore girlfriend to jail.' I think I called him a piece of shit and her a whore, which were both accurate.

But this kid is standing over there and he's like, 'Sir!'

Great, so now the kid's calling me 'Sir!' So I go, 'What?'

He goes, 'You can't say that.'

'Like, what are you talking about?'

He goes, 'You can't say that.'

I'm like, 'What the fuck? Are you kidding me?' Yeah, like I don't want to offend anyone by calling them 'whores' or 'pieces of shit'! The guy's a fricking meth cook – he's got dope, he knows I know he's got dope. His girlfriend *is* a whore and she has a warrant. So it is what it is!

Within two weeks of this incident, a different kid – although it may as well have been a carbon copy because, you know, they're pumping them out like Willy Wonka chocolates; he's a clone of this other kid – and I'm on a car stop. Well, this guy fricking hit me. So I grabbed him and bounced him off the hood and threw him up over the windshield and I'm putting the cuffs on him.

This kid's like, 'Sir! Sir!'

'What?'

'You can't do that.'

I'm like, 'What are you talking about?'

'You can't do that.'

'The guy fucking hit me! Absolutely I can do that!'

Apparently they're not teaching that. It's not allowed any more. Now it's, 'sir, what can I do to make you stop hitting me today?'

The difference between the old days and the new days! And all the guys who are enforcing these policies now – all our administrators – are the guys who used to, you know, sprinkle a little whiskey on themselves, take a few shots and then sit in the alley with the ten-dollar bill hanging out of their pocket, making like they're a bum so that people would come up and try and steal their money. And then they'd beat the shit out of them. These guys' careers were built around that; half of your assistant sheriffs and deputy chiefs now, that was what they did for amusement and law enforcement.

So that's probably a hack on a lot of people's asses – that 'do as I say, not as I used to do' programme.

****

The difference from when I joined eighteen years ago is that when you were put on the street, you were put on the street with a seasoned veteran. That was how you learnt and many times you would be in these situations where the seasoned veteran was, let's say, 'heavy handed', because he had already been on the job for twenty years.

I've seen guys get kicked in the ass just for drinking a beer in the street whereas nowadays you would just take his identification and write him a ticket. So things have definitely changed.

Policing has changed to a point where you use your mouth more as a weapon then you do your hands or your stick. You try to talk your way out of a situation or talk someone down from a situation more than you did years ago. That's the good side of it. The bad side of it is that people are not afraid of the police anymore. There is no retribution anymore because the courts have a revolving door system – you arrest somebody and they're in and out in a day.

Another problem is that police officers – who were once viewed in court as someone who would get on the stand and be truthful – are now looked at as liars and a lot of this comes from these past cases and the heavy handedness of police officers, especially with everything that was brought out with Rodney King and OJ Simpson.

You have to remember that the new officers who are joining the job now, they were the youth back then. They saw what was happening back then and they didn't agree with it – they were the rioters, the protestors and the college students. But now they're police officers and they look at us old timers and believe we were wrong in the way we were policing back then. Because of this, there is no camaraderie amongst us anymore. That so-called 'blue wall of silence' has broken down.

****

Camaraderie amongst officers is there but I don't think it's as strong as it used to be. When I came on the job we were all twenty-one, twenty-two years old and everyone drank together, everyone partied together, everyone worked together. It was fun and we were busy. We had bar fights every night. We had some tense summers and some tense moments. I equate it as being similar to somebody going off to war with a group of guys. You learn very quickly that you have to trust and like one another in order to work with one another.

We're still busy but it's not like is used to be. In the 90's there would be 10,000 people out on the street having a block party and you were vastly outnumbered. You don't get that now. It's not like that anymore.

Take away the volume of high-risk calls and you don't get the solidarity.

****

Prior to 9/11 I was doing high-end criminal intelligence. After 9/11, I somehow automatically became a terrorism expert. We were all suddenly doing counter-terrorism investigations. There was no training – it was just go out and do it. 'You're a detective, you know how. Just get it done.'

I think we are a little bit more refined now but still, there are lots of people who have no clue what they are doing. None whatsoever.

****

With West Coast policing, the culture is very, very different than East Coast policing. You don't have multiple generations of cops. Our police department, in its current form, started in 1973. Prior to that, there was a PD and a County Sheriff's that go back into the fifties. But our 'town' – for lack of a better term – really became a city of any consequence after the fifties, so we've only been working it sixty years.

You know, you've got New York and Chicago and Philadelphia, and some of these places where you've got generation upon generation of cops and a culture that is very, very different. Like New York, for instance – the NYPD has a very different culture in how they view policing and doing a favour for a fellow officer, or things that they would say. Like, back there it's nothing, you know, if you pull over another officer for a moving traffic violation, 'Oh yeah! Take it easy, see you later.'

I mean we've got people here on my own police department that'll issue you a citation in two seconds, knowing that you're a cop! Knowing that you're a cop on *their* department! Staggering. It's mind blowing to me but it happens.

That stuff doesn't happen with any regularity in New York or Chicago. But those cities have had major corruption investigations and major corruption identified and we as a young police department haven't gone through those same growing pains – and we're talking about sheer size as well. I mean, New York's got what? Fifty thousand officers? We've just peaked at 23 or 24 hundred. So the culture hasn't gotten around to the same 'taking care of each other' mentality, which is very common in New York and which is why for so long they've skirted the police and mobster association; because guys who are working foot beat in Manhattan, they're going to know every restaurant in their area. And the wise guy may say to a cop, 'Hey, come on in and eat at our restaurant – no problem.' And then that association builds over years and years and years and years.

I can't attribute that to corruption but I can attribute it to knowing your area and knowing the people in your area. And that leads to a kind of odd mutual respect for the other's arena, so to speak.

****

Are there policemen here that are taking bribes to protect drug dealers or major criminals? No. Are there people that are doing things that are a violation of our state ethic laws or taking gratuities that are questionable? Yes, there are. And it drives me nuts.

Someone in a mid-level position taking or aggressively soliciting tickets to a professional sports event or a free meal in a restaurant, for example. It's beyond perks of the job. Perks of the job are maybe parking illegally for five or ten minutes or some local person giving you a free cup of coffee – a de minimis perk. But when you start to get into things of value, of a couple of hundred dollars, and you're doing it frequently? Yeah, that's a little questionable.

People will give away things for free to curry favour with someone of high rank in the police department, maybe help them with a favour or get them out of trouble later on. Keep them off the radar if they are a particular establishment – a bar maybe – with some problems. There are a variety of reasons why somebody may do that.

****

When you have any organisation of 40,000 people, some are going to be corrupt. There's nothing you can do about it.

****

I don't like cops. When I was at the police academy they brought in this guy, he was a sergeant in the detective bureau and he was training us in 'police life', the police lifestyle, the police culture.

He actually said this, these words were his instruction to us at the police academy: 'Now, you need to understand that once you become a police officer, the only people who are going to understand you are other cops, so you need to make sure that all your other friends are cops. You only hang out with cops, because they are the only people who will really understand you.'

And all this 'be a wolf, don't be a sheep' bullshit and all this macho, testosterone-laced, 'we're the only people that can count on each other and you can't trust anybody or count on anybody else'.

I fucking work with people who believe that. I work with people whose only friends are cops. And they watch cop shows on TV all the time. When they're together all they do is talk about cop shit. They carry their guns with them to the bathroom. They carry their guns with them when they're mowing the lawn!

They make fun of me because I sometimes forget to carry my gun at work. Like, when I'm in plain clothes, I'll leave to go out and when I return five minutes later I think, 'Oh shit, I left my gun in my drawer.' You know? I'm more devastated if I forget my pen than my gun because I use my pen everyday; I haven't used my gun once. I've never fired a round.

They think I'm the freak because I don't have any cop friends, I don't watch cop shows, I don't talk about cop shit, I don't carry my gun with me everywhere I go, I don't wear my outer bullet proof vest when I'm leaving the station to go to Seven Eleven to get a Slurpee and come back; I'm not worried that I'm going to be shot all the time.

And another thing too, I'm a detective and I wear a suit either with or without a tie everyday – it's a different type of uniform. But most of the guys I work with wear khaki pants and polo shirts. I can tell that when they're speaking to people, these people that they're talking to are looking at them and thinking, 'Who are you, clown?' They look at me and there's a sense of authority and I get a little bit more respect because of the way I'm dressed. But of course my co-workers all make fun of me because I wear a suit every day. It's the opposite of normal thinking.

And here's another issue: most cops have never worked in the private sector. All the ones that I work with have never worked in the private sector. I worked in the private sector for fifteen years before I was a police officer, so I understand about dressing for success, dressing for the job you want, not for the one you have and all of the other subtleties that go into dealing with people and working for a business. A police department is a business in many ways, but they just don't get it.

When I go to somebody's house to interview them or I'm out talking to people about a case, I don't have my tactical vest that says 'POLICE', with my radio and my cuffs and all my stuff and my gun sticking out when I talk to 'em; I'm in a pair of slacks and a jacket. I've got a pen. I put them at ease. When I knock on the door, people answer because they don't see all that. But all my partners – all my partners in the detective bureau – they go out like they're on a SWAT raid. Just to talk to people!

They say, 'But it's for my protection.'

And I'll say, 'But aren't you worried that you're drawing more attention to yourself and if someone did want to target the police, you're identifying that you are police?'

When I'm out in my suit, with my badge under my jacket and my gun tucked in my pants, nobody knows I'm police. They might think I'm the door-to-door cable TV salesman or something. There's a low-profile way to do it, people. It's a different mindset. I'm completely different. I have always used the intellectual, methodical, thinking, talking approach. I don't do it by intimidation. Most of the guys I work with wear the big, thick boots; they have their knives tucked into all their shit; they've got the Oakley gargoyle, black glasses on, bald head, toothpick. They're trying to look as badass as they can. I would rather look friendly and have 'badass' in my back pocket. I can defend myself as well as any of these other guys can – I'm 6'3", 220 pounds, I'm trained like they are, I'm strong enough, I have the abilities to defend myself just as good as they do, I just don't need to portray that. Why do they do it? Either because they're insecure or they just think that's what cops do. Cops are supposed to look like ass-kicking Nazis. I mean, it's trained at the academy: be an ass-kicking Nazi.

****

We all hated this one guy. This guy – this cop – was ostracized. He was on his own and he ended up leaving the precinct. But even if you're an asshole, even if I don't like you and you don't like me, it doesn't matter. We both work here.

Here's one of the greatest sayings I was ever taught and I use it to this day: 'Protect your asshole'. They may be the biggest asshole on the planet but if you do not protect your own asshole nobody else is going to protect him for you. So it didn't matter. Anybody who legitimately needed help, got help. You never left anybody hanging or swinging in the breeze.

Protect your own assholes. If you don't protect them, nobody else is gonna. A guy with like a million years on the job told me that. And he was correct.

****

As a culture, we continue to divide – and many liberals will not agree with this but it's just my opinion – and this goes back to having the St Patrick's Day parade. Every single time we create a parade for a culture, we have created another divide. We're never going to be a melting pot or just one culture and all be 'Americans' when we have the St Patrick's Day parade or the Puerto Rican Day parade, for example. I truly believe that it continues to divide the cultures.

Now, instead of having the Latino Parade that all Latinos can enjoy, you have the Mexican day parade, you have the Dominican day parade and at these parades the youth fight with other youth that are not of the same culture as them. They say people just want to empower their culture but really, truly there is a division there that people don't see.

Gays have been fighting to get into the St Patrick's Day parade but have been denied. So, you have the Gay Pride parade now but the arguing continues about why they can't march in the St Patrick's Day parade.

Now, in policing we're bringing many of these people onto the police force and we're allowing them to recognise their culture rather than just be 'the police'. We have the German Society, the Italian Society, the Catholic Society, the Irish Society, the Gay Officers Action League, the policewomen – everybody's just separated. We're not working together and that is a reflection of society. We're doing it in society and now we're doing it in policing and it's going to continue to mushroom. We're allowing separation.

Everybody wants to represent their own culture. Well, you can represent your culture at home but you have to keep it separate from your job. How do you attend an anti-abortion rally but then also protect somebody who wants to get an abortion? How do you go to a Klu Klux Klan rally and protect the people of their First Amendment rights? You have to check your own beliefs and opinions at the door. The problem is, I don't think officers are checking it at the door anymore.

Officers are now complaining about investigations being carried out on certain organisations or groups; for instance, complaining about Muslims being investigated for terrorism. We have officers making complaints about that. They feel that the police department is creating a stigma – that all Muslims are terrorists. But the police department is not creating a stigma – you simply have to look at all avenues of investigations in order to police effectively.

Religious holidays are another problem. I can't be off on Christmas Day because, let's face it, not everybody can be off on Christmas Day. But for a Jewish holiday, all the Jewish guys get the day off. On Friday we have Jewish cops who are allowed to leave early and can't work late tours on Friday. How does that make other police officers feel?

They'll say, 'How come he can do it, but I can't? How come his religion is more important than my religion?'

There's the separation that I'm speaking of, because they're not acting as cops first. If you come on this job, you can enjoy your religion and you can have your religious holidays, but if you make a decision to become a police officer, you have to check it at the door. You're not a republican, you're not a democrat – you have no party lines because you effectively have to police all of them.

I'll have to go and work the Israeli Day parade but they give all the Jewish guys the day off so that they can attend it. Or they'll give the Italians the day off to attend the Columbus Day parade. But what if you're black and you want to attend the Columbus Day parade? Well, no, you can't get the day off because you're not Italian. So that is the divide I am talking about – a straight down the line divide.

We keep creating these ethnic barriers and then expect the cops to come on the job and police, but they're not. It's a very hard situation and I don't think there's any easy band-aid to fix it.

****

We've had an increase of police-involved shootings because nowadays, more often than not, if you come up to a gangbanger, instead of just trying to get away and pitching a gun, they'll shoot at you. They'll stand and shoot at you. I think it's just the lack of respect, but also the political climate. The gangbangers know that they have us on our heels; instead of being aggressive, we're backing up, and they know it.

They feel they have a little more power and there's also a lack of fear. I mean, years ago, the people would fear the police and you knew if you broke the law and you got caught or you ran, you got punched; so you'd fear the police. Nowadays they're begging you to hit 'em because if you hit 'em, they can sue you. You lock them up in the car or the van and they'll sit there and jaw-jack all the way back to the station trying to provoke you. So they know things have changed; they know there's a difference in policing.

Also, people now size you up on the street. If you walk up to somebody and they're dirty – they've got narcotics on them or a gun on them or they've just committed a crime – they'll size you up. They'll be thinking, 'Either, A) I'm gonna give up, B) I'm gonna try to run, or C) I'll shoot them.'

So they size you up. They take a look at you to see, 'Can these guys run? Are they younger? Are they older? Are they fat or over-weight? Are they small? Are they big?'

It's funny, I was working in patrol and on the radio we'd always hear these two cops – partners – call for help. It was like, on a weekly basis. So we'd jump in our cars and go and help them. No issue with that but I was just trying to figure out, how come these guys in par-ticular are always calling for help? I'm looking around and after a while I'm thinking, 'Man, I'm six foot tall. I have a partner who's six-four. Athletic.' And I realised, you show up to a job, whatever it is – a domestic, a battery, assault, anything, a theft, anything – you show up and the criminals, they size you up. These two guys I'm talking about are both about five-five, five-six. I mean, good police officers but if you get out of your car and you're both five-five, five-six, the crook's gonna think, 'If they grab me or if I let them grab me, I'm going to jail. So I'm going to go through them – either I'm going to try to run or I'm going to fight my way out of it.'

So you realise that it helps being in shape. Also your attitude tells them a lot – your reputation, your appearance, whether you're all dishevelled or not squared away. If you look squared away and you look fit and in shape compared to somebody who doesn't care about their appearance, or somebody who doesn't care about whether they're overweight or not, they know. The crooks know. They're thinking, 'I can get away from this guy.'

I'm not saying me and my old partner never fought with anybody – we had to fight with some people – but they were just a little more determined to get away. But after a while you learn you can't fight with everybody; you don't want to fight with everybody. It's better to use your mouth to get people in handcuffs.

But yeah, people don't fear the police anymore – not as they used to, anyway.

****

The job has changed; we've become much more liability motivated. There's a lot more knee-jerk reaction rather than common sense going on. I mean, somebody gets sued and it changes everything. We're becoming this kind of soft-gloved agency which at the same time tries to be hard-gloved. And sometimes it conflicts.

It may have always have been like that; I don't know if it's just that I've gotten older in the job and I'm seeing it more. I mean, our policy manual, when I came on, it was maybe three hundred pages. It's got to be close to eight hundred pages now. Everything is all about liability. We're very scared to do things that a police agency may have to do, in case it looks bad in the public eye. We would prefer to give the impression to the public that we are handling everything in the most civilised way possible rather than facing the fact that sometimes we are put here to be the enforcers of the law and sometimes it's not pretty, but it needs to be done. And the criminals see that.

The criminals, they're getting more violent. They're getting bigger guns. They're taking bolder steps. Even music and things like that are becoming much more violent towards the establishment and towards the police. It's becoming more acceptable to disrespect the police.

I always say, it's fine to question what the police are doing – in fact I'm always transparent. But now people actively go after the police and are openly defiant to the point where violence is being perpetrated throughout our society, whether it's on TV or in music.

The news is also becoming much less objective, and instead it's becoming more adversarial towards the police. When I was first hired, the news was kind of our ally. There were times when we would screw up and they would rake us over the coals for it but there's also times when we did OK or did good. Now, no matter what we do, there's always some controversy involved. If we get involved in a shooting, what's the first thing the media do? They grab the victim's mother or father and interview them and that goes on the news. Well, that's the first thing anybody sees or hears about the case and that then becomes 'the truth'.

So we're facing that environment – this society that's becoming much more adversarial against the police. And our department – and I'm sure it's happening elsewhere – is becoming a department who is creating policies and taking us in a direction where we are bending to it.

We'll say, 'Okay, don't rake us over the coals in the news. We'll change.' But we should be saying, 'No. That's just not the way it is. I don't care what you say or how badly you feel about this. We're enforcing the law and this is the way that we do it and that's the way it should be done.'

But we don't say that. Instead we bend towards the adversarial side and say, 'Okay, just don't sue us.'

****

The area where I work has got a lot of shit heads. I mean, there're good people that live there as well but there's a lot of shit heads that end up there too, so when you deal with them you have to get in their faces; you're swearing at them and cussing at them. You know, I'm 'mother-fucking' the guy and saying, 'Get the fuck outta here.' Stuff like that.

But then some officer that hasn't been on the job maybe five or six years shows up, looks at me and says, 'Oh my God! You're going to get into trouble for talking to him like that!'

There's been a couple of times when I'm 'mother-fuckering' some gangbanger up and down and some newer guy comes up and you can just tell – it's like a deer caught in the headlights – you can tell what he's thinking: 'Is he really swearing at that guy?'

It's totally different from when I was a young, newer officer working patrol. I mean we'd have contests every night to see who could arrest the most people, give the most warnings or find the most drugs or whatever. Now it's almost like who is *not* going to do the most. Who's going to do the *least*? Because the new officers are afraid and they have all been taught that they're going to get in trouble if they do anything.

We've had guys getting into trouble for swearing at a suspect! But a lot of the time, that's the only thing these suspects will understand.

If you're saying, 'Please sir, you just need to calm down and be nice.' They'll be like, 'Motherfucker! What the fuck?' You know?

If you 'mother-fuck' them right back, you're speaking their language. It's not like they're thinking, 'Oh my goodness! Those harsh words are hurting my feelings!' Finally they understand.

So you work to your environment.

****

I think in a lot of your major departments there're so many stopgaps that have been put into place that it's very difficult to have widespread corruption. At least, that's how I see it with our police department, because you'd have to have a number of people working together who would all need to be prepared to jeopardise their career and their potential future.

The opportunities for that are few and far between. I mean, I've worked on task forces where we've come into contact with upwards of two million dollars on narcotics cases. You would literally have to have about eight people in agreement on corrupt terms to do something with that or about that and the opportunities are just not there because there's so much knowledge surrounding it; so many people are notified and the culture has changed – at least it has here.

The culture is, it's not worth trying to grab a stack of cash from somebody and jeopardise your three million dollar, thirty year career (it is that much when you're talking earnings and pension) and I think our department has done a very good job of compensating the employees to avoid someone's need to be corrupt.

But I still think it happens elsewhere around the country.

****

We don't rely on the public. We don't expect anything from the public. We are the police and we police. We're not here to fix your problems; we're here to police you.

The public are a very limited resource – a very, very limited resource. People in general don't do the right thing. You can't trust the public; they only do things that are self-serving. There may be a small percentage that wants to help, but it's a small percentage. People walk with blinders on and they don't want to be bothered. It's hard to get them to testify in court even.

****

It needs to be emphasized sometimes, I think, that the public – that person who called for you – they don't care what you were just dealing with, they just care that you're there and that whatever their problem is right now, it is the most important thing that you have going on in your life. And you kind of owe it to the public to be that way.

You may have just been on some ridiculous call or you may have just gotten done with some internal affairs investigation and now you're going over to see an old lady who's house got broken into whilst she was out shopping and you're thinking, 'Oh, my God! Are you kidding me? I'm on a burglary call?'

You need to remember that this is an invasion of her life; someone broke into her house. She doesn't care that you just got chewed up or that you just saw someone get shot. All she cares about is that you – the police officer – show up and gives her the service that she deserves. And at times that can be extremely hard to do.

****

We get in trouble just for doing our job these days. The department – and I think this goes for lots of departments – they don't want you chasing cars because of the liability.

The state troopers, their policy is that they enforce all laws –

misdemeanour and felony. They will pursue you until the wheels fall off.

There's been pursuits in Tennessee that have gone all the way to the state line and they notified Kentucky state police that they were coming into Kentucky – you know, 'be prepared' – and Kentucky's like, 'Ten-four. But make sure you back off at least a quarter mile.'

So Tennessee backs off, lets the suspect keep going on the interstate and there sits Kentucky, just the other side of their state line, shotguns ready. And as soon as the car comes through, BOOM, BOOM, BOOM, BOOM! They just unload on the car.

So there you go; they can all do it but we can't.

****

Let me tell you about police work – it's 80 per cent boredom, 19 per cent paperwork and one per cent panic. Wait, change that. It's 80 per cent paperwork, 19 per cent boredom and one per cent panic.

14

9/11: One Officer's Story

I briefly considered placing this account in either the 'On The Job' or the 'Officer Down' chapter. Frankly, neither felt even remotely appropriate. Clearly it was no ordinary day at work - even by police standards. Dozens of officers were killed in an instant and many more have gone on to succumb to their injuries and illnesses in the years since. And even today, there are officers who are still fighting to survive the effects of that single tour of duty.

37 officers from the Port Authority Police Department along with 23 officers from the New York Police Department died on 9/11 in New York. Other officers from federal, state and local departments were also killed. One of the flight attendants of United Airlines flight 93 that crashed in a field in Pennsylvania was a former police officer, who had resigned from her force to become a flight attendant just a few months before the attacks. And there was a federal officer amongst the passengers. No police officers were killed at the Pentagon.

There are countless stories from that day, this is just one of them. It's the story of a cop - a New York detective - who came into work one

273

morning, and did his job.

I was there at 9/11. I almost got killed. The morning it happened, we were in work at 7am and normally we'd put the TV on but for whatever reason, we didn't that morning. I was working on a report; there were two murders, two days apart where the same gun had been used. I had very little computer skills at the time and we were still typing on carbon paper. I was struggling to do this report when somebody rang us and said, 'Do you know a plane just hit the World Trade Center?'

It was a gorgeous day and I remember riding into work that morning and thinking, 'Why am I here? I should be out on my boat.' And then you think, 'What idiot would hit the fucking building on a beautiful day like today?'

The initial stories were that it was a small plane or it was a news helicopter or maybe even a big plane. They told us to get ourselves down there but I went back upstairs to get something. There were about maybe eight or ten of us in the office at that time and they had all driven off before I came back down. I had the keys to another car so I jumped into that and I got myself down there.

I worked in an upper part of Manhattan, so I knew how to cut through Central Park and how to get to the Trade Center quickly, avoiding the avenues. By the time I got to 59th Street and Columbus Circle, it was coming out over the radio – the police radio and the news radio – that a second plane had just hit the other tower. So at that moment you know that this wasn't an accident. There can't be two pilots that are that fucking stupid in one day; it's just impossible.

So you knew something had happened.

Anyway, I got down there, parked the car and spent the next couple of hours trying to get back with all my people. The thing is, the police radios weren't working, because the transmitter was up on one of the towers. The cell phones weren't working either, so you'd have to use a hard line. I was right across the street from where the fire department was initially set up and the mayor and the police commissioner were there too.

I managed to get to a phone and called the office. They told me to call back in fifteen minutes. The guy in the office was keeping a log about where I was and where everybody else was and he was going to try and get a meeting point for us.

The fire department then decides that they're going to get closer and they're going to set up their Ops Centre in the lobby of one of the towers. There was a priest that turned up; the guy had on fire boots and jeans but he had on the black shirt with the white collar and I go, 'Look at this guy! A priest! A fire priest!' And I kind of had a little laugh about it. And then he put his jacket on that says 'clergy' and off he went. Within two or three minutes after he had walked off, he became the first casualty for the fire department. One of the bodies that came down from the top of the tower landed on him and killed him.

People called them 'jumpers' but that word is a bit of a misconception. They weren't necessarily jumpers as much as people hanging on to the outside. It wasn't like they made a conscious decision, like, 'Alright, I'm getting outta here and this is the only way.' Because you're not going to make it, you're not going to survive that jump. If you do look at the pictures that they show, it's just people hanging onto the outside and either they're overcome by the smoke or they're overcome by the heat or just... that's it, they let go. It wasn't like someone said, 'Get out of the way! I'm jumping.' I didn't see people physically stepping up and going, 'This is what I'm doing', like a jumper would.

Anyway, so we're still standing across the street and I'm seeing bodies coming down and when they hit, it was kind of like seeing a car crash – you don't want to look but you have to. And here comes the body, it's coming down and then it hit the ground and its head would go twenty feet this way and his shoes would explode right off. One particular guy was coming down and he was facing upwards and his arms were tethering. He hit a lamppost and split in half and when he hit the ground he just splattered and I just said to myself, 'Good God!'

I decided that, when we got this thing under control, I wanted to go over there. I just felt somehow compelled towards that particular person, you know? I thought that I'd try to get his property and give it to his family or... well, I don't know what I thought.

At some point, some boss comes over and told us – all the detectives – to follow him and we went into this particular building, which I believe was the World Financial Center and we went out the back door, by the Hudson River. We walked along the river to just south of the towers and stood under this bridge. We were standing under that just to keep out of the way of the glass that was breaking and the bodies that were coming out. I went to go use the telephone at the Marriott hotel because I had to call my wife to tell her where I was – to say that I was all right – and I told her what had happened; she was unaware because she didn't have the TV on.

She said, 'Don't go in the building.'

I said, 'No, I won't go in the building.' In the '93 bombing, some cops that went into the building got smoke inhalation. So I decide that I'm just going to wait for the fire department to put it out and then go in.

So we're all standing there and I went back to use the phone to find out if there was any update on where all the guys from my unit were but they couldn't find anybody and said, 'Call back in twenty minutes.'

Then, as I was halfway between the Marriott and the bridge, there was a noise that can't be described in any way other than it was the loudest noise I have ever heard in my life. You knew that it was not a 'look and see' noise; it was just 'RUN!'

I made it about a block – not even. It happened so fast. I was halfway down the block and my phone fell out of my top pocket from when I was running. So I turned to get my phone and then I saw that cloud you see in the news, coming at me. Within a second this stuff just overcomes you – this rush of air and dirt and dust. You didn't know what it was at the time, you just figure, stay low to the ground, stay low to the ground. You could feel a heat coming over you and it went from daylight to absolute black; you couldn't see a thing. But as I was running I kind of had an idea that I wanted to go into this one particular building, because I had seen the doors and thought I could get out of the way. So I crawled along the ground – in blackness – and found the kerb, found the building, found the door. I was throwing up because this stuff was getting in my mouth – it was thick. I was pulling it out in chunks, coughing, throwing up – it was shit. But when I found the door to the building, it was locked. I go, 'Fuck me!

I'm going to die here today. This is unbelievable.'

So I kept moving south, along the wall, because I couldn't see – it was black. I had to use the wall and as I was going, there was an alley-way and in that alleyway there were about thirty people and some-body had a flashlight and you could just barely make out a silhouette and I'm coughing and I'm throwing up and it was just sick. And a guy in the alley says, 'Cover your mouth! Cover your mouth!'

And I'm like, 'Oh, fucking good idea! Why didn't I think of that?' But you're just thinking about surviving, you didn't know what had happened or what to do.

It took about five or ten minutes before there was just barely enough light to see and I said, 'I'm a police officer.'

And another guy goes, 'I am too.'

And another goes, 'So am I.'

So there were three of us in there and I said, 'Look, we've got to get out of here; we've got to get these people out of here.'

So we made a human chain and there was some lady that was hurt, so we told these guys that they had to carry her. As we went down the street there was an ambulance and the crew were out of the ambulance, trying to shake off the dust, because they had their air conditioning on and everything got sucked into the vehicle. They were getting saline solution and passing it to us so we could wash our faces and gargle, trying to get this shit out of us and not really knowing what had happened or what to do other than we had to keep going south.

We found another building and we went in there to use the phone and to clean up in the bathroom and as we're getting squared away, they have the TV on – they have the news – and as we're watching what's happening a guy comes in with a bullhorn and screams, 'GET OUT! GET OUT! THE OTHER BUILDING'S GOING TO FALL! THE OTHER BUILDING'S GOING TO FALL!'

'Fuck that!' I said. 'I'm staying right here; I don't want to be out in that again. If the building falls and lands on me, I'll take my chances.'

I just knew that I did not want to be out in that again because, you know, you didn't even know what it was. You come to find out later that it was the whole building imploding inwards and it was all the concrete and all the asbestos and all the dirt.

So now the second building's down and we're like, 'Alright, we gotta get out of here.' But we wanted to stay away from the police plaza and we wanted to stay away from Wall Street, you know? You figure that maybe there's going to be more attacks, with what's going on.

We're just south towards Battery Park and then you hear this roar of a jet and you go, 'Fuck! Again?' And then you come to find out that it's the military jets.

We ended up in the fish market and they had hoses and we're using hoses to clean off and again to gargle. Plus they let us use the phones. Eventually we got a muster point where we all went to and that was it.

Later that day and that night, when we were able to go back over there and see the area where we had been standing when the first building had come down, the whole top of that building had fallen into the building where we had been standing and the glass atrium was all collapsed; it was all gone. Every one of us that was standing there would have been dead. If some guy didn't say, 'Let's go over here,' we would have all been dead.

One way or another, every single person in that police department somehow, some way, ended up either digging down there or working down there – even if it was just directing traffic. At some point you were going to be there. I would know guys who would work their whole day and then they would go there and work for five or six hours – digging, helping.

During the initial searches after the buildings had collapsed, you never saw a desk, a chair or a filing cabinet; you never saw anything that looked like anything. It was just dust, debris, wire, concrete, parts of planes, parts of this and parts of that. I mean how many desks and chairs do you think were in those buildings? 110 storeys but there was nothing. It was surreal.

The only people that were going down to the site were police. We were working twelve to eighteen hours a day. They eventually shut the road, the West Side Highway. There was no traffic into the city for the first couple of days, so you were the only people on that road and when you're going down there, there'd be folks lining up with water bottles and flags and banners and waving to you. It was incredible, the people that turned up and the support. It was an amazing first week, almost a month. Even bad guys weren't really bad. It's like it just stopped and everybody was supportive.

They had us posted on the Intrepid – that's the aircraft carrier by 42nd Street. We were using that as a temporary headquarters. We were working from either 4pm or 6pm, 'til like 6am or 8am the next morning. I didn't know what was going on; you're kind of in a zombie state, so to speak. You're just getting on with it. But it was surreal. You'd come in and you'd be on the flight deck of this thing and you'd get your daily briefing and your assignment of jobs that you had to do that day and then you'd look to where the towers used to be and all you saw was the smoke billowing.

You used to see the buildings no matter where you were in the city. Whenever you came out of the train or the subway, if you didn't know that particular neighbourhood you just had to look up and if you could see the World Trade Center, you'd say, 'Oh, okay, I know what direction I need to go now.' It was surreal to see that they weren't there anymore; it was just smoke. And then to go down there and physically see the carnage... it was just horrendous.

I knew quite a few people who were killed there that day. I knew one of the firemen, because he was a cop who had become a fireman. I knew quite a few cops who were killed. One of them was my best friend's neighbour and he said that he had seen him that morning and they were scheduled to have beer at five o'clock that night at a local pub. Then there was a fella who was in my academy class; they had pictures of him on the news. He had carried two women out from one of the buildings – not physically, but they needed help and he helped them out. He wasn't a big guy but he was fit. He carried them out and put them on the kerb and then he ran back in. That's when the building came down. I don't think they ever found him. They'll never find him. So there were a lot of people I knew killed that day.

At the time, nobody warned you of any dangers of what it all was – the debris and dust. Now people are coming up with cancer and stuff. I have a spot on my lung and some sorts of spots on my lower abdomen. They're monitoring it to see if it's cancerous. They say the ones in the abdomen aren't but the one in the lung, well... they're hoping it's just scar tissue but they're monitoring it.

I have gotten so much radiation from MRI's and x-rays and everything that they didn't know whether they were doing me more harm than good. They don't know whether what I have may kill me or whether they've hit me with so much radiation that I may just die of radiation poisoning instead. So they've stopped. It was fucking crazy. I'm just hoping for the best on that one.

Everybody has a story from that day – every single person; they were there when the towers came down and almost got killed one way or another. But I can tell you that on that day, nobody cried.

So there you go. That was a weird day.

15

End of Tour

I could have gone to almost any country in the world and collected stories from officers and they would have still been funny, absurd and fascinating but with the American police there is just something else. If any cops in the world have an x-factor, then surely it is them. I mean seriously, chasing after a gorilla called 'Little Joe'?

Cops don't care who you are. It doesn't matter what your skin colour is, what religion you are, what sex or age you may be, what social background or class you are, or even if you're a gorilla. Despite all the bullshit we hear about, the bottom line is this: if you're in trouble, a cop will come to your aid. A cop will help you. You may be a complete stranger, you may even be someone who hates the police, but a cop will willingly risk their own life to save yours. They are an amazing bunch of people who to me have become, after researching and writing this book, a little bit more special. They don't always get it right but for the most part, the vast majority are decent, honest human beings who want to serve their communities. I don't know what you will come away with after reading this book, this collection of stories and opinions, but I hope at the very least that you now have a broader understanding and respect for the law enforcement officers of the United States. I know that I do.

Thinking back to my own experiences with the American police and reading back through these tales, I have to wonder, would I still have wanted to join the NYPD, back when I had telephoned the American embassy in London? Do I still wish I could have had a go at being an American cop?

Hell yes. Now where did I leave those Ray Bans?

The final words I am leaving to two female officers - one at the end of her career, the second just starting.

As a cop, I think you do the best you can everywhere you go. Did I change the world in my career? No. I didn't change the world but hopefully along the way I helped some people. I put some bad guys in jail, I changed some people's opinions about cops, I treated people with respect – unless I had to do otherwise – and I like to think that I left my city a little better place than before. But I don't know if that's true. I think it's a continuing job that I will be handing over. But I'll look back at my career and I'll be proud and I'll be happy and I'll feel as though I've accomplished something in my own small way.

But, is it measurable? Probably not. But I did the best I could every day. I went to court prepared to testify against the bad guys; I showed up to work, ready to work and gave a hundred percent whilst I was there. I helped people where I could, arrested people when I had to and helped my fellow officers whenever they needed me. And I think that's it.

If you're looking for a medal for doing all that stuff, you're not going to get it. You have to have the satisfaction in yourself that you did a good job. People aren't running around, patting you on the back. To me, I have to look back on what I did and say I'm proud, I'm happy I did it, I was lucky to have had the opportunities that I had and I worked hard. If that's not enough for me, well, I'm not getting anything more than that. I loved it all.

****

I wish I had some more exciting stories. Talk to me in another fifteen years.

EPILOGUE

When I first reached out to contacts I had made with police departments across the country to tell the officers that I wanted to interview them about their work, their lives and to get their opinions so that I could write them down and put them into a book, I had no idea what their reaction would be. There was, perhaps unsurprisingly, some scepticism about what I was doing. Officers were naturally concerned about being identified; speaking about their work wasn't illegal but they were worried about how it would be viewed by their departments, their colleagues and their communities. For this reason I made a rule that everyone would be speaking to me anonymously. Although I would know who they were, their names and details would not appear in this book. Some (I'm thinking particularly of the NYPD here) didn't care, but the rule remained. Once they felt assured that this would be the case, officers opened up to me in surprising ways. I met many officers only once and was often with them for just an hour, and sometimes even less than that.

When officers spoke to me about the effects of the job on their personal lives (countless divorces, suicide attempts and alcoholism) or, as some did, broke down in tears as they recalled particularly distressing incidents from their past, I realised that these men and women had given me their complete trust and really believed in what I was writing, which is a record of what it is like to be a police officer in today's America; the good, the bad and, at times, the downright outrageous.

I conducted a couple of interview over the phone across the Atlantic but it quickly became obvious that to get the best out of these conversations, I needed to actually meet the officers face to face. So I jumped on a jumbo and crossed the oceanic divide. I didn't embark on one, single journey, I did it in two main segments – West Coast and Midwest followed by more Midwest (they had a lot to say), the East Coast and the South, with little bits done here and there in between, such as meeting American officers when they were in London or catching officers while I was in the States for other reasons, such as vacations. It became something of an obsession, a crusade even. I'd travel across the country simply on the off chance that an officer would speak to me and in the end I interviewed everyone from street cops to Chiefs of Police.

As I said, many of these officers were meeting me for the first time and there were occasions when they were given just a few minutes warning of what they were about to be asked to do. Often, I would have arranged to meet with an officer who would suddenly remember a friend who had an interesting story to tell or who would see a colleague walking into the room and the friend or colleague would be told to sit down and speak to the guy with the strange accent (which they often took for being Australian) and tell him all about themselves. Officers in the South, in particular, thought I sounded funny. But if they thought I sounded strange to them, they should have heard how they sounded to me.

These interviews were conducted in patrol cars with sirens wailing, secluded offices, bars, homes, honky-tonks (whatever they are), restaurants (from the best to the worst), bars, police bases (on one memorable occasion, a police cell), bars, parking lots, hotels, bars and even outside the White House. The bars were my favourite; it was always interesting listening to wild police stories while surrounded by intoxicated chaos.

In the course of collecting these tales I ate everything from alligator (the South) to hot dogs (everywhere) to excellent gumbo (oddly, because it's a Southern dish, in the Pacific Northwest) with lots of lobster roll when I could get it (New England). I drank plenty of beer but greater amounts of coffee than I care to recall. I was never offered tea. Not even once.

There were times when the research didn't go as planned and contacts would suddenly disappear or perhaps hide when they found out exactly what I was doing. On more than one occasion I was left stranded in a city or town without an officer to speak to, and day after day would slip by where I would spend hours sending out emails and checking my phone instead of carrying out interviews. On these occasions I would sometimes simply walk up to an officer in the street and tell them what I was doing. Most of the time, the reaction you're probably thinking I got is exactly what I did get. But occasionally an officer would nod their head and start talking. On other occasions I would make frantic phone calls to good contacts across the country who would then start making calls themselves to ensure my trips were not wasted. In fact, that is how I came to find myself in Baltimore, after things had not gone as well as planned on one of my trips to DC (the last time I was there was during a mass-shooting, which tied up the entire department). But almost always, I was greeted with genuine kindness and was once even given a house and a car (and twice, a gun) for my personal use.

I visited small towns, large cities, mountain communities, desert communities, places everyone has heard of and places no one has heard of. The result, I hope, is a book that will give the reader a completely honest and intimate view of American law enforcement.

Each individual cop is shaped by the people they meet, the officers they work with and the calls they attend. The very nature of the job can, on occasion, spawn a very dark sense of humour and it is no cop-out to blame this dark humour and behaviour on the stresses of the job and see it as a coping method. Having said that, I have genuine fears that this book, or at least some of the stories within it, will lead to serious criticism of the police, or even lead some police officers themselves to become angry with what I have written. It should be pointed out that some of these more shocking stories relate to a very different time. Things have changed for the better, and are still changing.

Looking back, there were times when I was truly horrified at what I was being told, but I have included all the stories, no matter how unpleasant or how badly they reflect on the cops involved, because it is important that readers understand the realities of the job; it is tough and it can be dangerous and though it may sometimes be hard to understand the way officers behave or the things they do, it is also important not to hide from the truth. As Thomas Jefferson once said, 'Honesty is the first chapter in the book of wisdom.' Cops seem to understand that instinctively, because when I questioned the officers I was interviewing, expressing my concerns about recording what they were telling me, their reaction was always the same: 'I don't care. Put it in.'

THE END

ACKNOWLEDGMENTS

I have been visiting the United States regularly for a number of years now and I am always overwhelmed by the generosity of the people I meet. I know of nowhere else where I could simply arrive, often out of the blue, and be so well looked after and welcomed.

One of the conditions when I started researching this book was that officers would remain anonymous within it. For this reason it is not possible to enter the names of all the officers throughout the United States of America who spoke to me or else helped me in other ways with the completion of this book. They all know who they are and to them I say a very special thank you. Thank you so much for your openness, your honesty, your kindness and your friendship. Without these officers there would simply be no book. I cannot thank the police officers, sheriff department officers and deputies and state troopers who helped me, enough. They humble me to the point of embarrassment.

Everyone has people in their lives who in one way or another, helped them along the road to reach the point they were hoping for. Sometimes this advice and help can be huge, sometimes it can be something small but without them, things may have been very different. Support of various kinds has come to me from Robert Dinsdale, Elly James, Eleanor Lang, Bob Howe, Morgan, Ellen Datlow, Anthony Moore, George and Marie, Bruno, Andy Soutter, and Neil Cumming together with Kurt and his wonderful family.

In addition I would like to thank my agent and publisher Humfrey Hunter who was enthusiastic about this idea as soon as I presented it to him and who has been a genuine joy to work with. He was, quite simply, everything a new writer could hope for. Thanks also to David Boa who designed the amazing cover.

I would like to thank my mother who has always supported me, my father who gave me an interest in both policing and writing to begin with and my brother David, who has always been enthusiastic about my ideas. I would also like to thank – though it pains me – my good friend Guy, whose belief in me has always helped me move forward. I must also say a quick hello to Jake, Evie, Dexter and Nathan, and Bonjour to Ethan.

Most importantly I want to thank my wife Lisa, without whom, I simply wouldn't be able to achieve anything. She is understanding, calm and patient, often listening to my – sometimes foolish – ideas without complaint as well as helping with editing and proofreading. I don't deserve her. Lisa, thank you. I love you.